STAY UP

racism, resistance, and reclaiming Black freedom

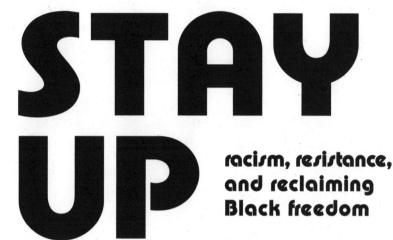

KHODI DILL

ART BY STYLO STARR

annick
press
toronto · berkeley

Cover art by stylo starr, designed by Cleopatria Peterson and Sam Tse
Interior designed by Cleopatria Peterson and Rachel Nam
Edited by Claire Caldwell and Khary Mathurin
Expert read by Karina Vernon
Copyedited by Mercedes Acosta
Body text proofread by Dana Hopkins
Sources formatted by Erin Chan
Cree translations reviewed by Dorothy Visser
Indexed by Siusan Moffat

Pages 259–280 constitute an extension of this copyright page.

We acknowledge the support of the Canada Council for the Arts and the Ontario
Arts Council, and the participation of the Government of Canada/la participation
du gouvernement du Canada for our publishing activities.

Canada  ONTARIO ARTS COUNCIL
CONSEIL DES ARTS DE L'ONTARIO
an Ontario government agency
un organisme du gouvernement de l'Ontario

Library and Archives Canada Cataloguing in Publication

Title: Stay up : racism, resistance, and reclaiming Black freedom / Khodi Dill ;
     art by stylo starr
Names: Dill, Khodi, author. | starr, stylo, illustrator.
Description: Includes bibliographical references and index.
Identifiers: Canadiana (print) 20230158390 | Canadiana (ebook)
     20230158730 | ISBN 9781773218076 (hardcover) | ISBN 9781773218083
     (softcover) | ISBN 9781773218090 (HTML) | ISBN 9781773218106 (PDF)
Subjects: LCSH: Racial justice—Canada. | LCSH: Racial justice—United States.
     | LCSH: Anti-racism—Canada. | LCSH: Anti-racism—United States. | LCSH:
     Black people—Canada—Social conditions. | LCSH: Black people—United
     States—Social conditions.
Classification: LCC HT1563 .D55 2023 | DDC 305.896/0971—dc23
     Classification: LCC PZ7.1.T36 Sam 2023 | DDC j823/.92—dc23

Published in the U.S.A. by Annick Press (U.S.) Ltd.
Distributed in Canada by University of Toronto Press.
Distributed in the U.S.A. by Publishers Group West.

Printed in Canada

annickpress.com
thegreygriot.com

Also available as an e-book. Please visit annickpress.com/ebooks for more details.

"I hope I can live up to my ancestors'
expectation of me because I really believe that
I have a duty to all those who have come before me,
to all those who lie at the bottom of the ocean, to all those
who lost their lives, whether it's in cane fields or the cotton
fields or, you know, hanging off some
tree, to continue this struggle, and to continue
to love and to continue to believe and to
continue to try to be human."

—Assata Shakur, *The Eyes of the Rainbow*

For my children.
—K.D.

Dedicated to you.
Thank you.
—S.S.

contents

the land

The anti-racism work and the writing that I do take place on Treaty Six territory. Without the solemn agreements of treaty, I could not do the work that I do, nor live the life that I live here on the beautiful prairie lands of Saskatchewan, Canada, where I raise my children and dream for their futures. Saskatchewan is located on the traditional and ancestral territories of several Indigenous Peoples, including the Dene, Cree, Saulteaux, Lakota, Dakota, Nakoda, and Métis Peoples. Many of these nations have their own names for themselves in their own languages. It is on these lands where I was educated about anti-racism by some of the world's leading academics, most of them Indigenous women scholars, whose brave practice here has improved both education and society in our country and our world. Here, I affirm my commitment to support the important work of decolonizing this land, our society, its institutions, and its minds, and to support the difficult but crucial work of truth-telling and amends-making, now and in the future. Colonization is ongoing here, and so too must be our resistance.

author's note

The memories in this book are accurate as I remember them. Occasionally, the names of those involved have been changed or omitted in order to protect their anonymity.

At times, a racial slur used historically to target Black people appears in this book. Trust that I don't take including it here lightly. But the suppression of stories of anti-Black violence has been used to silence and discredit our people for hundreds of years. As Black people we must reserve the right to tell others the names that people have called us in order to diminish, demean, and dehumanize us. They created a word to help distinguish us from them and have used that word and its consequences to this day to justify our ongoing mistreatment and our deaths the world over. That is the story that I am telling in this book, and so I've decided to include the word here in full wherever it is relevant. It should go without saying that not everyone in the Black community will agree on this issue, but know that many within the community do agree on one thing for certain:

If you're not Black, **don't say it**. That goes for read-alouds and sing-alongs, too.

introduction

Have you checked your news feed lately? It's overwhelming out here. It's beatings and murders and shootings and demonstrations and wrongful convictions and wrongful deaths, and hell, even wrongful acquittals going on. And all this has been happening damn near cyclically for decades. It's easy to let it all catch up to you, overtake you, immobilize you. That's exactly how I felt when I watched the police killing of Philando Castile, a 32-year-old Black man, in Minnesota in 2016. Castile was driving one night in July when police stopped him and killed him in front of his partner, Diamond Reynolds, and her 4-year-old daughter, who were both in the car.

No matter the details of the incident, the motive for the killing, or the fact that Castile had been stopped by police a total of 49 times in the 13 years leading up to his death, watching the incident on video from my home in Canada changed a lot for me. First off, it changed *me*, like who I was, at the core. Immediately after seeing it, I fell victim to that same old immobility; I curled up in a fetal position and remained there, mentally and emotionally, for months. I stopped engaging with anti-racism for a time, withdrew socially, and stopped writing and creating as well. It was the first time that I had experienced a setback of such magnitude. It made it clear to me that anti-Black racism was a trauma that could impact me and all Black people even from a great distance. And its painful blows stay comin' relentlessly.

Because of that, I've realized that our work in fighting racism must be relentless too, though not without rest. That's why now, during a time of both ample motivation and sufficient means, amid increasingly rampant racial injustice and division, I've decided to write this book. Thank you for joining me, for showing interest, for wanting to listen and maybe learn a little bit too. I believe that when we make the decision to truly listen to each other, we become like family, so I hope you don't mind me thinking of you as such and calling you that, too—family. It's a term of endearment, respect, maybe gratitude for what we can all accomplish together in the future, or what we can *transform* in our lives and our society. Those of you who are young readers are aptly poised to take on this work—full of promise, creativity, and, possibly, angst over the alarming state of the world. Trust me; that angst is a normal human response to what is, at times, a dreadful reality. The state of the world *is* alarming. So please, don't try to stifle that angst. It's a necessary feeling, a feeling *everybody* should have in the face of injustice, and one that we can use as fuel for our ever-important fight.

We wouldn't be like family if I didn't introduce and locate myself for you. I live and work on Treaty Six territory in what is currently widely known as Saskatchewan, Canada. I identify as biracial and Black. My

2

father is white and my mother is Black. I am middle-aged, middle-class, straight, and non-disabled. I identify with the masculine gender I was assigned at my birth, which took place in Nassau, Bahamas, in 1983. Not long after my arrival, my family relocated, and I was raised alongside my older sister Chrissy here on the Great Plains of Canada, in Saskatchewan, a province whose name is derived from a Cree word, kisiskāciwuni-sīpiy, meaning "swift-flowing river."

In my hometown of Saskatoon, the South Saskatchewan River cuts the city in half, in many ways marking a racial divide between its inhabitants. The central west side is home to many working-class Indigenous and immigrant communities, alongside some working-class and middle-class white communities, with many people living in poverty. On the east side, predominantly white and middle-class (or even richer) folks reside there. Some of these east-siders hardly dare to enter the west side, let alone think fondly of it. So you see, while they've written racial segregation out of policy, it still occurs economically and geographically, here and almost everywhere else too. My town and many others like it are perfect symbols of race relations in Canada, where people are largely separate, tense, aloof, suspicious, and unflinching in their entrenched beliefs about "the other," no matter how loud or quiet they may be about these beliefs.

But it's here in Saskatoon where I also learned that those entrenched beliefs aren't entirely static; there are people working tirelessly at all levels of our community to change them. It's here where I decided that I wanted to join these efforts. I received my master's degree in Educational Foundations from the University of Saskatchewan, working under the close supervision of renowned anti-racism scholar Dr. Verna St. Denis. In my thesis research, I focused on the anti-oppressive power of artistic practice—spoken word poetry in particular, which is one of my great passions in this life. Within my own spoken word circles, I noticed that poets from marginalized communities who performed at poetry slams in Saskatoon were helping to change and better the arts community here. I learned so much from them and from my professors of anti-racism over the years. What I share in this book has been inspired by the ideas and art of all these powerful people. I can only hope to do them justice. In writing this work, I have also drawn on my own lived experience as a biracial Black man on the Canadian prairies, and my formal training in anti-racist, anti-oppressive, and decolonizing education.

I certainly don't have all the answers, but I've got a whole lotta questions, and I hope that this book can be a way of posing them to the world. Perhaps you can help answer some of them, or answer the call to join those of us who are fighting for the liberation of Black people, Indigenous people, and people of color everywhere. There's no perfect strategy. Even our terminology is often insufficient. In this book, I do my best to use terms that are widely acceptable at the time of writing. But times and terms change, as they should. Please forgive me if, one day, the language I've used here becomes out-of-date. Just as words change, so do people. I could not have thought to write this book 10 years ago. And 10 years from now, I may have changed some of my thinking still. In fact, I hope to have done so. Anti-racism is a lifelong process of unlearning, involving continuous personal and social transformation and betterment, which should forever be among our top priorities. Just know that the spirit of this book is one of justice for all people.

There are those who will say, "Well why would you write about race anyway? Race doesn't matter." But in the words of Dr. St. Denis, "Race matters because members of society have internalized racist ideas about what skin color tells about the value and worth of a person or a group of people." It's a privilege to be *able* to believe that race doesn't matter; usually, to hold such a belief means that you have simply never been the target of true racism. As racialized people, our lived experiences are quite different. If you're somebody who truly believes that race doesn't matter, maybe reading this book will help to change your perspective. If you're already racially conscious, whatever your age, I hope you'll find some validation here. After all, anti-racism is for everyone.

I want to stress that my particular version of anti-racism is not the only version, nor may it be the *right* version at all. I simply want to share what I have come to understand in the hopes that it might be helpful to others. I fear that sometimes today, we become far too focused on *who's* right and *who's* wrong, even among social justice advocates. Holding each other accountable is important, but when we work to divide ourselves, it is only ourselves whom we conquer. Our time would be better spent in striving to understand *what* is most right and wrong with our society and getting on with the important work of uniting to *do* right; that is, fighting the racism that stays killing us regardless of our divided attention.

Today, I hesitate to watch recordings of police killings. For years I suffered flashbacks of Castile's killing, of the voice of Reynolds's daughter in the backseat. Considering that I wasn't physically there for the incident, it's hard to explain the post-traumatic stress that witnessing it on video gave me. But history has shown us that racism and colonialism cross borders with brazen ease and entitlement. Anti-Blackness stretches like a suffocating blanket from Europe to Africa, from Africa to the Caribbean, from the Caribbean to Canada and the U.S.A., and well beyond. It has been held within people's minds, carried on their slave ships, transmitted through their words and violence, all without a care in the world for precise geography. And so on a spiritual level, I *was* there for Philando Castile's killing; my Blackness, which is Castile's Blackness, which is Reynolds's Blackness, which is her daughter's Blackness, was there. The harrowing reality is that Castile could have been me, or any Black person.

At the time of writing, my own daughter is four years old. And she's a luminary. The thought of her having to learn about Castile's shooting death, let alone witness one like it, haunts me. She and my warm and sensitive 2-year-old son (himself a young sage) are among the main reasons I'm writing this book. Because I dream that their world and your world will be better, and a little less cruel and unjust than mine.

I fought hard to emerge from my state of immobility in 2016 because I realized I may have been hiding from the truth, that racism is a real and present danger still, one that restricts our movements, our knowledge, our words, our happiness, our dreams, our futures, and our breathing. Racism threatens our *lives*. Meanwhile, there are lots of things that can stifle our action in fighting this threat: our social division, our fear of dying, our collective trauma, our exhaustion, or even our numbness to it all. Whatever the cause, when we are able to muster the strength and the courage, we must come together bravely to face our future and make sure that it is bright. When we can do that, we will do as the incomparable James Baldwin encouraged. We will "cease fleeing from reality and begin to change it." *That's* revolution, family.

How might we achieve that, you ask? Well, let's talk about it.

SECTION I
the know-up

I

the gut knows whussup

you mighta never heard of it,
but i call it bsp.
it's a built-in sorta radar
that finds the enemy.
so don't be tryna sell no apps
or decoders to me
when black sensory perception
smell racism for free.

the chocolate dinosaur

Tyrannosaurus rex, brontosaurus, brachiosaurus, velociraptor, the chocolate dinosaur, stego—Wait, *what?!* That's right, I said it—the chocolate dinosaur. Doesn't fit with your encyclopedic knowledge of dinosaur species, does it?

Yeah, that's how I felt when I first heard about it too. And no, I'm not talking about some kinda delicious novelty treat neither. Nah, what I'm talking about . . . is me. *I'm* the chocolate dinosaur, and the situation in which I became that? It's probably my earliest memory of experiencing racism.

I was in first grade. My classmates and I were outside for recess, out in that cold, snowy abyss that is winter in Saskatchewan. It was my first year at that school and I hardly knew anybody there, but the truth is, I was a bit of a loner kid; I hardly *ever* knew anybody back then. Everybody called me shy, even my own family. Looking back, I'm not sure how much of my shyness was an inherent personality trait, or if much of it stemmed from my self-consciousness about being Black, and so often being the *only* Black kid outside my household. I wouldn't have thought about this connection back then though, and no one would have really helped me to. That lack of racial guidance was part of the way it was in those days. For a lot of young racialized people, that's the way it *still* is. And that's exactly what I want to undo.

Growing up in the 1980s and 1990s in the predominantly white southern Saskatchewan towns of Regina and Moose Jaw pretty much guaranteed that I wouldn't hear or take part in *any* critical conversations about race, let alone about racism, ever. Even the frequently mocked town name "Moose Jaw" is an anglicization (more like *erasure*) of a Cree term, moscâstani-sîpiy, meaning "a warm place by the river," an origin that few who live there know about. From what I could tell in my youth, the grown folks around me dealt with race and racism using the very same strategy: ignore, ignore, ignore, unless something bubbled over. See, back then, as with now, something often had to *pop* before the topic of racism ever

10

came to the surface, at which time it *might* be addressed, usually with an attempted quick fix. For something to pop in the first place, though, someone would have to complain about racism. And in order for someone to complain about racism, they'd have to be able to understand it, recognize it, *and* feel valued and empowered enough to speak out about it.

For a 6-year-old Black kid in Saskatchewan, good luck with that.

Like a lot of young Black kids, I had no deliberate guidance for my Blackness. While my folks taught me well enough not to judge anyone by their skin color or background, I had no real understanding of the concept of race or what it meant in our society, nor did I have any real terminology for race or racism. Within my household, between my mom, my sister, and me, Blackness was ever present, and therefore not questioned. However, it was also seldom spoken of. My parents instilled in us kids their strong values for compassion, justice, and equality through their actions more so than through their words. When I went out into the world, I tried to take those values with me, but I quickly developed an obscure sense of being very different from my overwhelmingly white peers, many of whom made that difference well known. Eventually, I developed my own cold shell of shyness to protect me from the cruel intentions of some of these kids. I reasoned that if I avoided getting close to them, they couldn't hurt me.

Facing racial hostility back then, I thought that my racist peers, and even my *potentially* racist peers, were the real enemy, rather than a racist society that constantly churns racism (and racists) out. The system we live in is designed this way, setting whiteness on a pedestal that is both invisible and starkly obvious at once. I didn't consciously see this pedestal, nor understand systemic racism as a kid. I simply focused on avoiding racist individuals. And since I could never quite be sure of who was or wasn't racist, I decided to just not speak to anyone I didn't already know and trust, which of course made making friends difficult.

Still, there were times when I could temporarily overcome my shyness. Role-play games helped, likely because they let me become somebody else, somebody *raceless*, whether it was a Transformer, a Ninja

Turtle, or whatever. Stepping into these roles meant I could at least try and leave my glaring visible difference behind, if only for a few minutes. It's likely no coincidence that my affinity for shedding my skin like that came about just as I started developing a low self-image, which I now know was caused by anti-Black racism. There were lots of times when I much preferred acting like someone else instead of being me. I took up theater acting in high school, and even pursued the craft well into adulthood. I wonder, was this self-escapism, self-preservation, or both?

Whatever the implications of my humble acting career, it may have all started on that snowy day in Regina. It was sunny out; I remember that, but everything was still cold—it usually is in Saskatchewan. I watched quietly as a white classmate stomped his boots hard on the ground and declared that it was a great way to keep your feet warm. I decided to copy him and try the technique myself, as did some other kids. It did help, and I *still* use that slick move to this day, so whoever you were, kid—thank you. You've kept a Caribbean brotha's toes toasty for life!

Anyway, all that foot stomping led to some white boys in my class

pretending to be dinosaurs. Besides the fact that I was a huge dinosaur nerd and likely had every dinosaur book out from the library at that time (from both the children's *and* the adult sections), the game seemed like another welcome way to stay warm out in that frozen schoolyard. Somehow, I was brave enough to try and join in the fun.

"I'm a T. rex!" I declared as four or five of us roared and stomped about.

"No!" snapped one of the other boys. "You're brown like chocolate. So you're a *chocolate* dinosaur. That means *we* have to eat *you!*" I guess the other dino-boys liked the idea; they converged on me, and I quickly succumbed to something like a pig-pile. Besides struggling to breathe under the weight of it, I gotta admit—it was pretty warm underneath all them kids (I was serious about the cold weather, family). But the truth is I had been singled out for my skin color, and stripped of my right to make my own decisions because of it. And so for all my joking, it wasn't funny. The seemingly innocent label of "the chocolate dinosaur" quickly proved right all my insecurities about being Black—that is, being different—in the first place.

*ℬ*b**sp**

I'm grown now, and educated in anti-racism; I can now articulate that what I was experiencing in first grade was the feeling of being **othered**.[1] But back then? Nah. I just felt *bothered*. And in the moment I had no idea why, although in retrospect, this BS was likely one of my first experiences with BS*P*. It's like ESP (Extra Sensory Perception), except Black; *Black* Sensory Perception, like when your gut tells you that somebody or something around you is racist, no matter how subtle, nuanced, or unprovable the racism may seem.

---

[1] **othered:** the result of being ostracized by someone or a group, because of a perceived difference (racial or otherwise) from "the norm."

I should note that the BSP acronym here is meant to be playful and is by no means exclusive. All racialized folks, not just Black folks, likely have a similar intuition for racism, as all people who experience any sort of **oppression**[2] likely have the same. It's hard not to notice a weapon when you're the target of it, no matter how concealed that weapon may be.

Black Sensory Perception may sound like a gift offered in parcel with the curse of oppression. But the problem with BSP is that like any super-power, until you've learned how to use it and harness it, it's useless and potentially even dangerous. Without knowing the many names and faces of racism, all you might be left with after a racist encounter is confusion, and the enduring feeling of having been gut-punched (definitely *not* a gift). And although racialized folks are often able to *feel* this pain, without anti-racist education, we are often unable to understand or precisely explain the source of it. No doubt that pain with an unknown source is the hardest kind of pain to treat, and the most dangerous kind to let be. It's a catch-22. I mean, how are we supposed to change the things that hurt us while we're still hurting? At any rate, healing ourselves starts with one thing: trusting that the gut knows whussup.

I mean, you ever walk past a house or a business, or even just get a look from somebody, and you *know* you better not linger?

Yeah, you know that gut feeling.

If you're Black, or from another racialized community, you've probably gotten that same sort of feeling from other sources too, like school officials, security guards, or the police. No lie, Black kids every-where are very likely to sense racism from these authority figures, sometimes because of terrible past experiences with people in these roles, and sometimes just from a serious gut feeling, maybe based on

---

[2] **oppression:** generally, the dominance of one or more social groups over others, creating advantages for the dominant group(s) and disadvantages for the group(s) experiencing oppression. Racism is one of many forms of oppression.

the way they watch you, follow you, or talk down to you like you're nothing. All of that can get your guard up, make you wanna lash out, or make you want to avoid people in these positions. That dynamic alone prevents a lot of us from speaking out about the racism we experience.

Of course, the lack of complaints about racism is partly why the leaders of organizations and institutions will often proudly declare: "There's no racism here!" In fact, people who make these types of ignorant declarations—in schools, on sports teams, in places of worship, wherever—are often the very reason why racism goes unreported, as they make it known up front that we will not be supported or believed.

There are other reasons why we sometimes don't complain about racism. I think one of the reasons I stayed silent during the Chocolate Dinosaur Fiasco, as it shall henceforth be known, was that my fellow prehistoric playmates were the first group of kids at that school who welcomed me into their recess play at all, and deep down, I wanted to make friends, in spite of my perceived shyness. Hell, these kids were being *nice* to me before this all went down. What's worse? I think they probably felt like they were *still* being nice even while (b)othering me. Talk about confusing! Racism often works this way, as racist people will conceal their (sometimes unconscious) attitudes of superiority in things like politeness, kindness, or charity, and all that can make racism very difficult to pin down, let alone confront.

It's like, what was I to complain about on that fateful winter day at school anyway? Should I have run and told the teacher that some kids had invited me to play with them? Hell, those kids were nicer to me than some of the teachers. I remember one recess in the same grade, I was standing alone, picking up gravel and letting the rocks slip gently through my fingers back onto the ground. While I might have been viewed as a loner for doing so, the truth is it felt nice. It still does. You ever tried it? You *should* sometime. I mean I was basically in peak mindfulness! Anyway, this middle-years teacher, a white man (I don't remember any racialized teachers at that school) was standing just outside one of the school doors, quite far from where I was. His class of rambunctious white eighth graders were assembling around him like a school of fish looking for food. I got the sense that he was one of the most well-liked teachers at the school, but I didn't know him from anybody.

"Hey!" I heard him shout. I looked up, and to my surprise, he was looking back at *me*. He had his hands cupped around his mouth so he could project his voice. "You, over there by the slide! If you wanna play with rocks, try using the ones in your *head*!"

I don't know what hurt more, the teacher's cruel comment, or the uproarious laughter from the horde of students around him. Yeah, with teachers like that, I'm not sure who I would've gone to with a complaint about racism, even if I'd had the ability to fully perceive or comprehend it in the first place. And besides, who could I have complained to about that teacher's grown ass? And what would have happened if I had?

No lie, when I was a kid, it was easier to just try and ignore racism, like everybody else. Besides, complaining about racism at a rate equivalent to experiencing it? That would be absolutely exhausting—ask any racialized person—and that's *before* being undermined or gaslit by those to whom we might complain in the first place.

how we know

It's easy for people to **gaslight**[3] you about your gut feelings when our society has conditioned (or programmed) us to rely heavily on Euro-Western

---

[3] **gaslighting:** this term originates from a 1938 play called *Gas Light* by Patrick Hamilton. In it, a woman tells her husband their home's gas-powered lights get dimmer each night. He tries to convince her she's hallucinating due to mental illness. In fact, the husband is dimming the lights himself and is deliberately lying to her. When somebody gaslights you, they're trying to manipulate you into thinking you're wrong or mistaken about a situation, about someone's intentions, or about your whole reality. Think: "This isn't about *race*!" Gaslighting is a well-known abusive behavior in relationships.

notions of logic, objectivity, and measurability for understanding our world. These ways of knowing dominate education systems in North America, often at the expense of more emotional and intuitive ones. That means we get the impression from very early on that Euro-Western ways of knowing are the only ones to be truly trusted. Obviously, it helps racist institutions to position intuition as not real and therefore not worthy of study, and to position emotion as irrelevant or unimportant; both intuition and emotion help you *understand* when you're being targeted because of your race—and those institutions don't want you to understand that. Arts classes are often the spaces where you're most encouraged to think holistically and explore your intuition in schools. But these are always first on the chopping block as governments increasingly claw back public education budgets.

School districts often prioritize math and science offerings in high schools, usually at the expense of electives like art, music, or creative writing. And as for mental health, emotional learning, and spiritual education? They're often nonexistent in our public education systems. What a shame. When we're taught *out* of using our intuition, we may learn to misread it, mistrust it, or lose it altogether, and that makes it easy for us to even gaslight ourselves when it comes to racism, giving people all kinds of free passes to diminish and dismiss our humanity. Sadly, emotional and intuitive ways of knowing don't have to be at odds with fields like math and science. I once had a professor who told me he hated math until one of his teachers taught it to him as a philosophy rather than as a set of strict rules. Others have described math as an art form because of the patterns within it. These illuminating ideas can help shift perspectives about math completely. Yet they rarely reach students in our Euro-Western public education systems, where there seems to be little room for holistic approaches to teaching and learning.

But here in North America and beyond, before European settlers arrived, Indigenous cultures lived from time immemorial, and for many, intuition was not only real, it was an important part of their lives and an integral tool for their decision-making. For many Indigenous people, it still is. Yet Indigenous people's advocacy for recognition of their distinct ways of knowing is often ignored by a society that is focused on securing only the measurable scientific evidence for every new idea. Even Indigenous scientific knowledge is often dismissed until it is routinely (re)discovered by Western scientists.

Like a lot of us who've been oh so colonized, I struggle sometimes to trust my own gut instincts, even when they're slapping me across the face. In our society, though, we're not meant to trust our intuition—far from it. We men especially are conditioned to repress our feelings, and everyone is discouraged from trusting the supposed hocus-pocus of intuitive thinking and feeling, because by Euro-Western scientific standards, if it's not measurable, observable, or provable, it ain't even worth the time. As you can see, this suppression works conveniently in favor of colonialism. If people experience racism and perceive it on an intuitive level but can't "prove it" when we're so often called upon to do so, that makes our complaints very easy to dismiss entirely.

Many Black people are connected to or part of the Indigenous cultures in which intuition plays a central part. It took me a minute to come to terms with that notion for myself—that my own Black identity could be conceived of as Indigenous. See, I had built up my entire conception of Blackness around a version of it that was distinctly North American, if a little bit Caribbean, but one that was completely separate from an African **diasporic**[4] identity, which I now see as critical to who I am and to Blackness in general. My earlier understanding of Blackness had been based only on the Blackness that I knew and had seen firsthand or in popular media—a Blackness that, while rich and distinct in its own right, had been colonized, contorted, and held hostage from its true roots.

---

[4] **diaspora:** any group that has been dispersed outside of its traditional homeland, especially involuntarily, as with African peoples during the transatlantic slave trade.

Through my mother's lineage, I am Bahamian. But I am African, too. That is, my mother's ancestors, *my* ancestors, were Indigenous to West Africa. The fact that they were forcibly removed from Africa and forcibly relocated to this side of the Atlantic Ocean does not make me any less African, nor any less Indigenous. These terms are identifiers of people as much as place. Of course, forgetting our ties to Africa and the brutal ways in which they were severed is again advantageous to **white supremacy**, and therefore encouraged in our society. As our own Indigeneity is colonized, erased, we may even feel inclined to participate in anti-Indigenous racism and colonialism within North America, with no hint of irony or hypocrisy; that is, without understanding that racism as internalized self-loathing. Trust that our connections to Africa are not obscure, only *obscured*, and are by no means ancient history.

white supremacy

All ways in which traditionally white ways of knowing and doing reign supreme and are maintained as supreme in our society. Examples range from what we think of as "flesh color" when it comes to crayons or bandages, to the ways institutions favor and uphold whiteness, right down to the very worst of hate crimes and cross-burnings.

Around fifth or sixth grade, I was tasked with a family tree assignment at school. We were asked to interview our parents and trace back our family history as far as we could. I was excited about the project, and especially about researching my mother's (Black) side of the family. Despite having been born in the predominantly Black nation of The Bahamas, I was raised almost entirely in Canada. Therefore, I was very familiar with my white Canadian relatives, and even some of the family history surrounding them. Even though I felt very welcome and comfortable around my extended family in The Bahamas whenever we visited, because of my long absences, I sometimes felt like I didn't truly know them all that well, let alone who their (and my) forebears were.

For my school assignment, I first sat down with my father, who is white, to interview him about his ancestors. My dad has always had a keen interest in genealogy, and some of his family members had done research over the years to compile the Dill family history. I had a big tan piece of construction paper and began to draw the branches of my dad's side of the family tree. I nearly ran out of room for it all, as generations upon generations of well-documented names sprang forth.

Then I sat down to interview my mother, and something happened.

We got stuck. We'd gone through the members her immediate family, most of whom I knew, and all of whom had European-sounding family names. But by the time we'd reached but one of her grandfathers, my great-grandfather, suddenly, there was nothing more to report. Damn, my tree was gonna be lopsided. Over-full on one side, and all sparse on the other—like a pruning job gone bad. My mom explained that she simply didn't know any more about her lineage, and that there was no genealogy book to go looking in either. Eventually I made the connection to slavery. With its violent uprooting of people and destruction of families, its murder of resistors, and its complete lack of documentation around the births, deaths, and purchases of human beings, this long-normalized institution had effectively erased my Black family history. And it had sealed the deal by forcing my family to take on all-new British last names with which to hide our *true* names, and make us forget them. To make us forget our ties to Africa. To make us forget ourselves.

I didn't go around advertising to folks that the reason I had a lopsided tree was because of slavery. I just remember looking at that big gap in that tree, looking at all that *emptiness* there on the upper righthand side, and feeling it too. How was I supposed to know what my roots were if I couldn't even find my branches?

With a longing like that—an emptiness in your identity—you can try and pretend that it's not there. You can even try and mask it or fill it with things that lean your identity more into whiteness; perfect English, straighter hair, or "dressier" clothes. But the ghosts of your true history may never go away. For me, although I didn't know their names or faces, I could always feel them, hanging from my family tree.

Having some validation or some guidance for my intuition in my youth would have been helpful, but today I don't need a teacher or anyone else to tell me that my intuition is real, valid, and should be trusted. This I know. I've learned to validate my own intuition, including my gut instincts. Whether it's interpreting a dream, or understanding that I'm being slighted or threatened based on my race, or even sensing those ghosts from my family tree, I have stopped second-guessing myself. That urge to always doubt ourselves is rooted in white supremacy.

There's a whole lot more to this intuition thing—I'ma come back to it. For now, just go on and trust yourself as you explore this particular way of knowing. And trust that the bad feelings you get from being insulted, downtrodden, belittled, or shamed are real, are valid, and are most likely the result of some serious cruelty. For Black people, Indigenous people, and people of color, if you attribute your experience of this cruelty to racism, trust that racism and its perpetrators are to blame. And don't let nobody tell you different. Not even the police, as they've been known to do.

in *the* trouble with the law

I've always felt nervous around police.

It's hard not to. In light of today's widespread sharing of traumatizing videos of police brutality against us, Black people everywhere have been conditioned to associate police with the imminent threat of death. But when I was a teenager in Moose Jaw in the late '90s and early 2000s, fresh off o' gettin' my license, there was no YouTube, no Facebook, no Twitter on which to share and view videos of police brutality. Hell, the closest thing we had was the nightly news, and wasn't nobody watchin' that (they hardly ever covered stories of police brutality anyways). We heard the odd thing about police misconduct, but we were far from bombarded with it. For example, I remember hearing *something* about the Los Angeles Riots, but all I really understood was that the city was on fire, and that it was caus-ing traffic issues for a bunch of white people. Nobody told me until much later that the so-called riots—more accurately called an upris-ing—were a response to the police killing and beating Black people with no repercussions. Back then, the only opinions I had about the police were based on my own encounters with them. And my very first personal encounter actually wasn't too bad.

Would you believe me if I told you that my mom called the cops on my ass when I was eight years old? I know what you're thinkin'—I musta been *seriously* bad to deserve that. To this day, I plead innocent! We were in The Bahamas, chillin' in the food court with all my aunts and uncles and cousins. My mom was trying to order some chicken, but I wasn't havin' it. And yes, I mean that as a double entendre; I wasn't havin' any of her trying to tell me what to eat for lunch and I most *definitely* wasn't havin' no chicken. Thing is, I'd seen a photo of a juicy-ass cheeseburger on the menu at another spot in the food court. I *needed* that cheeseburger. I knew just what to do, and immediately began flexing the only super-power I had over my mom: sulking.

Unfortunately, my mom wasn't havin' any of my sulking that day either.

"Khodi, you see those policemen there?" I looked down the corridor and saw a group of five or so Black Bahamian cops walkin' the mall. The cops in Nassau, Bahamas, were seemingly always Black men, and they always rolled just like that, walkin' the beat like a squad, batons danglin' off their belts at the ready. I have to admit, I normally thought they had a super cool vibe, but not if the vibe was finna be turned on *me*. "You better smarten up," my mom told me, "or I'm telling the police you're being bad."

For most kids, the threat woulda been enough. But most kids weren't Khodi. Nah. I straight up sulked my way into *actually* gettin' the cops called on me. Damn, criminalization starts early! As my mom summoned a young cop over, it didn't take long for my tears to spring out like a fountain. At eight years old, my only knowledge of police was that they would throw you in jail if you were bad. Since I was being bad, in my mind the only logical outcome of the encounter was that I was going to jail—possibly forever.

"What's the matter, son?" the police officer asked me. I could hardly get the words out through my wailing.

"She won't buy me a cheeseburger!" I cried, pointing at my mom in a desperate attempt to have *her* arrested instead of me.

"*What*?" replied the cop, incredulous. He turned to my mom. "Why you won't buy the kid a cheeseburger?"

If you're surprised right now, imagine my eight-year-old, tear-stained face. My eyes probably got shiftier than an ass in a hard seat trying to figure out what the hell had just happened. I don't remember if I ever did get the burger (I probably did). But I also got much more than that. I got

a. the relief that I would not be going to jail for the rest of my life, and

b. the short-lived belief that police could be kind and gentle souls who would always have my back.

I held onto this belief that cops were dope well into my early adolescence, not because of anything that Canadian cops did, but all because of what them cool, beat-walkin' Black cops did back in The Bahamas. Back home. I know they weren't perfect either, but it's amazing how much one experience in your youth can influence your whole perception. Eventually, my perception would change, and my later encounters with police in the U.S.A. and Canada would sway the tide entirely.

"What's your name?! When's the last time you were arrested?" the cop yelled at me as soon I stopped my car. This was about a decade after the food court incident, on a quiet night in Regina, Saskatchewan. The cops had set up a routine stop-and-check along a busy street in town, likely to check drivers for signs of intoxication. But those questions caught me off guard. I mean, I didn't know this cop from anywhere.

"Uhh . . . never," I answered, confused.

"*Never?!* We'll see about that," she said as she went to run my file. I don't know why I was worried. It was true; I never had been formally arrested or charged with anything. "Move along!" was all she said as she returned and gave me back my license. *Nice meeting you too*, I thought. But damn, did that encounter bother me. I knew sure as hell that she wasn't askin' *everybody* that question. She'd given me an immediate presumption of guilt, not the presumption of innocence to which every North American person is supposedly entitled. The same energy came at me a few years later from a U.S. border guard—basically a cop too. Border guards also wear a badge, carry a weapon, and work to uphold **carceral**[5] systems.

"When's the last time you did drugs?" this imposing guard asked me. I suddenly got that déjà vu type feeling.

"Never."

"*Never*?" I guess the U.S. border patrol agency and the Regina police used the same training manual for dealing with Black people. Nothing makes you feel more dehumanized or taken down a peg than **prejudice**,[6] especially when the person pre-judging you has a gun on them.

---

[5] **carceral:** relating to jails and other institutions of human confinement and/or detention (like jails, prisons, and immigration detention centers). The word "carceral" is a good replacement for "justice" in "justice system," since within that system, justice is often hard to come by for racialized people.

---

[6] **prejudice:** the premature passing of judgment, without any real evidence, often based on preconceptions and/or misconceptions about others or the social groups to which they belong.

By today's standards, the harsh greetings these officers gave me might be thought of as microaggressions, a term we'll look at more closely later. While their terse words may seem insignificant to some, for me they were very impactful, and not in a good way. I was only just beginning to understand my own Blackness, let alone the implications of being Black in a racist society. I was hardly able to understand these chilling encounters as evidence of racism, only as . . . well, chilling. Could I have proven it was racism at play? No. Did I *know* it was? Yes, I did. You feel me?

Things all came to a head when, as a young university student, I was just chillin', catching up with some non-Black friends at a pizza place in Moose Jaw. You wanna talk about being caught off guard? I probably still had my mouth around the straw in my root beer when two policemen approached our table in the middle of the busy restaurant.

"Excuse me," one began. "Can we see some ID?"

"What?" I said, confused as all hell. Was he lookin' at *me*? Was he *talkin'* to me? What was happening? I immediately started going back through my recent memory to make sure I hadn't committed any high-profile crimes. Nope, couldn't think of any!

"Why?" I demanded, indignantly. I sensed people starting to stare. Moose Jaw was a small-ass town, and since I was one of very few Black people there, and a prolific athlete, a lot of people knew who I was. I felt . . . compromised.

"We can't disclose the reason," the officer said in a low voice.

"Well I'm just having some food with my friends," I replied defensively.

"Okay, would you just show us your ID so we can get out of here?" he said through his teeth. His second, the cop standing a little behind him, was staring at me, silent and unflinching. What the hell was I gonna do? I stood up and took out my wallet, which I thankfully had on me, and gave them my drivers' license (remember, I was drinking a *root* beer). The leading officer didn't look at my ID for but two seconds before he gave it back to me and left, with his silent partner following behind.

It was dead quiet in the whole spot, and it seemed like every person at every table was staring at me. I'm sure I recognized some of the faces too, but I willed myself not to, and tried to avoid eye contact as I slinked back down into my seat. I had never been so humiliated or felt so publicly slighted in my life. I lost my whole appetite immediately.

I learned later that the cops who had hassled me that night had been looking for another Black guy they already knew, and it wasn't like there was a whole lot of us in Moose Jaw anyways; they should *easily* have been able to tell us apart. But instead, the cops used a longstanding police mechanism for racial profiling—carding. The practice is not much different than it was in the era of slavery, when authorities would often demand to see the "free papers" or other documentation of any Black person who was out in public unescorted. Similarly, an unlawful colonial pass system was used to control the movements of Indigenous peoples in Canada. The government gave "Indian agents" the power to grant (or deny) permission for people to leave First Nations reserve communities for any reason. Authorities could demand to see people's permission forms and would often arrest anyone unable to produce one. Modern carding only differs in that almost everyone has ID now, but police still routinely demand identification without cause from mostly Black and Indigenous folks—racism with the illusion of equality.

Few white people will understand the impact of carding, having little to no experience with it. Personally, even being asked to show my Costco membership card makes me stiffen up, as I wrestle with flashbacks of the indignity and the nagging feeling shared by a lot of Black and Indigenous folks in North America that I don't belong in the spaces I'm expected to exist in.

These are just a few of my negative experiences with the police; there are many more. I know mine may pale in comparison to the experiences of many other racialized people, a lot of whom didn't live to tell about theirs. But my experiences were dehumanizing and demoralizing still. Following each experience, all I was left with, as usual, was a complicated feeling, that BSP type feeling, of painfully futile indignation. I had no outlet for this feeling, and no closure for it either. It's the type of forced repression that will eat you alive from the inside. But outlet or no outlet, those who experience racism don't need anybody to tell us we're experiencing it. Like I said, we *feel* it; we *know* it. The welling of our angry tears tells us, our quickening heartbeats tell us, the pits in our stomachs tell us, our breathlessness tells us, the stares of those who witness tell us, and we know. We just know.

We must trust these gut instincts and not ignore them, in spite of the routine dismissiveness of others. So too, we must express these feelings and *act* on them whenever possible, because when feeling meets action, that's when change becomes possible.

resist.

Something I didn't quite understand when I was younger is that for racialized folks, there's really no such thing as ignoring racism, that deep down, doing so is impossible. There's only denial, which, just like in the stages of grief, does not change the underlying issue, nor curb its ongoing effects on one's self-esteem, mental health, daily life, or future outlook. Nah, I *tried* to ignore racism because that's what felt easiest to me. But by believing I was ignoring racism, I was actually stewing in it. Each new experience with racism turned up the temperature in the stew all around me, and in my own body. Eventually, I got to the point of feeling like my blood was boiling. Some days, I still feel that way.

Like my blood is on a constant simmer.

Our society has a way of discouraging expressions of anger, especially among Black people, almost as if the emotion itself is unhealthy. But having emotions is never unhealthy; keeping them in is. Besides, the type of anger I'm referring to is the healthiest type of all, and the most righteous. It's the type of anger that will speak back to injustice and help break down systems that cause injustice in the first place. Those who try to stifle our anger are only trying to maintain *in*justice.

27

Hard as they may try, righteous anger always finds a way, just as I believe that one day, true justice will find a way too. Whenever our anger breaks silence, we truly threaten the oppression that constantly threatens us.

For Black folks, one of the ways righteous anger can come out is through art and music. You can hear it in Ms. Lauryn Hill's "Black Rage." You can feel it in N.W.A.'s "Fuck tha Police." Sometimes, racism makes you feel like you could just lose it and unleash, truly. But like with any problem, racism's crushing blows are tempered somewhat through understanding how racism happens and being able to articulate that. Once you can know, name, and understand a problem, you can begin laying plans to try and overcome it. Perhaps that's what anti-racist music and art are all about—naming and overcoming racism, in *style*.

One way to help decipher racism is to apply a little enlightened retrospect to our own memories. This strategy stems from the ideas and research of feminist scholar Dr. Frigga Haug, who called it memory-work.

WERE THERE TIMES WHERE YOU FELT TARGETED, OTHERED, EXCLUDED, OR OTHERWISE PUNISHED BECAUSE OF YOUR RACE?

YOUR GENDER? YOUR SOCIAL CLASS? YOUR SEXUAL IDENTITY? YOUR ABILITY? YOUR AGE EVEN?

The idea is to apply the concepts you've learned about oppression to your own memories and see if doing so changes anything. So, go ahead and think back on your life and your experiences.

It may help to write these experiences down, even in third person if you'd like, to help you see them from a fresher perspective. Thinking about your memory, what sort of power dynamics were at play? That is, who held more or less power in the situation? And where did that power come from? Did you experience a loss of agency, voice, or value in that moment? Though these dynamics can often be invisible in the heat of the moment, hindsight combined with critical thinking may illuminate them brilliantly.

Whatever the details of your specific memory, trust that you were right to feel what you felt, even if somebody tried to make you deny it. As I alluded to about BSP, the sensory perception of people who experience oppression is definitely *extra*. Even if you were mistaken, even if your feeling of being othered, bothered, demeaned, or discarded was all because of some terrible misunderstanding, what others need to realize is that these "misunderstandings" hit differently for folks who experience oppression. They feel like part of a repetitive pattern; a design even, since we're so accustomed to being targeted. Let it be known—that whole dynamic itself is one of many palpable disadvantages that oppression creates for us.

We know our experiences, even if we may struggle at times to understand them. But knowing without understanding is not paradoxical. Trust me, family; I teach English Language Arts, and one thing I tell my students when we're looking at the much-dreaded grammar lessons is: "You *know* this stuff already. If you can speak a sentence, you know your grammar. But I'ma help you *understand* it. I'ma help you know and name all the parts and pieces." Because of our lived experience, even in the absence of anti-racist education, most people who suffer racism are often completely competent in realizing it exists and that it's everywhere. It is those who are neither oppressed nor educated in anti-racism who tend to be *in*competent in this area and who, ironically, are often in charge of making important decisions affecting racialized and other marginalized communities.

Thankfully, it doesn't have to stay this way. Anti-racist, anti-oppressive education is a field of knowledge that anyone can learn from, whether they're from an oppressed group, an oppressor group, or any combination of the two. Anyone who takes part in this kind of learning will become not only competent in *recognizing* racism, but also in being able to analyze and articulate how it functions. So, like I told my young grammarians, I'ma help you understand it—in the next chapter of this book.

There, I hope we can discover the true roots of our angst, our anger, our sadness, our whatever. For Black people, Indigenous people, and people of color, discovering the reasons for the negative feelings we have about our experiences is crucial. Lest they worsen. Lest they lead to self-loathing, mental health problems like depression, anxiety, addictions, and more. To truly work against these unfavorable outcomes, we've gotta dive into some real-deal anti-racism theory. We've gotta understand what we're up against before we can begin the important work of resistance. And once we do understand, that's when we can begin to quench the thirst of our frustrations with the righteousness of justice.

For myself, learning from my esteemed past professors about how racism really works helped me look back on my whole life with new eyes. In changing my perspective on my own history and identity, my identity and my history actually changed. My *life* changed. I became charged up with a fiery enthusiasm for social justice, began shouting from the rooftops about the need for resistance. And once I started to share my new understandings of racism and how to fight it, I noticed something: some of those people with whom I shared began to change also.

Could this be a way to make the whole world change?

It's dope, you know, the way social consciousness can spread like wildfire. I hope it ignites something for you too. Maybe together, we can burn some shit down.

2

Black ain't a color; it's a concept

with my english perfected
and my shirt buttoned up,
with my afro trimmed down
and a step that don't strut,
when i be feelin' low
in some high-waisted slacks,
they gushin',
"we don't even think of you as Black."

whiteboy?

I was asleep in my bedroom when my dad came and woke me up one morning. I was living at home, but 20 years old—too old for it to be normal that he'd wake me. Instantly, I knew something was wrong. "Khodi," he whispered. "It's your grandmother back home. I'm sorry, but . . . she passed away last night." It was a hell of a way to wake up. There was no real transition for me; I went from sleeping soundly to bawling my eyes out.

I regret to say that I didn't well know my grandma Lottie, of Nassau, Bahamas.

In Canada, I rocked my Bahamian roots, adorning my teenage bedroom with Bahamas flags and a poster featuring a white sandy beach, pristine aquamarine waters, and swimsuit-clad models boasting the country's slogan, "It's better in The Bahamas." That shit is hard to *argue* with, family. But my relationship with my relatives there—all warm and incredible people—has regrettably never been super tight-knit. Like I said, I rarely had the opportunity to visit growing up; in fact, my run-in with the Bahamian beat cops might have marked my last trip out there until my twenties. Pre-social media, and too caught up in my own shenanigans to pick up a phone, I just wasn't keeping up with everybody's lives, including my grandmother's. When her death came upon us all too soon, I was walloped with a self-inflicted guilt trip, and a hole opened up inside me that I knew I'd never quite be able to fill. My grandma was gone.

Returning home for her funeral became something of a pilgrimage for me, a chance to truly reconnect with my family and my roots. I knew I owed Grandma Lottie that at least. Stepping off the plane back home in Nassau is always a trip. As soon as you step outside, that air feels more like steam as it fills your lungs. Warm, muggy, and heavy. It forces you to slow down, chill, and understand . . . you're in The *Bahamas* now. Reuniting with family there has always been an animated and vivacious affair, no matter how bittersweet. I'll never forget my mother's reunion with some of her dear sisters on that somber trip. There was screaming and smiles and laughter and the usual jumping up and down, and then swiftly, silence, a tight group hug, and tears as the weighty truth set in; they were together again, but motherless.

Eventually, we found ways to settle into the usual upbeat rhythm of our visits. There was soca and reggae music and uninhibited dancing. My mom and her siblings laughed and busied themselves cooking our favorite dishes: yellow grits, curry chicken, peas and rice, dumpling soup, johnnycake, fried plantain—you name it. The little ones played hopscotch and jump-rope outside in the hot sun while me and some of my older cousins would shoot hoops—where there was no basketball net, a milkcrate and some plywood nailed up on a light post would do. Then to beat the heat, we'd all hit up the neighbor's house like a squad to buy "some cup," frozen juice served in disposable plastic cups, which a lot of folks sold straight out of their living room windows. In *that* heat, their business was booming.

When my grandmother's funeral came, it came with a bang. Coming from the solemn Lutheran funeral services I'd witnessed in Canada, I was in for a shock at this Bahamian Pentecostal one. The Black pastor at the church spoke with the zeal of MLK *himself* as he encouraged us all to "be a *worker*!" in the church, like Lottie had been. As the minister sang along emphatically with the powerful voices of the swaying all-Black choir, he literally bounded all over the stage, veins popping out of his temples and sweat covering his entire head. People in the congregation called out constantly, stood up, raised their hands, wailed with grief, and some even moved to the aisles to dance and let loose as they caught the holy ghost. Later, at the burial, one mourner ran toward my grandmother's grave and attempted to jump inside; two suited funeral home employees guarded the grave and calmly restrained the person, as if nothing about the incident was out of the ordinary.

The emotions on display were shocking to me, but not unreal; Lottie Almace was a phenomenal human being, after all. More shocking per-haps, in retrospect, is the degree of emotional repression I'd become so accustomed to at many of the funerals I'd seen in Canada. Until then, I don't think I'd understood the pressure we feel here to sit quietly and to sit still when someone we love has died. The emotions of my family and my community in The Bahamas were some of the realest and most cathartic and in that place, the most *normalized* that I'd ever seen or felt. And those moments with my Black family in that Black neighborhood in that Black city on that Black island in that Black country had me feeling more deeply connected to my roots than ever; feeling *Blacker* than ever, and freer than ever too. More whole personally, in spite of the great loss at hand. At my grandmother's funeral, I finally got to *know* her and her community, which were both a part of who I was and who I am. It was as if I'd discovered an element of myself that had never properly had a chance to breathe before that moment.

Then a day or two after the service, I was in a Bahamian convenience store, looking for a Coke. "Look at this whiteboy," a little voice said. I glanced over and noticed that it was a little Black Bahamian girl who'd said it; when I realized she was looking in my direction, I had to do a double take. *Where?* I wondered. *Where's a white boy?* Only thing was . . . she wasn't talkin' *to* me. She was talkin' *about* me! The young girl and her friend were both staring straight at me and snickering to boot. The girl who'd spoken couldn't have been but five years old; her dark skin contrasted starkly against the oversized white men's undershirt she wore as a dress. I smiled, maybe even let out an amused "hmm," but the truth is she had taken *all* my words away. I finished getting my Coke and left the store, but you know what? That moment never left me. She had really shook my grown ass. For real. It wasn't that I felt like the target of racism—far from it. I just felt confused as hell.

The thing is, in spite of my lighter skin tone, back in the predominantly white town of Moose Jaw I had grown accustomed to being "the Black guy." But this little girl in The Bahamas saw me as, relatively speaking, snow white. Despite feeling a little slighted, I had to love that girl's confidence, knockin' a 20-something down a peg like it was old hat. So why was I so shook? Well, I think it was the uncertainty that the moment left me with.

Here I'd been feeling more Black than ever, and then *BAM*! Whiteboy city.

I musta ruminated on that incident for weeks, family. Honestly, I *still* come back to it sometimes. I mean, how could a person go from being Black in one place to white in another, without problematic face paint? Lemme tell you; it took me a while to figure out. Back then I didn't have the language or the background information to understand the race dynamics at play, to understand how I was too Black for Canada and too white for The Bahamas. But after a few socially conscious, brave, and intelligent educators helped me learn about anti-racism and the social construction of race, I think I got it.

My education in anti-racism didn't cure racism for me, but it definitely cured my confusion about racism and about race itself; it helped untangle my tangled-up mind, helped redirect my misdirected anger and my angst. See, BSP works best with AOE, anti-oppressive education. That's the real one-two punch, the perfect combination.

race-making

They say black is not a color but rather the absence of light. In that sense, black is not just *not* a color, but rather, it's no physical thing at all. What it is instead is a concept, an idea. The same goes for what we think of culturally as Blackness, and for race in general (so too for gender, class, sexuality, and ability). See, what early European scientists like Johann Friedrich Blumenbach and Carl Linnaeus attempted to do in creating race-based categories of human beings has since been categorically debunked. That's worth some celebration.

Blumenbach divided humans into five races based on skin color and described white people as the most beautiful of all—go figure. Linnaeus's taxonomy of race in his 1735 work *Systema Naturae* created a very clear hierarchy of race, at the top of which were again, you guessed it, white people. And as Ibram X. Kendi explained in *How To Be an Antiracist*, "The Linnaeus taxonomy became the blueprint that nearly every enlightened race maker followed and that race makers still follow today." These hierarchies were used to help justify everything from enslavement to **colonization** to **eugenics**.

colonization

This occurs when a new group of people enter an already inhabited geographical area and work to take control of that area and of its Indigenous inhabitants, establishing a new ruling "colony" (e.g., Europeans in North America). Colonization is an enduring process, not an event, and has historically involved the brutal suppression and oppression of Indigenous peoples, voices, and rights in various ongoing ways.

eugenics

Referring primarily to state-sanctioned policies and/or practices of sterilizing or otherwise preventing reproduction among people deemed by those in power to possess undesirable characteristics (historically including but not limited to: Indigenous and other racialized groups, people with physical and mental disabilities, and those whose gender or sexuality does not adhere to established conventions). Eugenics is far from ancient history; disturbingly, the forced and coerced sterilization of Indigenous women has been documented in Canada as recently as the 2010s.

Personally, I like Kendi's term: race maker. You see, in reality there is more genetic diversity within single racial groups than across racial groups. So, since race categories do not exist biologically, they must be made and manufactured, even imposed at times. In anti-racism theory, we refer to this sort of race-making as social construction. It can be a tough concept to grasp, especially when race, which we often think of as visible at the very least, can seem so physical in nature.

But think about it—is race a physical trait? Is it just skin color? Well, some may be surprised to learn that some groups whom we think of as white today were not always considered as such. Several lighter-skinned ethnic groups from Irish to Ukrainian to Italian and beyond have at some time or another and in some place or another been excluded from the umbrella of racial whiteness and its privileges, often facing harsh persecution as a result. When it comes to those of darker complexion, I can tell you that my Cambodian friend Rotha and I match up pretty close there, despite being racialized differently. Back in high school, we used to always compare skin tones—especially in the summer when the tans would set in. For some reason it was always a point of pride for *any* of my friends, even some of my white friends after they got back from a tropical vacation, to say, "I'm Blacker than you, man!" While this was all meant in good fun, it most definitely contributed to how I was **racialized**,[7] along with many other things that went much further than skin color.

I mean, when I was a teenager, complete strangers would just come up to me and ask if I could *break-dance*—I couldn't! And after admitting that to these inquirers, I would actually feel less Black than before, and like I had let them down somehow. I guess you could say that when I was a kid, my Blackness always seemed a little precarious against the backdrop of other people's expectations and interpretations of it. White people have told me more than once that I wasn't Black at

---

[7] **racialization:** the social construction and negotiation of racial identity. While we may contribute to the making of our own racial identities, society and its oppression contribute to racialization too, whether we agree with their contributions or not. Racial identity is not fixed, but dynamic, and can change depending on a variety of factors.

all, but rather mulatto. When I first heard that term, I had to look it up in the dictionary, and my discovery was less than esteem-building. I learned that the word *mulatto* described a person with one Black parent and one white parent, and that it was derived from the Spanish word for a young mule, due to the animal being the product of cross-breeding between a horse and a donkey. Talk about adding insult to injury. *Damn.* If anyone out there is still using this term, please stop it—it is literally dehumanizing.

I had always known I was biracial, but everywhere I went in my mainly white hometown, I was Black. The **individualized racism** (see page 43) I experienced assured me of as much. When a second-grade classmate told me God musta burnt me when he made me, I was Black. When a fourth-grade classmate called me a nigger, I was Black. When a stranger said to my white father, in front of me, that my dad must've adopted me, I was Black. And when the police, security guards, and border guards from Moose Jaw to North Dakota followed me around or hassled me for no good reason, hell-bent on ruining my day, my ass was most definitely Black. If I suffered all this racism in light of my Blackness, in a society that would never see me as white, couldn't I at least call myself Black? Though I never consciously thought about it, it was a question that hung over me like a raincloud, eating away at me quietly. I didn't have the racial literacy to really articulate such a question, let alone pose it to myself. All I had were feelings of ugliness, inferiority, and *uncertainty* about which racial group I fit into, if any.

race-dividing

This sort of racial tightrope walking is common to people of biracial or multiracial identities, even to anybody who walks in more than one cultural community. And not knowing which racial side you're going to fall into at any given moment, if you do end up falling, is most certainly a trip. But I do have to temper my complaint. I know full well that my relatively lighter skin tone has afforded me privileges and platforms not always afforded to those with darker skin, and it has also afforded me favor among white people by comparison, whether I recognized it at the time or not. The phenomenon of shadism—or colorism—might have been a part of why my white friends would sometimes tell me, "We don't even think of you as Black," and expect me to be grateful. Still, experiencing anti-Black racism and then being told that I'm not Black at *all* amounts to some next-level gaslighting, I'll tell you.

My friends' message, affording me "honorary" white status, was meant to be benevolent, complimentary even—but was it really? If I had to let go of my Blackness in order to be accepted among my white peers, what did that say about my Blackness, or about Blackness in general? About me? After all, my Blackness is a part of me. This is exactly how **internalized racism** (see page 43) starts to germinate within a young Black mind. And in our society, that's almost inevitable.

This whole social construction thing is pretty complex, but I hope that my reflections here have helped to show that race is far from merely skin deep. Nor is it bound up solely in a person's physical appearance, language, culture, nationality, community, or religion, though some of these can be connected to racialization. Importantly, while race *is* socially constructed, it is still very real, as are its implications. Race is both tied to and constructed in part by social hierarchies. And although the modern-day hierarchies are often unspoken, they are still very well known and enforced, and they're not much different from the ones found in those early pseudo-scientific theories I mentioned.

Admit it; you can see them, can't you? Those racial hierarchies? You wouldn't be racist to admit it. In fact, it's important that you do. To beat racism, we need first to acknowledge all of the ways our society, which is largely controlled by white people, upholds white superiority. We need to see and understand that it was designed to be this way in order for white folks to maintain favor, maintain advantage, and maintain power over others—meaning that in relative terms, it was designed for racial-ized folks to experience disfavor, disadvantage, and disempowerment. Of course, there are all sorts of exceptions to this social dynamic, but the fact that it *usually* happens this way is key to observing and understanding racial inequity.

When identifiable racial groups are disproportionately disadvantaged on a social level, that's what we call systemic racism. And seeing this **systemic racism** in action and admitting its existence is the foundation of anti-racism work. It can be hard for some people to come to terms with because we have become so conditioned to understand racism as only individualized acts of meanness based on racial prejudice. And while this sort of racism does hurt people, systemic racism hurts the lives and well-being of entire racial groups in ongoing ways, even if it doesn't always manifest visibly as hate or hate-fueled.

Hierarchies are all about power. And power, like race, is largely socially constructed. While physical power is generally easy to observe with your own eyes, social power requires a little bit more flex to read. It's doable, though. Think about it—in our society, which racial group holds the most wealth? The highest-paying jobs? The most CEO positions? The most seats in government and in other high-level decision-making sectors? If you guessed white people, you'd be right. This inequity might seem easy to explain away through the fact that white people make up the majority of the North American population. But white people are still disproportionately overrepresented in these positions. Trust that racism doesn't care about group population ratios—only established racial hierarchies. Just look at South Africa.

During the several decades of **South African apartheid** (see page 44), the white people who colonized that country and designed its laws held the most wealth, the best jobs, the most CEO positions, and at times *all* government seats.

For much of apartheid rule, Black South Africans (a population once subjected to slavery there), weren't allowed to vote for their own

individualized racism

Acts of cruelty or meanness targeting individuals or small groups, based on negative attitudes about racial groups held by the perpetrators. Individualized racism is often highly visible or emotionally charged and can look like racial slurs, stereotypes, hate speech, or hate crimes, to name a few examples. Social power is a key element of individualized racism, which can be understood as both the result of systemic racism as well as a contributor to it.

internalized racism

This type of racism happens when you view yourself or your own racial group, consciously or unconsciously, as inferior to those in a more dominant racial group. This perceived inferiority often stems from past experiences with individualized and/or systemic racism, such as a culmination of microaggressions, exclusion, or other discriminatory and even traumatic events related to your racial identity.

systemic racism

Also called structural, systematic, or institutional racism, this type of racism is so normalized that it's often invisible, especially to those who are not its targets. It refers to the ways in which white superiority is embedded into our society's laws, regulations, social norms, and institutions, generally resulting in disadvantages for Black people, Indigenous people, and people of color, and resulting in relative privileges for white people.

43

South African apartheid

The term *apartheid* comes from the Dutch-derived South African language Afrikaans, and means "apartness." This unjust system of apartness was brought about initially by the all-white National Party, who took power in South Africa in 1948 and began to enforce segregation laws that endured until the early 1990s.

government, making it virtually impossible for them to transform their unjust society. But there was one major difference between South African apartheid society and contemporary North American society. In South Africa, white people were the minority by *far*, rarely reaching above 20 percent of the total population. Yet they ruled the country. It's worth noting too that Black South African opponents of apartheid rule were often labeled as terrorists, including worldwide civil rights icon Nelson Mandela. But despite spending 27 years of a life sentence in prison for his anti-apartheid efforts, Mandela was eventually released in the wake of a swelling Black resistance in South Africa. Incredibly, Mandela would later rise to become president of the very nation that incarcerated him, and would work to extinguish the bitter legacy of apartheid rule, which had effectively outlawed interracial marriage, barred Black people from government participation, and dispossessed Black Indigenous groups of their lands, relocating them to government-designated areas.

If all this talk of segregation or dispossessing people of their lands and confining them to reserves sounds familiar to you, you're not wrong. Governments in both Canada and the United States have historically enacted their own apartheid-like policies in their efforts to control the lives and movement of Black and Indigenous peoples alike. There's evidence that the South African government even looked to Canada's own Indian Act as a model for how to address Indigenous affairs in South Africa. This sharing of the colonial playbook has had grave consequences. Whether we use the word apartheid in North America or not, many of the inequities we see today, including poverty among Black and Indigenous populations, stem directly from the legacies of apartness policies, some of which endure in today's laws, however surreptitiously.

the hard-work hoax

It's easy to assume that because we don't currently live under officially named apartheid rule, everyone in our society has an equal opportunity to succeed, and that those living in poverty are to blame for their condition. This problematic mindset is a prime example of what we call deficit thinking, and it only works to further rationalize and fuel oppression. While we may assume that if people simply worked hard enough, they *would* succeed, this belief is based on the idealistic notion that our society is a meritocracy (where those who deserve to succeed based on their individual merit will do so). In the reality we live in, the idea that equal opportunity for success exists for all people is as far-fetched as any fantasy novel.

The term "meritocracy" was actually coined with ironic intent by British novelist Michael Dunlop Young, who used it to criticize the English education system at the time. It was a system that streamed, or divided, students into separate types of high schools based on test scores. The guy wrote an entire dystopian novel about meritocracy, arguably to demonstrate the *dangers* of falling for such an idea, and in spite of that, people everywhere didn't just fall for it, they fell in *love* with it. Today, countless institutions still employ, with great enthusiasm, the same educational streaming practices as those criticized by Young. Oops.

The truth is that we do live in a racist society, officially or not. And contrary to meritocratic beliefs, our society is designed to make it harder for racialized people, women, and any people who aren't **cis**[8] men to succeed. Throw in the fact that our society is also homophobic, transphobic, classist, ableist, and then some, and you see where this is going.

From Florida to the Yukon, people today still use meritocracy to explain social and personal problems alike, and to try and motivate young people to subject themselves to strenuous, unforgiving, and low-paying labor with little room for self-care. "If he'd only worked harder, he coulda *been* somebody!" "Just pull up your bootstraps and you will succeed." "You can do anything if you put your mind to it!" "Rise and grind!" Sound familiar? Even some of Canada's most highly regarded political figures point to the poor decision-making habits of individuals as among the main causes of poverty. Such an attitude exemplifies deficit thinking at its finest, implying that anyone in the country not living in relative comfort and safety must have simply made bad choices. In Canada, poverty disproportionately affects racialized people; this deficit thinking implies that for some poor people, their first bad decision was being born the wrong race.

What narratives like these fail to recognize is the finite nature of wealth in North American society, and how that wealth is distributed, held, and *with*held.

A 2020 report by the Canadian parliamentary budget officer showed that in Canada, the wealthiest 1% of people own over 25% of the wealth, and the poorest 40% of people own only 1.2% of the wealth in this country. History shows us that these wealth gaps between the top and the bottom were not earned fairly, and that they tend to increase over time rather than decrease. For decades, our society has made it harder and harder and harder for the average young person, regardless of race, to succeed. And racism only exacerbates this challenge for racialized people.

---

[8] **cis or cisgender:** used to describe people who identify with the gender category they were assigned at birth (typically correlated with their biological sex).

Poverty is an imposed structure and not a personal choice. Given the systemic formula, as the rich get richer, over time, poverty is designed to get worse. That makes escaping poverty virtually impossible for most people who find themselves in it, regardless of how hard they work. Yet dominant narratives will wrongfully position people living in poverty as only misfortunate or perhaps even lazy, and will position laziness as the most detestable of human traits. Greed, however, is not scrutinized, regulated, or punished within this system of inequity, which only ever posits riches as *earned* and therefore deserved by those who hold them. This fallacy is continuously used to justify ongoing inequality, as well as to bolster public faith in meritocracy, which cruelly positions poverty as deserved by those who experience it.

TOTAL WEALTH IN CANADA

1.2% — OWNED BY THE POOREST 40% OF CANADIANS

25% OWNED BY THE WEALTHIEST 1% OF CANADIANS

Ironically, many of the wealthiest people in the world inherited their riches and do not need to work at *all* or need only to work very little (often to manage their finances). Meanwhile others live in poverty despite working multiple jobs involving hard physical labor. Those physically taxing jobs often come with little pay, poor treatment, and few opportunities for career advancement. Committing to this sort of work is a necessity for many Black and other racialized folks, but often comes with great sacrifice to one's health, to one's ability to spend time with family, get enough rest, or even enjoy life outside of work. Meanwhile, the underpaid hard labor of people in the working class often allows wealthier folks to stay wealthy or get *wealthier* while enjoying all the rest in the world. So where's the laziness at again?

Due to historical and current wealth hoarding by mostly rich white people here in North America and beyond, the suggestion that hard work is the solution to poverty is entirely baseless. Creating the illusion of equal opportunity not only sets up large groups of people to face unforeseen barriers, but also encourages a mass competition for which there is little to no reward. And the scarcity of this reward is exactly what they want to keep secret—or at least downplay—while encouraging *everyone* to just work harder all the time! I'm not sayin' don't work hard for what you want in this life, though you'd better make damn sure you really want what you're working for first. Both capitalism and white supremacy have ways of tricking you into thinking you want things that *they* really want from *you*—trust me. All I'm saying is, we got some hard work to do before everyone can benefit fairly from their own toiling.

Unfortunately, because public faith in meritocracy is so widespread, those who work hard but hit barrier after barrier can end up feeling as if they are just not good enough, and that perhaps they never will be. Factoring in the overrepresentation of Black people, Indigenous people, and people of color living in poverty in North America, it's easy for this sort of internalized classism to intersect with and worsen the effects of internalized racism, contributing to low self-image, feelings of hopelessness, and prevalent mental health problems within our communities. That's unfortunate; in reality, no one deserves to live in poverty, and it is *not* an inevitability. It's a design. And designs can change.

There is a lot more to the current design, though, than just money and meritocracy.

standard supremacy

Our entire society is built around social conventions, traditions, and norms, most of which are based on the common Euro-Western—or white—way of doing things. Everything from physical appearance to household living arrangements to pastimes to attire has a set standard of acceptability in our society. These standards are not only normalized through the amount of people practicing them, but they are also often forcefully policed, whether they're written somewhere or not. As I mentioned in Chapter 1 many of these standards are embedded in the Euro-Western education systems that dominate our society and mold the bulk of human beings living within them.

Strict dress codes, for example, should be ancient history. Yet today they're everywhere, in schools and other public institutions—hell, even in nightclubs, and they go beyond impinging on our freedom of expression.

They are deeply rooted in classism, racism, colonialism, sexism, and other forms of oppression. In some parts of Canada, dress codes have even become laws that disallow public servants from wearing traditional religious and cultural attire such as the turban or hijab. Such laws do not adversely affect white Christian people, though, whose traditional attire is meant to become the supreme standard for all of us.

Even where there is no official institutional dress code in place, racialized people are still regularly policed for our attire—be it a du-rag, a ribbon skirt, the height of the waistband on our pants, or our traditional hairstyles. Even when we're not breaking someone's arbitrary rules, we are often ostracized simply for straying from what is considered normal

for clothing and appearance. And because people tend to conflate whatever is "normal" with what is right, they also tend to think whatever hasn't been normalized must be wrong, including some skin tones. It's a damn shame, and this mentality actually affects everyone, not just racialized people. It works to reinforce racial hierarchies, and places us all in competition to adhere to imaginary ideals of "respectability" or "professionalism" regarding our appearance.

Patriarchy plays a prominent role in dress-code policies. How many girls have been spoken to, covered up, or sent home from school because their clothing has been considered a distraction to the boys in the class? The school policies that create these scenarios obstruct freedom of expression and objectify feminine-presenting students, and they do nothing to dissuade other students from participating in that objectification.

Dress-code policies aim largely to enforce our competitive assimilation into white society and its gendered, patriarchal norms. But surely, true freedom cannot only mean having the ability to do as *they* do and become like *them*, but rather to be able to do as we *wish* and *be* who we *are*. For generations before now, assimilation into the dominant culture was a necessary means of survival for Black, Indigenous, and other racialized folks of all genders. But there is a great cost to assimilating, as we are forced to repress our own humanity and our identities in the process.

To hell with that. We must no longer accept conformity to white patriarchal standards as a prerequisite for our success or our belonging here.

Across the Western world, racialized people are working hard to overturn outdated institutional dress codes and other vestiges of assimilation policies. For example, Indigenous students in Utah recently secured their right to wear tribal regalia at high school graduation ceremonies in the state. But why should Indigenous and racialized people have to fight for these changes in the *first* place? Institutions should be making these changes now, proactively, removing policies and focusing instead on instilling and upholding values of compassion, respect, and equity within their ranks. I'll bet you can think of a few ways that school dress codes or schools in general could be more equitable. Stick with me; we'll look a lot more closely at schools in Chapter 6.

how they hide the bigger picture

Dress codes are only one of the ways through which white standards are upheld in our society. Standardization is everywhere in our daily lives and can seem so normal that it's difficult to decipher the ways in which white supremacy, sexism, and other forms of oppression often inform these standards. Upholding and *policing* the standards helps reproduce and reaffirm that oppression within our society. This is a dangerous cycle that, if left unchecked, will go on reproducing itself forever. These are the very workings of institutional racism. And while this racism creates conditions of privilege for white people, it simultaneously creates inequity and disadvantage for racialized groups, a dynamic underlying almost every aspect of North American society.

One of my former university professors, the brilliant Dr. Alex Wilson, used to remind us students frequently that we are all marinated in systems of oppression. I think that's why forms of oppression like racism can be so hard for some people to see, because white supremacy has simply become the lens through which we see the world, or the lens which blurs our view of it. Then there are those who deny that racism exists because they have something to lose by admitting that it does, be it subtle, intangible forms of privilege or more observable power and resources. For this reason, a lot of folks don't *want* to see racism or privilege at all. Willful ignorance is truly bliss for them. But for most racialized folks, ignorance is impossible—we don't just see racism; we live it.

You've gotta admit that racism, one of the most destructive elements of our society, is quite simply *normal* here in North America. And by normal, trust that I don't mean right. Racists often come across as some of the nicest people. And as their "polite racism" (be it condescension, microaggressions, or **saviorism**[9]) is often served with a smile, it rubs our faces in the already suffocating pretense of equality all around us.

Contrary to popular understanding, all a person really has to do to participate in racism in North America is . . . well . . . nothing. Inaction, or apathetic participation in the current state of affairs, only keeps things the way they are. In that respect, there is no such thing as

---

[9] **saviorism:** occurs when people in positions of privilege believe they can save individuals who are experiencing oppression from their "misfortune." Saviorism ignores real social barriers to equity, does nothing to change those barriers for others, and co-opts the agency of those experiencing oppression.

neutral, whether couched in niceness or in silence. Racism is embedded into the fabric of our society—it's a part of the well from which almost everybody drinks. So yeah, polite people can be racist too. Anyone can.

Straight up, you do not have to be actively curb-stomping a Black person to be participating in racism, nor even calling the cops on a Black bird-watcher for that matter (a contemporary real-life example). Yet individualized acts of personally mediated racism like these are the only kind of racism that most people will admit still exists today. That's partly because nobody wants to think of themselves as evil, and I don't believe that most people are. But many tend to be oblivious to systemic forms of oppression that may influence their own beliefs, words, and actions, and this obliviousness makes them confident in denying their own racism. And when it comes to the way that *institutions* deny systemic racism, well, there's a reason for that too.

When I was a kid in school, my classmates and I were only taught to look out for individualized racism. Participating in events for the March 21st International Day for the Elimination of Racial Discrimination, we got stickers in the shape of an open-palmed hand saying something like *"Racism. Stop it!"* and plastered them everywhere. That same day, our teachers taught us casually about how it was wrong to call people bad names based on their skin color. This was something that *everyone* could agree on: teachers, students, and educational institutions alike. Hell, it even made "anti-racism" feel fun! Meanwhile, in the same school systems that peddled these lighthearted activities, expressions of systemic racism like racist dress codes, white-washed curricula, and an ever widening racial "achievement gap" (a serious misnomer) flourished unchecked.

It would be easy to believe that the broader systemic racism in our lives sustained itself in spite of things like our *Stop Racism!* stickers, but it was more likely that the stickers helped to sustain that racism, by keeping our critical focus very narrow. Institutions and politicians alike will distract us with their efforts to highlight or curb only individualized racism in order to keep us from becoming aware of racism in its more insidious forms. And as systemic and institutional forms of racism persist without acknowledgment, they catalyze internalized racism too. Even without white people telling racialized folks we are less-than, we often *learn* to feel that way simply by existing within the current system. That feeling is only worsened by being taught from a young age that the system that *makes* us feel that way isn't racist at all! And those disadvantages and feelings of inferiority we're experiencing? They must be *our* fault, inherent to our lives and bodies, because it's equal opportunity out here! Please.

When institutions fight only individualized racism, they can say, "Hey, look, we're doing something about this very important issue!" But if your biggest goal in anti-racism work is to keep somebody from calling me the n-word, then you best get back to the drawing board, because I can go for years without being called a nigger to my face but usually only days without being made to feel inferior. Like I said, even without racial slurs being hurled all around, white supremacy is palpable, everywhere. We don't gotta conjure up images of white-hooded Klansmen to be subjected to white supremacy in North America; we need only to step out of our front doors, go to the movies or the mall, enroll in a school, interact with security guards or the police, exist here.

Without question, systemic racism in North America is often felt most deeply in institutions like schools, partly because most of our institutions are involved in different forms of social gatekeeping. Our educational institutions decide who gets to succeed financially. Our carceral systems, like the prison industrial complex, decide who gets to be free. And our systems of policing often decide who gets to die. All of these systems work together to effectively make these decisions—and the outcomes of these decisions negatively impact racialized people at alarming and disproportionate rates.

See, the effects of whiteness being normalized, made *standard* and therefore supreme in our society, create an environment that generally reaffirms the identities and the very lives and rights of white people.

That's the basis of white privilege. Meanwhile, Black people, Indigenous people, and people of color experience an environment that is generally negligent or hostile toward our identities and our lives, and that often *denies* our rights and freedoms.

In 2021 in London, Ontario, a 20-year-old white man was alleged to have deliberately struck a family of five with his pickup truck, simply because they were visibly Muslim. That means someone saw this family, and without seeing their humanity, saw only their difference, their noncompliance with Euro-Western standards, and decided that they should be punished. Decided that they should be terminated, erased. Four members of the family were tragically killed in the incident in London. And while Canada grieved publicly for a moment, as it often does after such highly publicized displays of hatred, we seem to have yet to collectively understand that racism and Islamophobia are never just a one-time event; they're a part of how North America *styles* itself. Mosques are routinely targeted for attacks and arson. Hate crimes targeting Black Muslim women are on the rise in our cities. Racially motivated mass shootings abound in the U.S.A. Imagine needing to be ever fearful of going out in public in your own town simply because of your race or religion. That ever-present potential for unprovoked suffering? *That's* disadvantage. *That's* racism. Not needing to be fearful of the same? *That's* white privilege—and if you're white, you typically can't help but benefit from it, whether or not you care to see it or admit it. White people and racialized people in North America live in different worlds. And nobody can blur my view of that.

the role of white tears

The irony of white North America's reactionary tears, thoughts, and prayers is that a lot of folks here subconsciously relish the opportunity to display such grief. Why? In doing so, they can avoid addressing the ways in which Islamophobia and racism pervade the fabric of our everyday society and give them privilege in return. It's another example of why a focus on only individualized racism can become a great distraction tactic. All people have to do is feel bad *publicly*, often on social media, to distance themselves from racism and maintain their own innocence. But white folks' very public grief over individual hate crimes pales in comparison to the shared grief, public or not, of marginalized people who experience those hate crimes as part of the collectively *hated* target, experiencing *real* anguish over a *real* loss and a *real* wound to their collective identity. Plus, those in the targeted group experience a real threat to their own well-being and the well-being of their families and communities, often inciting enduring anxiety and a pervasive sense of doom not shared by all groups.

When white folks respond to hate crimes by crying out publicly in sympathy or simply sharing their own denouncements of individualized racism, they tend to let themselves off the hook for any hard engagement in anti-racism work in ongoing ways. As we've already discussed, through inaction, they actually contribute to the white supremacy that breeds hate crimes in North America. White folks need not do anything but exist in order to benefit from the racial hierarchy under which we all live—and some of us suffer. Without anti-racist intervention, many can convince themselves to sleep soundly at night so long as they assure themselves that they "love everyone," that they are "not evil." That they're not like those killers and shooters and "sick people." But without a doubt, ongoing self-reflection and active participation in anti-racism are crucial for all white people who wish to be true allies.

If it's not obvious enough, trust that I'm not calling every white person racist out here. But I'm definitely not calling every white person innocent. Many might think that means I'm calling them all guilty. But let me trouble that too. Guilt, and especially so-called white guilt, can be a very counterproductive disposition to take on. Typically, people who are made to feel guilty for benefitting from racism will sort of shut down, turn off, and stop moving forward, immobilized by the weight of their newfound culpability. That inaction is the exact opposite of what is needed to defeat racism. Nor do we want folks who feel guilty to simply get emotional out loud and then seek forgiveness from racialized people so they can call the issue closed.

That forgiveness is exactly what Canada seems to have been looking for in its contemporary efforts around so-called reconciliation with Indigenous peoples here. As Indigenous writer Jesse Wente has advocated, Canada should really be striving for *conciliation* rather than reconciliation, since the latter term implies that the country once had a "functioning relationship" with Indigenous peoples. The historical record tells a different story. The Truth and Reconciliation Commission was established in 2008 to document the bitter history of **Canada's Indian residential "school" system.**

Over six years, the TRC heard harrowing testimony from thousands of residential survivors. In 2015, it released its final report, including a list of robust and important calls to action aimed at creating amends for the atrocities perpetrated by the government and its agents. But Canada's "reconciliation" efforts have had very little to do with actually making amends. Most have focused primarily on cultural responsiveness and inclusion efforts; making moves to try and include Indigenous cultural content or perspectives in our institutions. Unfortunately, institutions often attempt this inclusion without much care or genuine intention, and it can end up becoming mere **tokenism,**[10] more like lip service to conciliation than a truly anti-racist or decolonizing act.

Cultural responsiveness is important work when handled properly, but it alone is insufficient for dismantling the systematically racist

---

[10] **tokeni/m:** the careless practice of including a nod to a group that is typically underrepresented in a given context. As an example, the sudden inclusion of "ethnic" sounding names to mathematics word problems in the textbooks of the 1990s was extremely tokenistic as these inclusions did nothing to address the systemic barriers that lead to underrepresentation in the first place (thereby reinforcing those barriers).

impacts of colonialism. As Indigenous scholar Dr. Pam Palmater pointed out, "essential social services for First Nations people to alleviate crisis-level socio-economic conditions go chronically underfunded" even now. While including Indigenous cultural knowledge and content in today's schools is important, that inclusion simply will not fix these enduring problems. Not by a long shot.

Indian Residential Schools in Canada

Canada's church- and state-run residential schools affected over 150,000 children and subjected many of them to atrocious emotional, physical, and sexual abuse, and even physical death. The colonial government forcibly removed Indigenous children from their homes and families and sent them to boarding schools, whose specific aim was to strip Indigenous children of their languages, cultural identities, and spiritual practices, attempting to impose Christianity upon them. The schools ran from 1883 through the late 1990s, when the Canadian government ended its official sanctioning of the system.

It is widely known that what took place in this country's residential school system constituted genocide. But for some, the grisly concept only sunk in after ground-penetrating radar was used in 2021 to locate thousands of unmarked graves at former Indian residential school sites across Canada. That distressing reality is why some, like Anishinaabe writer and educator Jana-Rae Yerxa, have powerfully noted that Indian residential schools are not accurately described as schools at all since ". . . schools do not require graveyards." It's also worth pointing out that these graves only confirmed what many, like the Tk'emlúps te Secwépemc community's Elders, already knew and had been telling about for decades. And again, for a brief moment in time non-Indigenous Canadians shared their shock—itself proof of ignorance or prior dismissiveness—their grief, their thoughts and prayers, and then went back to their everyday lives.

Even as the search for more grave sites endures, Canada and its governments continue to flout the rights of Indigenous peoples. In 2021, the national police force here continued to forcibly remove Wet'suwet'en hereditary chiefs and other peaceful land defenders from their own territory, which is unceded to this day (meaning its original inhabitants never agreed for it to be used or occupied by Canada). Police arrested them to allow large oil companies to advance ecosystem-threatening pipeline projects on their land. The brave actions of the Wet'suwet'en land defenders are worthy of respect, admiration, and support. Had it not been for Canada's illegal occupation of their territories, they would not have been forced to wage a resistance nor defend anything at all, but because they did resist, they were criminalized for it. The truth is that these defenders were only attempting to protect their own land, yet Canada, its police, and its corporations collaborated to make criminals out of them. Convenient for them because in doing so, they worked to self-justify their own illegal and environmentally reckless activity, and their continuing occupation of this part of North America.

So yeah, I'd say colonization is ongoing here.

Once people among white settler groups see the true depth and breadth of colonialism, racism, and other forms of oppression in our society today, it can be easy for some to become immobilized with guilt, as I mentioned. But I suggest we all try feeling and *showing* something much more actionable: responsibility. The word literally means "the ability to respond." A little bit of guilt is okay, but with it, we've gotta resist the urge to rush toward tearful apologies. Guilt, and any search for absolution that stems from it, must be backed up by responsibility and accountability for real atonement and amends. This comes through a lifelong commitment to action and allyship, through which even those among oppressor groups can join the fight against oppression. Considering such a fight requires strategizing, planning, and collective action, many anti-oppressive thinkers have moved to recoin "allyship" as "co-conspiratorship." As a first step for any rookie co-conspirators from oppressor groups out there, may I suggest a little self-reflection?

check your privilege

People's lack of awareness of the unearned power and privileges they may have can become a major obstacle in their engagement with activism. Because so few among dominant groups are aware of their privilege, that privilege itself, and the racism it stems from, become very easy to deny. You will often hear white folks who made it from rags to riches report proudly that they never experienced *any* privilege, and that they had to work *hard* for every single penny they ever got. Remember our chat about meritocracy? Well, while I'm not one to gaslight anybody about the amount of hard work they may have done in their lifetime, I'm also not one to *be* gaslit about the very real disadvantages that Black people, Indigenous people, and people of color have experienced and continue to experience due to racism. The existence of white privilege doesn't preclude white people from ever having to work hard in their lives, or from facing adversity. Capitalism alone guarantees such conditions for most. White privilege simply means that the adversities white people face in their lives are not the results of systemic racism.

It's been this way for a long time. Both in the U.S.A. and in Canada, white people got one hell of a head start in accumulating wealth through the exploitation of Black and Indigenous people's forced labor, and through the ownership of "property" in both humans and land (slavery was practiced within Canada's pre-confederation borders until 1834). Though I'm sure many of them worked hard to manage all those people who were forced to work for 'em!

History shows that many European immigrants to the "New World" were given *free* land on arrival, which North American governments had effectively cleared of Indigenous peoples in preparation for just such a giveaway. As Indigenous peoples were removed to government-controlled reserves, they were (and still are) legally prevented from owning land there, a stipulation that heavily restricts wealth accumulation. As Dr. Martin Luther King Jr. once explained, while the U.S. Congress was helping white European immigrants to America secure plots of land for free, Black Americans already living in the country were being denied land there. The government even offered agricultural skills training and financial assistance for farming equipment to those European newcomers—easily and unfairly setting them well ahead of Black and Indigenous peoples in their personal, economic, and agricultural endeavors. As for Canada, Black would-be immigrants from the U.S.A. were dissuaded from settling *here*. In 1911, proposed federal legislation even warned that Canadian winters were too hard for Black folks to endure. No lie. The legislation was aimed at banning "any immigrants belonging to the Negro race, which is deemed unsuitable to the climate and requirements of Canada." I guess they wasn't trying to tell us about that foot-stomping trick!

I understand; the pioneers worked hard, sure. But as scholars like Dr. Sheelah McLean have shown, the white families who were gifted property in North America did little to earn their initial ownership of it, and in many cases, their descendants are still holding onto that property and *then* some in the form of wealth today. This fact alone renders the modern-day wealth gap between white and racialized peoples in North America entirely illegitimate, and in need of serious reparation. As white settlers were out here getting swag, Indigenous peoples were being displaced, the labor of racialized people was being exploited, and their collective attempts at wealth accumulation or even livelihood were actively restricted and undermined. Oh, and they still are! That's privilege and disadvantage in a nutshell.

We've also gotta look at privilege and disadvantage through an intersectional lens; it goes far beyond just whiteness. Certainly, some white folks do experience systemic disadvantages in their lives, and these may be related to other forms of oppression. So too, some racialized people experience privileges (and again, disadvantages) related to other forms of oppression. I identify as a man, and typically express my identity in ways that are traditionally viewed as masculine. As I mentioned earlier, that all lines up with the gender I was assigned at birth. While there have been times that I was at a disadvantage socially because of my race, I must acknowledge that I experience immense privilege in light of my gender identity and expression (among other factors). Admittedly, this took me a while to understand, even after I began studying anti-racist education back in 2005. See, cis male privilege, like white privilege, is just so ubiquitous and normalized that it is almost perfectly deniable by those who experience it. It's easy to think sexism doesn't exist when you've never been the target of it. Hell, if you're in that boat, you may even become angry or defensive upon seeing women and people who are gender nonconforming working for equity. If so, I hope my own reflections here might encourage you to reassess those reactions.

Recognizing privilege of any variety means trying to stay conscious about how much space one takes up, both physically and metaphorically. It means deeply considering when to share your opinions in conversations, or whether you should even *have* an opinion. And it means actively listening to and supporting people and communities whose oppression you benefit from, be they racialized people, women, people from the 2SLGBTQ+[II] community, people who live in poverty, people with disabilities, or others in *their* efforts toward equality and in *their* quests for justice.

I don't claim to be an expert on all forms of oppression; as a person without lived experience as the target of most forms, I shouldn't try to. No doubt there's a lot to the complex issues of sexism, classism,

---

[II] **2SLGBTQ+:** two-spirit, lesbian, gay, bisexual, transgender, queer or questioning, and additional gender and sexual identities (not including cisgender and heterosexual).

homophobia, transphobia, and ableism that I will never fully know or understand, even though I do benefit from them. But I can still make an effort to move *toward* understanding. As a part of that journey, I'm trying my best to take what I know about racism and use it to better understand and to try to break down these other forms of oppression, to unlearn and learn anew, hopefully forever.

I believe that that's what allyship (or co-conspiratorship) in all its forms has got to be: an ongoing, everyday, lifelong process of personal transformation and commitment to social equity. The pathway in supporting any group or community is not quick, nor straight and narrow. It is winding and sometimes cyclical and can be rife with setbacks and mistakes—I've definitely made my fair share of them. But the most important element of allyship, I believe, is to try and maintain a humble position of learning, of listening, of trying to do good, and if you come to understand that you're doing wrong, trying to do *better* next time.

Ain't that what we should all try and do? Be better for each other than we were yesterday?

the stories we tell

One of the easiest ways to recognize privilege and disadvantage is to listen for beliefs, attitudes, and narratives (or stories) that may serve to uphold inequity. In the field of anti-oppression, we call these dominant discourses. Sometimes, they are values statements, or convictions about the way the world should be, and they inform many political ideologies. Sometimes, dominant discourses are just plain stereotypes. And as scholar Dr. Kevin Kumashiro has cautioned us, promoting a racial stereotype can cause a lot of harm. Each time we do, our words are both strengthened by and simultaneously *strengthening* racism. Therefore, calling out stereotypes and other problematic discourses when we hear them is an important part of combating oppression.

In the thick of my formative years of anti-oppressive education, I got to the point where I couldn't *stop* hearing these troubling discourses *or* pointing them out. It didn't matter if I was in school, at work, or at a party, as soon as somebody let something foul come out they mouth, which happened often, I was right there, sayin', "Discourse!" I even got sing-songy with it like "Diiiis-cooouuurse!" and pointed at the perpetrator. Most people had no idea what the hell I was on about until I explained, interrupting their own stories and jokes and further annoying them. Well, it wasn't long before that shit earned me the nickname Buzzkill Dill. No lie.

It's like, "Yeah that's a great joke, Barrett, but have you thought about how it both buys into and reproduces a problematic belief about _____ people as inferior to other humans?" I could shut down a good time fast, family. *Trust* me!

Eventually, I had to step back slightly from my eagerness to point out these dominating narratives, if only because I found them (and still find them) to be *so* ever present that many conversations couldn't even last two minutes without me interrupting with another "Diiiiscooooourse!" I share this story to point out just how legitimately popular stereotypes and problematic beliefs about racial groups and other groups of people are in our society. These stories often impact how we think about, act, and feel toward people from social groups outside our own.

But combating oppression isn't just about pointing out these harmful dominant discourses; we also have to interrupt them, disrupt them, and *replace* them with other, more accurate ideas about the causes of inequity. Since my Buzzkill Dill days, I've found this option to be much more welcome at parties, especially. So, let's say someone repeats the now worn-out discourse that a Black victim of police murder "got what was coming to them." An effective initial response might be something like, "But they were a human being, though." In some cases, this will be enough to get the discourse-dropper to shut up. But if not, you can at least keep the conversation going by getting into the historical and ongoing inequities experienced by Black people in police encounters, which lead disproportionately to their injury or death. After all, it's hard to argue with facts. In the U.S.A. today, Black people are 2–3 times more likely than white people to be killed by police. Based on available race data, the situation within Canada is not so different. Here, Black people form only 2.92 percent of the population but 8.63 percent of police killings. Indigenous people form only 4.21 percent of the population but comprise 16 percent of police-involved deaths (annualized over 20 years).

If that problematic partygoer still needs convincing, take it further. Tell 'em that as people recirculate the morbid belief that most of these victims likely deserved to die, they bolster widespread public investment in that same mythology. Tell 'em they're contributing to the criminalization of *all* Black people within the imagination of white North America and its police, within its prisons, and within its cemeteries. Ask 'em why they feel a need to rationalize and justify the unwarranted and disproportionate killings of Black human beings in the first place. Ask 'em if they believe our lives matter.

Where we live, the social construction of Blackness itself is tied up in rampant narratives of criminalization and justification. Remember, Nelson Mandela was a "terrorist" and even Rosa Parks was a "criminal" just for sitting on a bus. Keep an eye out for the variety of means they'll use to criminalize and discredit today's freedom fighters, too.

Ongoing false conceptions of us as lawless or even dangerous are borne out of enduring systems of power and privilege. These are real systems with proper gears and cog wheels and all, which operate beneath the surface of a real-seeming but in fact illusionary day-to-day reality. A reality with car rides and pleasant small talk and great schools and universities, cities with vibrant arts districts and greenspaces and great transit systems, houses with leak-proof roofing and watertight basements. But underneath it all, racism expands like a pool of water from a leaky tap. And oftentimes, only racialized people can hear its dripping, feel its wetness and its cold, experience its heaviness in the breaths we struggle to take.

A human body should be free from such hindrances to comfort and freedom. But Black bodies have rarely ever been free. From the exploitation of our labor during the slave trade to the exploitation of our labor today in prisons, the job market, athletics, entertainment, and even anti-racism work; from the abhorrent abuses and assaults of Black women then and now to the control of Black people's reproductive rights then and now; from the way we were once told to kneel before our so-called masters to the way we're now told to stand up before our so-called flags, Black bodies have rarely ever been free. We may not be drowning in overt racism like we were before the modern civil rights movement of the '50s and '60s (though, some days it sure feels as though we are), but trust that racism still drips from every wall of every institution in North America, and its dampness still has a way of working its damage slowly, of seeping into the air and into the lungs, of killing us still.

the roots of resilience

There's trauma in all that. And I have heard mental health experts refer to trauma as resulting at times from a loss of control over one's experiences. There is even an entire category of trauma, called chronic trauma, to describe what comes with prolonged or *repeated* experiences of highly stressful situations. Damn. That sounds a lot like what Black and racialized people are prone to experiencing in North America just by living here. Yet how many of our increasingly public conversations about mental health have been paired with conversations about systemic or even individualized racism? In my experience working in schools, the answer is almost none.

What a shame it is.

Asian-American scholar Dr. Mimi Khúc has advocated for decolonizing mental health care with a more holistic, contextualized approach. As she put it, "Therapy is wonderful and it's one tool but it also does not capture the extent to which suffering is experienced. . . . Therapy cannot explain to me—or at least most therapists can't explain to me—how racism shapes my daily suffering." I believe that an untold number of mental health problems may be related to various forms of oppression. Focusing only on individualized treatment plans for those suffering will never amount to social changes that might prevent some mental health problems from beginning in the first place.

There's no hiding or sugarcoating Black trauma. Since before **Emmett Till** to the days of **George Floyd** and beyond, our trauma has been ubiquitous, often gruesome, and almost always highly publicized, just like the white tears that often swiftly follow and then evaporate. The publicity of our hardships handily retraumatizes members of the Black community over and over and over and over and over and over again. Though it shouldn't have to be this way, it always has been.

Emmett Till

Lynched at 14 years old in Mississippi in 1955, after allegedly trying to flirt with or whistle at a white woman. A widely circulated photo of Emmett's open casket, portraying his disfigured and brutalized face, helped fuel momentum for the Black civil rights movement of the 1950s and '60s.

George Floyd

Murdered by police at 46 years old in Minnesota during an arrest in 2020. Minneapolis police officer Derek Chauvin knelt on Floyd's neck, restricting his airways, for almost 10 minutes during the public killing, a video of which was widely circulated online, fueling momentum for the ongoing Black human rights movement.

Unfortunately, these public displays of our suffering are often the only catalysts for conversations about change in the broader society. Why? Well, that goes back to gaslighting, plain and simple. Racialized peoples have been telling the stories of our suffering for centuries; it's just that typically, we aren't believed. High-definition videos of police officers shooting unarmed Black people at point-blank range, body-slamming young Black girls onto concrete floors and schoolyard pavement have, at *times,* gotten folks' attention. But dishearteningly, despite the clear pattern of racial profiling, many have responded to these videos by dismissing them as evidence of only isolated incidents. That narrative serves to justify people's continued inaction and thus only refuels systemic police violence both on- and off-camera.

Certainly, racialized people have developed a resilience toward the social factors that infringe on our mental, physical, spiritual, and emotional well-being. So much so that our resilience is often mythologized, commended, applauded, *studied* even, and usually without an eye toward changing the conditions that require such resilience in the first place. Schools can be especially guilty of this. But think about it; resilience itself is only a relative term. It cannot exist without suffering, desperation even. I often wonder whether such emphasis on studying and building resilience actually justifies the ongoing mistreatment of racialized people, since it reinforces beliefs like "oh, they're tough; they can handle it." Some have even proposed teaching resilience strategies to young Black and Indigenous people as a way for them to deal with poverty, racism, and "intergenerational trauma." But when using that term, remember one thing: we did not inherit this trauma from our parents, our grandparents, or any of our ancestors. We got it from colonial oppressors, from racism and white supremacy, from colonization itself. It is these scourges that are better described as intergenerational, and not our trauma, because these scourges have persisted to exist across multiple generations. So don't be pointin' fingers at us.

As a social goal, instead of striving to build resilience in racialized people facing colonial violence, how 'bout we focus on reducing the need for that resilience in the first place? How 'bout we focus on ending the violence instead?

resist.

People's tendency to view Black and other racialized communities as inherently traumatized, unwell, or "broken" is precisely why I am compelled to provide y'all with a framework for really unpacking and understanding racism. If we rely solely on intuition (or BSP) and don't have any terminology, critical lens, or guidebook for interpreting our experiences of racism, then we likely won't be able to identify the *source* of our pain. And like I said in the previous chapter, that's dangerous— that perpetual mystification, that lack of understanding of why we're hurting. It is all potently damaging to the human soul, even sometimes after a single experience of racism, a single so-called microaggression, a single experience of not getting to be the dinosaur you really wanted to be at playtime. Oftentimes, the racism we experience hurts us because it robs us of our agency and free will (that robbery is a prominent goal of racism, the legacy of which reaches back to slavery). No doubt, today, many of us experience this theft of agency to varying extents throughout our daily lives. Big or small, these experiences may amount to traumas, and their impact is cumulative. But these impacts are far from inherent to our communities—they are inherent only to racism.

Without knowing the source of our pain, we are bound to carry around unresolved trauma. If left unknown or ignored, trauma may result in mental health problems that can affect every part of our lives, including, at times, our very will to live. I can't begin to know the exact source of every racialized person's pain. But I'll tell you one thing: if you are carrying around pain and you're not sure why, know that it ain't your fault. Those who may claim that it is are only missing the bigger picture.

The full impact of white supremacy on our lives is hard to measure, though it is easily felt. Its intersection with capitalism and other forms of oppression creates an atmosphere in which we are all driven to try to live up to false and often unattainable standards. Meanwhile, deep down, each one of us is a unique individual that is exceptional, powerful, and worthy of love and validation, despite the narratives that surround and story us.

To the young racialized people out there right now, peep this: you have been through a lot, family. Even if you never truly realized it before. That hidden kinda trauma is one of the toughest kinds of trauma to resolve. Until you uncover it, it's *un*resolvable, but steady keeps eatin' away at you, and your sense of identity and self-worth. In all this, know that you are resilient, yes. *So* resilient, whether you realize it or not. And your resilience is commendable; worthy of a standing ovation, no doubt. But your resilience isn't who you are. It is the armor they made you build in order to protect yourself. The armor you built and showed in the face of their violence, their pushing, their prodding, their dirty looks and judgments, their dominant discourses, their name-calling and humiliation, their exclusion and subjugation, their mythical meritocracy, their power and abuse and control, their stories and nooses and bullets and uncaring.

Their *racism*.

Go on and name it, blame it, and change it.

And heal from it too, by taking back your agency, and reclaiming your freedom. Reclaiming a life without any need for armor.

What has always been in you, family, independent of and predating all this great suffering and all of this resilience, is strength. Inner strength. Inner power. Black power. Brown power. *Human being* power. This is the power that defines you. It is who you are.

And it alone shall form the basis of your liberation.

70

SECTION II
personal liberation

3

don't be hatin' (yourself)

hair like pubes, hair like pubes,
you be lookin' all crude with your
hair like pubes.
hair like pubes, hair like pubes,
you gon' never be the dude with your
hair like pubes.

"relaxer"

It was hot that day in Moose Jaw. There probably wasn't a cloud in the whole sky, 'cause there was no escaping the sun. I was gathered with some kids from the block, just chillin'. This much older kid, Trent, was out there too. My friends and I were around 10 years old but Trent had the body and the presence of a grown man. I remember trying to look up at him but the sun seemed like it was right behind his head, glinting off the looping red locks sticking out from his baseball hat. I had to squint. I'm not sure what he was doing hanging out with us, honestly. But he came up to me, close.

"Holy crap! Look at Khodi's hair," he announced to everyone as he pulled gently at my locks to test their spring. "His hair's as curly as pubic hair!" Everyone laughed. Trent had said it like he was genuinely incredulous, and perhaps he was. I had grown used to people touching my hair, usually without asking. They'd often compliment me on it in fascination. But the pubic hair reference definitely caught me off guard. I mean it didn't leave me in my finest moment, though it seemed to leave Trent in his. He marched off shortly after his quip, with his chest all puffed out and a pep in his step. I wonder if he'd rushed off to avoid anyone taking note of his own hair, which curled conspicuously out from under his cap in all directions.

The group of kids around me moved on quickly enough, and I guessed my friends still loved me, but the thing I started to ask myself after that comment and more comments like it was . . . did I love *myself*? If this had happened today, Trent's insult would have been called a microaggression. Stacked up over time, microaggressions can cause serious and enduring harm that the prefix "micro" is simply insufficient to capture. And while the racism they carry may be unintentional at times, these daily offenses are often deeply felt by the targeted person. Black Harvard professor Dr. Chester M. Pierce, who coined the term, intended it to be understood that the effect of even *one* microaggression could be severe, and that the cumulative social effect of microaggressions could be so great as to impact the stability of the world we live in. And that's exactly why the alleged good intentions of many who deliver these aggressions are irrelevant. When it comes to racism and other forms of oppression, it's not the intention behind someone's words or actions that matters; it's the *impact* that they may have that is crucially important.

Around the time of Trent's insult, I started asking my mom to help me straighten my hair.

I knew what so-called hair relaxer was. I'd witnessed my mom and my sister using the stuff multiple times. It was always a big ordeal when Chrissy got her hair straightened with it. My mom would wear rubber gloves to protect her hands from the abrasive chemicals as she rubbed the sought-after product into my sister's scalp. Then it was a waiting game. How long could Chrissy survive the burn? It was always this thing where my mom was like, "See if you can wait longer," and my sister was like, "No!" and my mom was like, "No pain, no gain!" Then, when it got to be absolutely too much for my sister to bear, my mom would rush her over to the kitchen sink and plunk her head in it while she ran cold water all over to get the "relaxer" the hell out, trying for dear life not to get it in Chrissy's eyes! I mean it was hard-core for real. But it was by no means unique. Black people have been going to great pains to straighten their hair for ages.

While individual people make choices about their appearance for a variety of reasons (not always related to internalized racism), white supremacy is clearly at the root of our society's compulsion to uphold and maintain Euro-Western standards of appearance. Malcolm X explored this dynamic in his autobiography, explaining that, at one time, the iconic civil rights activist had made a habit of chemically straightening his own hair (again, painfully so), as did millions of other Black men and women in North America during the mid-1900s. Later, Malcolm X spoke out against the sweeping popularity of the trend, which he had come to view as a symptom of internalized racism within the Black community.

But I'd never even heard of Malcolm X when I was 10 years old. All I knew then was that I didn't like my hair. As the sole Black kid in my grade, and at times in my whole school, my hair didn't match the way the popular boys' hair (or any boys' hair for that matter) flowed in the wind, could be swept nonchalantly by hand, or parted easily to one side. I do remember my father trying his damnedest to part my little dry-ass afro for church on Sundays, though. Try as he may to form a neat crevice in there, he mighta got a temporary dip for his efforts. My hair's inability to cooperate with "normal" hairstyling techniques frustrated *me* as much as it frustrated hairstylists. Don't even ask me about the time I requested a mushroom cut at the barber's! Damn.

The thing is, I didn't *need* comments like Trent's to make me feel less-than. That messaging was all around me, and it wasn't just to do with my hair. From the cool kids at school to my teachers to celebrities, almost everyone I saw who was successful and beloved in the world around me was white. Unconsciously, for a younger me, this meant that even my skin tone was a problem. How could I be like *them* if I looked like *me*? I became saddened at the idea that there was no way for me to change my skin tone. But I was just a kid. I hadn't thought about doing what many brown-skinned people feel compelled to do today— avoiding the sun for prolonged periods so as not to darken themselves further (I've had students skip outdoor field trips for this reason). I also hadn't considered using toxic skin-bleaching creams, which are known to cause skin problems, kidney issues, and mercury poisoning in the grown folks using them worldwide, and especially in Africa, the Caribbean, and Asia. The success of companies promoting these products in predominantly non-white countries speaks to the global reach of white supremacy, and its ties to capitalism.

It's worth mentioning that I never did straighten my hair. And today my sister Chrissy, a truly socially conscious person and a role model for me, rocks a variety of innovative Black hairstyles on some queen energy.

I'm not here to judge anyone's hairstyles or anyone's appearance. A word of wisdom, however, comes from the fictional character Ida in Jael Richardson's dystopian novel *Gutter Child*, whose gripping narrative examines issues of race, capitalism, and colonialism. In it, the warm and motherly Ida advises the protagonist Elimina, "I tell all you young ones that when it comes to beauty, don't go looking for your reflection in someone else's mirror. You hear me? You are lovely as you are."

the reach of whiteness

Although it may come as a surprise to some, many independent and predominantly Black nations within Africa and the Caribbean are still wrestling with the impacts of white supremacy, which came to them via colonization. Many of these countries have ties to the so-called **British Commonwealth,** whose aim was never actually to make wealth common.

British Commonwealth

A collective of 54 countries spanning the globe. Almost all countries within the Commonwealth, including Canada, were formerly colonized by the British and to this day maintain political affiliations with Great Britain.

The Bahamas is in the same boat. Upon returning there as an older kid I was shocked to learn that their national system of government is essentially the same as Canada's—British-based. And most public schools there are still based on the British schooling model. Little Black kids of all ages can be seen running around in neatly pressed school uniforms: shirts, ties, and slacks for boys; and shirts, ties, and skirts for girls.

Now some students love their uniforms, and there may be some benefits to school uniforms that I won't go into here. But there are problematic elements that are worth exploring. As we've discussed, rigid gender-conformist clothing policies, wherever they are, clearly impinge on both cultural and gender expression. In The Bahamas, outside of school, people wear all manner of clothes, including colorful dashikis and dresses and headwraps and tams and other garb with ties to Mother Africa. But in schools, it seems the only ties allowed are ties to colonialism.

Anyone can grow up and go through this type of education system without ever consciously thinking about the negative messages it delivers them about their own culture daily, but subconsciously at least, it will have an impact. Clearly, the specter of longstanding British-based colonial assimilation policies haunts many schools even today.

The fact that we so often follow colonial dress codes without questioning them speaks to the insidiousness of white supremacy, and its many bait traps. It's not uncommon for people experiencing oppression to begin to buy into the ideals and ideologies of their oppressors. In fact, it's one of the surest ways in which oppression reproduces itself. And as South African anti-apartheid activist Steve Biko noted, "The most potent weapon in the hands of the oppressor is the mind of the oppressed." Think about it; what better way to keep a group of people in check, to keep them down, than to have them keep *themselves* in check and keep themselves down? The way to do it? Suppress them, demean and restrict their ways, their arts, their culture, and passions. Their clothes. And make them fall in love with your clothes, your ways, your standards, your expectations. Make 'em think that's what freedom means—conforming to fit a mold that erases their own identities.

This dynamic certainly affected me. Like I said, when I was a kid, the prevalence of whiteness around me, as among popular superheroes and media stars, sent me a strong message about what it took to be successful and loved in North America. Between that and what my church was tellin' me about striving to be like a supposedly white-skinned, straight-haired Jesus, you can predict the effect: more self-loathing. Even if I could "relax" my hair, lighten my skin, whatever, I knew deep down that I would never look like any of those superheroes and other icons. Not even my eyes were the right color. Today, when I see the way my little nephew looks up to Black Panther, I give thanks.

good talk, bad talk; white talk, Black talk

White supremacy is about far more than just color. The very concept of whiteness describes a whole matrix of ways of knowing, doing, and being in our society. As we've already examined, it's from within this matrix that standards are set around everything from attire to behavior to knowledge to career paths. Even communication itself is often defined by these same sorts of standards. Hell, that's why they call the English they teach you in school "standard English."

For me, from a young age, I was drawn to language. I've always been compelled to perfect it, even to perform it. I had my first public speaking gig at about six years old, as part of a concert for the local Caribbean Association. I had to put my mouth up to this microphone and read a couple lines of a poem to this big dark room full of grown folks. Even though I was nervous as hell, with the spotlight on me and all that, I'll never forget the sound of my voice being amplified through that PA system. I almost couldn't believe it was me who was makin' such a big sound. It made me understand something crucial—that under the right circumstances, even one small voice can make a whole lotta noise.

Looking back, that experience may have laid the foundation for what would later become my passion for spoken word arts. Even back then, I wanted to know and understand language deeply, learn its supposed rules, and practice it all until I got it right. And I was surrounded almost entirely by native speakers of standard Canadian English at school, among friends, even in my home. Except for one person: my mother.

My mother has retained her Bahamian accent for the better part of 40 years living in Canada. The sound of it is simply magnetic. Her voice has a higher pitch and a rhythmic flow; its brightness is outmatched only by her pealing laughter, which could often be heard echoing through-out cavernous Moose Jaw auditoriums during my school-age years of theater performance. It wasn't uncommon for people to come up to me after a play and say things like, "Great job tonight, Khodi. Your mom's laugh is amazing." I swear one year, her laugh almost made the perfor-mance review in the local paper. People thought it was remarkable, and they must have been, on some level, jealous of her unfettered enjoyment of those high school plays. My mother and so many of my relatives from The Bahamas display this unrestrained joyfulness and this readiness to laugh in their communication with each other; a refreshing change from the emotional repression that Euro-Western norms seem to dictate in our society.

There are other standout features of Bahamian English too. The "th" sound as we know it in colonial English is very different in the English of Bahamian people. In a word like "there," it sounds more like the way most North Americans pronounce the letter *d*. And in a word like "three," it sounds more like the way the letter *t* is pronounced here, which is why, as a child, I often became frustrated with my mom. I'd say, "Mom, what time are you done work today?" She'd say, "Tree-tirty." I'd say, "Mom, it's *'thhhree-thhhhirty.'*" She laughed at the time, but let me ask myself something right quick: where in the *hell* did I get off? After only a few years in Canada, I'd become the damn language police. Obviously, my ass needed some discipline, but even more than that, I needed to decolonize my mind.

What I didn't see then is how my mother, who has been so isolated from her place of birth and her family for so long, carries that place and her family with her, within her speech, like medicine. North American society works hard to erase non-white cultural identities, including linguistic ones, but when my mom's words come out, they are healing; they are remembering and retelling a legacy. No doubt, some linguists point to a lack of "th" sounds among West African languages as the very reason for the alternative pronunciation of this sound among many Black communities today. The same goes for "er" sounds, as in words like "brother" (does "brotha" sound familiar?). It stands to reason that Black English varieties are blended, not broken, as so many assume. Nobody calls English broken when it's spoken with a French, German, or other white-coded accent. In fact, people often enjoy hearing such accents, whether "th" sounds like "zz" or not. In British English, native speakers of most dialects rarely pronounce "er" sounds themselves, and some will actually add in an *r* sound where there *is* no *r* so as to verbally link two vowel sounds together. But we in North America don't accuse Brits of breaking the language. If that's because they "invented" it, then speakers of standard North American English have altered it too, and have no right to point fingers elsewhere.

Today, it's not uncommon for me to switch into a Bahamian-esque accent and cadence when I'm conversing with my mom or my extended Bahamian family. In fact, at times I feel awkward about my speech not sounding *more* like theirs. But I have spent so many years trying to "perfect" my English that I've strayed far from the already perfect speech patterns of my own family. Because of that, in my experience with public speaking, some listeners have been moved to remark incredulously about how "articulate" I sound. As someone who was raised almost entirely in Canada, I'm shocked at their shock. But white people say this sort of thing all the time to Black folks, especially if they believe that those Black folks sound white.

Not only is it inherently racist to uphold Black people who master the standards of colonial English as exceptional or exemplary, but it buys into problematic myths about so-called language purity. As renowned linguistic expert Noam Chomsky affirmed, "There is no such thing as a language," only lots of "different ways of speaking that different people have which are more or less similar to one another." Chomsky also noted that the correctness of one's grammar or speech can only be measured within the language group in which it's being used. In light of this fact, there is no such thing as correcting the English of someone from a different language community than yours. Their way is correct already, just as yours may well be. In other words, if you ask a Bahamian what time it is, it just might be tree-tirty, family. So deal with it.

Besides, how well would someone who speaks only colonial English fare in trying to understand a group of Bahamian people conversing in their own dialect? Such a person may even need to study and practice Bahamian English for years before coming close to emulating the local language forms—even I struggle at times. But resisting the impostor syndrome that comes from trying to converse with my own community, I now understand my reclamation of Bahamian English and **Ebonics**[12] as equivalent to decolonizing my communication patterns, which have been powerfully assimilated against my true will. When I speak Bahamian English or Ebonics, I'm not putting on an accent or "dumbing down" my speech, as some may criticize; I'm actively resisting the impacts of white supremacy. I'm decolonizing my speech.

I now see—and reject—how white supremacy helped put the "standard" in so-called standard English. But I have to admit that, as a young person, I often enjoyed the surprised-sounding compliments people would give me about my command of the language. I even thought such a command made me smarter, or at least made me appear that way. These compliments made me strive to study language harder, perfect it even more, enroll in university as an English major and then go on to teach colonial English to young people of all races and cultures. I even studied French intensively, largely because of the advantage it gave me in decoding English grammar. Now I see that in working to collect all this incredulous praise, I wasn't making myself smarter at all, only whiter. And by reproducing and reinforcing colonial English conventions in my own classrooms as a teacher, I was upholding white supremacy. I'd become a cog in its machine, and all this as a by-product of people's low expectations of my ability to speak well—that is, their low expectations of my Blackness. Damn. Steve Biko was right—my mind *was* a dangerous weapon in the hands of the oppressor.

I have based my life and my career around having a command of the English language. And here I am today, using all that language-loving gusto to write this book. Having the opportunity to write it is a privilege, for certain. But the journey that got me here came at a cost.

[12] **ebonics:** from "ebony" and "phonics," literally meaning "Black sounds." Ebonics is an alternative term for dialects collectively referred to by some as African American Vernacular English, though distinctly Black dialects also abound among communities outside of the United States, and across several other language and cultural groups throughout the world.

Whiteness and Blackness relate to one another through unequal power structures and through systems of privilege and disadvantage. So, by privileging the white colonial form of English in my life and my work, I was simultaneously demeaning, restricting, and disadvantaging Black English forms, which are themselves more than worthy of study (we'll talk more about this idea in Chapter 6). And as I demeaned and denied the legitimacy of Black language groups, I also demeaned and denied my own Blackness. And I did every last bit of it eagerly, albeit unconsciously, losing my ties to my home, my community, my own *self* along the way.

Internalized racism is a trip.

Elements of Blackness that I didn't deny in myself, others denied for me. During my youth, some of the few positive Black role models that were in the media were athletes. Even my non-Black friends couldn't help but drop their jaws in amazement at some of the athleticism that Black athletes displayed, from track and field to football to basketball and beyond. And on my schoolyard basketball court, every white kid and their uncle thought they were Michael Jordan, or if they didn't think they were Michael Jordan, they at least thought they were Black.

By the time we were 12 years old or so, our pick-up games on the outdoor court had suddenly transformed into "street-ball," and movies like Spike Lee's *He Got Game* provided the perfect role-play formula as my non-Black schoolmates and I began to push, shove, foul hard, and most definitely trash-talk each other. And rest assured, trash talk was one of those realms of speech where Ebonics was preferred. I felt like *I* could at least make it sound authentic; my white friends mostly knew they was clownin'.

Was it weird being the only Black kid in a sea of white kids talkin' Black and talkin' smack? Yeah, looking back, it really was. Everybody seemed to enjoy it though. For me, I felt like I had a chance to use Ebonics in my hometown for once. I can't tell you what my white friends got out of playing Black, but history shows that it is a popular pastime for some.

Back then I had hops, and I could ball a little bit, so I made my school's A-team for basketball. It was all white kids, except for this one South Asian dude, Nav, who was a year older than me. In the first practice, he made a point of shaking my hand and telling me sternly, "Khodi, congratulations on being the *second* Black man on the team." Dude was dead serious too. It seemed that the liberties my schoolmates of all ethnicities took in co-opting Blackness precluded me from receiving proper recognition for my actual Black identity.

I couldn't be mad at Nav though. While my school community may have situated Blackness in problematic and appropriative ways, Nav's own race and culture were essentially omitted from representation there. It's easy to understand why a racialized person would grab on to aspects of another culture when their own cultural identity has also been suppressed by white supremacy. And while even today many are compelled to grab onto whiteness and assimilate as a means of survival, I get why moving toward Blackness becomes an attractive alternative for others. After all, Blackness *is* beautiful, and our culture is intertwined with a well-documented history of protest and resistance against oppression. But here's hoping for a world where none of us are compelled to hide our own cultural identities, where we are all embraced for the beauty inherent in all our cultures, all our peoples, all our faces and features and souls.

dash of confidence

As I said, I had hops back in school. And athletic endeavors like basketball and track became new arenas in which I could find success. And these sports, unlike studying English, afforded me some semblance of Blackness, of *feeling* Black, which I rarely experienced elsewhere during my school days.

The few Black role models I found within the athletic sphere felt like they were truly for me. My goodness, I remember watching TV and seeing the Jamaican-Canadian sprinter Donovan Bailey smash through the world record for the hundred-meter dash like it was yesterday. Dude was at the 1996 Olympics in Atlanta. It was the summer right after seventh grade. My whole family was gathered around. Even watching the pre-race interviews was a marvel, as several young Black athletes like Bailey, Ato Boldon, and others each declared themselves the fastest man on *earth*, calling BS on all other claimants and channeling their best GOAT energy. The strangest thing was, each of them talked like they believed it too, like they truly believed in themselves *and* in their greatness. I had never seen such confidence, such pride, such unapologetic boss energy in my life. I needed me some o' that! But then, to see Donovan Bailey? a Caribbean man? like me? runnin' for Canada? the country *I* called home? after a bad start even? come from behind and absolutely surprise-*annihilate* them other dudes? Well, my mom screamed, my dad hollered, and I damn near had a heart attack! Lemme tell you.

If I had plans that night, I cancelled 'em. I was *vibrating*. The combination of Donovan Bailey's confidence, success, and Blackness was hypnotizing. I'll never forget his expression when he crossed the finish line; Bailey held his mouth and his eyes way the hell open as he relished in the victory. It was Black joy epitomized. My next few nights were not spent partying but rather compiling a scrapbook of all the Donovan Bailey news clippings I could find and trying to figure out how to *become* Donovan Bailey. It was the beginning of my deep love affair with track, and the real beginning of my exploration and my claiming of my own Blackness, a life phase Ibram X. Kendi has concisely referred to as "racial puberty." Overnight, your boy was a Black flower, blossoming.

By then, I already knew I was a fast runner, but the time had come to get serious and start proving it. I knew I could easily beat anybody in my grade in a foot race, and straight up just started challenging people left and right. This became a great confidence builder, and a good way for me to overcome my usual shyness. I'd just be like, "Yo, what's your name? You wanna race?"

One of them races did set me back, though. And not because I lost; I won. It was what this dude told me afterward. "Yeah, but Black people have an extra muscle though," he groaned in front of all our peers. "*What*?" I said. "Yeah," he said. "It's not fair, 'cause Black people have an extra muscle in their leg."

I was a kid. I don't know why I gave my classmate the credibility of a biologist with a Ph.D. in human anatomy, but I did. I didn't talk back or refute his bogus claims. It wasn't no smartphones back then—hardly an Internet—so I couldn't Google it and be like, "Not true! See?!" I just had to wonder about it—half-*believe* it, be embarrassed about not knowing it in the first place, and then, worst of all, feel bad for "cheating." Whether he meant to or not, this sore loser classmate of mine had taken one of the few elements of myself that I attributed to my Black identity, and that I perceived as positive, and turned it into a negative. Well shoot. I went back to bein' shy for a minute.

Myths about Black bodies as inherently powerful aren't all that uncommon or new. They can be traced all the way back to the days of the transatlantic slave trade, during which traders selected, captured, and sold African people for their perceived potential to endure strenuous physical work and produce offspring who could do the same. If this sounds a lot like how workhorses are bought and bred, you're not wrong. And modern-day narratives about Black people's inherent athletic advantage are no less dehumanizing. In fact, they contribute to white North America's fearful imaginings, its nightmares, and its persistent stereotypes about Black men especially as potentially dangerous animals. These stories, which position Blackness as both superhuman and subhuman at once, work to justify now the same things they did during slavery: the enduring exploitation of Black labor, and the ongoing dehumanization and systematic killing of Black people.

The trouble was, as I grew, I had begun gaining confidence in myself and my Blackness where there had previously been none, and routinely, people would dash that confidence right out of me. I did persevere, though, and kept at my athletic endeavors, even as people routinely tried to take me down a peg. And white people taking Black people down a peg was nothing new either. From before emancipation and right through the segregation laws of the Jim Crow South in the U.S.A. and the widespread segregation policies here in Canada, the perceived social and economic inferiority of Black people has always been rigidly reinforced.

Having a society whose very laws uphold white superiority bolstered some white people in asserting that superiority for hundreds of years. For instance, it certainly helped white people to look down on a Black person if that Black person was not legally allowed to drink from the same water fountain as them or eat from the same lunch table or sit in the same section of a theater.

Viola Desmond

In 1946 in New Glasgow, Nova Scotia, Black entrepreneur Viola Desmond was arrested and fined after refusing to move from the whites only section at a local theater. Although Desmond's story of protest in Canada predates Rosa Parks's similar protest in the U.S.A., it was suppressed or decades (historically, Canada has rarely admitted its own racism in a timely fashion). In 2010, she was pardoned posthumously by the government of Nova Scotia. In 2018, Viola Desmond's likeness was featured in commemoration on the ten-dollar bill in Canada

Under these rules, posted via signage at every turn, white people would appear, feel, and *be* legally justified in demeaning, degrading, and even killing Black folks. The power imbalance was truly tangible. It wasn't written in fine print. It was posted in ALL CAPS.

See, the system of white supremacy needed and still needs to constantly teach and reaffirm the supremacy of whiteness. Why? Because that supremacy is false, and the manufactured illusion of it is very fragile. To maintain it, laws were drafted, policies were written, signs were painted and posted, people were maimed, and examples were made. Today, while most laws and policies that explicitly uphold white superiority are gone, white superiority still lives on in many social and economic policies—it's just not as blatant. And the attitudes around such superiority remain too, as do the lynchings that often accompany them. Throughout history, racist lynchers have often been self-styled authorities, vigilantes targeting those who dare challenge the system of white supremacy. And while it was perhaps more common in the past for white civilians to take on such roles, today's authorities often wear badges in the act of lynching. I wonder, how did we get here?

overseer/officer

Some time ago, I had the pleasure of going to see hip-hop legend KRS-One in concert in Saskatoon. Indigenous activist, emcee, and spoken word artist Zoey Roy had worked hard to compel the emcee to visit the town that most high-profile musicians skip over when they're on tour. KRS-One gave the most hype, most electric live performance I've ever seen, and his voice boomed like Thor's hammer on the stage. At one point, after a sick freestyle, he performed his song "Sound of da Police." Through his lyrical wordplay and intonation, he slickly pointed out the similarities between the sounds of the words "officer" and "overseer," the latter of which refers to the hired disciplinarians of slavery-era plantations. To be sure, the very formation of police forces in the U.S.A. was based primarily on preserving slavery.

Here in Canada, our own national police force, the Royal Canadian Mounted Police, was founded largely to control and displace Indigenous peoples by various methods such as containing them on reserve lands and forcibly taking their children for placement in residential schools. And those Indigenous people who resisted the government's policies of segregation, control, kidnapping, and assimilation were often met with harsh punishments, including government-coordinated starvation and other means of murder. More recently, the attempts of militarized police to suppress the Wet'suwet'en people's uprising in western Canada proves that the government's control and displacement of Indigenous peoples from their own lands is ongoing to this day. In recent cases in the U.S.A., even the National Guard has been called in to help curb various forms of Black and Indigenous resistance.

Since colonizers first set foot in North America, there have been grave consequences for racialized human beings wishing to assert their humanity and their freedom here. Isn't being human all that Ahmaud Arbery was doing when he decided to go for a jog one afternoon in Glynn County, Georgia, in 2020? Spotting the young unarmed Black man running through their neighborhood, three white men followed Arbery for five full minutes, and one of them, Travis McMichael, shot him dead. According to witness testimony, McMichael called Arbery the n-word immediately after shooting him. Noteworthy: police in the area made *no* arrests until months after the incident, as the hard work of social activists resulted in unignorable public pressure.

So many of our iconic freedom fighters throughout history were murdered also. Others, like Arbery, Breonna Taylor, and George Floyd, lived outside of the limelight until the moments of their murders and have only become iconic in their martyrdom. They are complex symbols, representing both great hope for our communities and proof that no Black person is ever truly safe in our society. Other Black public figures like NFL quarterback Colin Kaepernick, who ignited the #TakeAKnee movement to help shed light on police brutality and systemic racism, have had their livelihoods threatened and diminished after making public statements in favor of Black human rights. The same happens regularly at all levels of the job market across the continent and beyond, regardless of one's public status.

People maimed; examples made.

See, for Black people, there have always been consequences for what some see as our audacity, be it the audacity to go for a jog or to the grocery story, or to not stand up for the anthem of a country who enslaved our ancestors and still won't recognize our rights. Some people just can't stand us having any sense of free will. They can't stand our confidence, since, to them, it appears to threaten white supremacy. There's even a derogatory term to describe a confident Black person: uppity. This term is *still* used on occasion to invoke negative ideas about Blackness without referring to Blackness directly, a technique known as dog whistling or coded language. Politicians and laypeople alike routinely use these techniques when they wish to skirt around political correctness norms without *actually* coming correct.

a pledge to ~~her~~ *your* highness

While the methods and the language have somewhat changed, the efforts to demean and control Black people, and take them down a peg, persist. Despite Canada's independence, our country, like all those in the Commonwealth, maintains deep ties to the British monarchy. The face of Queen Elizabeth II is on damn near every coin, her picture in damn near every public school. And now that King Charles III has taken the reins, I'm sure his face will begin to populate our lives also. During my early school years in Regina, they used to have us students sing "God Save the Queen" on the daily. New citizens of Canada must pledge to "be faithful/

And bear true allegiance" to the British monarch. Upon being initiated as a Boy Scout, I had to pledge to "do my duty to God and the Queen." The whole thing surprised and confused me; I had only joined Scouts because I wanted to go camping. It seems like everywhere you go in Canada, people are trying to get you to bow down to her royal highness, but I never really felt like bowing down to anyone. Making somebody bow down, in any context, is only a way of *keeping* them down. Besides, to invade any and all nations and suppress and kill and colonize and enslave local populations just to elevate yourself? That's nothing to be proud of. To me, that speaks to a certain *low*ness, and no highness at all, in fact.

If there's one thing I can ask of young Black and racialized people, it's that y'all bow down to your *own* highness, not someone else's. And trust that you have that highness within you. If you don't feel it, I would venture to say that it's most likely been suppressed, though not annihilated, by the white supremacy that we are so subjected to throughout our lives. And you can get your highness back. As renowned Black artist Kadir Nelson noted, history's prominent Black icons have all "been able to overcome great obstacles by becoming the hero that dwells within them." Nelson went on to state that "we all have the potential" to do the same.

Whether it's through clear expressions of self-love or mastering the art of trash talk, many Black sprinters and other athletes today clearly know their inner heroes and embody their own highness. So do most rappers. In fact, the self-confidence-boasting (and boosting) modeled in hip-hop may be one of the genre's greatest benefits for young Black listeners, a good counterpoint to those who dismiss it as being too violent or containing too much foul language for young ears. Then again, rap's often playful element of **braggadocio**[13] may be one of the reasons why

---

[13] **braggadocio:** a prominent element of rap music in which emcees claim prowess or superiority over others in any number of areas, including artistic ability. Despite the level of intensity that it can inspire in hip-hop, many emcees employ braggadocio as well as "dissing" with playful rather than malicious intent.

the genre has been so historically derided, dismissed, censored, and outright banned by colonial bodies. Like, how dare all these Black folks be so confident! We've got to put a stop to this!

The truth is that the stark confidence, the not-so-humble brags, and even the dissing trends found in hip-hop culture connect back to long histories of Black resistance. Consider slavery-era games such as the dozens, in which enslaved African folks would playfully insult each other while boosting themselves up, often using wordplay or rhyme, as a means of entertainment and to vent frustrations. It's not as if they could vent those frustrations to their captors. Avoiding upsetting the ones who wielded whips and nooses was a matter of survival back then. But so was having some sort of emotional outlet. So, compelled to bite their tongues or face consequences, the enslaved African people would often let their would-be retorts fly in the riskless fury—and occasional fun—of the dozens. Interestingly, there is evidence that similar games may have even pre-dated slavery, with verbal contest rituals being part of the rich oral tradition in parts of Africa. So yeah, Black rappers come by it honestly. But the confidence they tend to display lives in *all* of us. For Black painters, doctors, nurses, teachers, students, programmers, CEOs, animators, translators, politicians, and writers—all of us, whoever we are—our confidence is integral to our success.

It has been said that we Black folks living today are our ancestors' wildest dreams. I expect that that's true. And in thinking about those ancestors, beleaguered, beaten, and bruised as many of them were, and in thinking about their dreams, about the fact that they *had* dreams, *had* hopes, you gotta be in awe of their confidence too. I mean, what are dreams and what is hope without confidence anyway? To me, the courage and determination of my enslaved African ancestors is hard proof that confidence, though it can be tested and tempered, can never truly be taken away. It is innate.

In that regard, confidence is not something that you should have to build, but rather get out of the way of. For racialized folks, this often means getting *others* out of its way, putting their negative comments, their troublesome portrayals, their racism out of your mind (or on your list of things to overcome). It means that if they won't value or validate you, your freedom, or your highness, that *you* and your community must be the ones to do so. We must love ourselves even if they will not love us. I can't overstate the importance of doing so. Self-love is a true invincibility shield for hatred, family. In fact, it is impossible for them to hurt you with their hate if you love yourself. The great abolitionist Frederick Douglass clearly loved himself, fighting so hard and so fearlessly for his own and his people's liberation. The formerly enslaved orator and writer once said of his haters, "They cannot degrade [me]. The soul that is within me no man can degrade. I am not the one that is being degraded on account of this treatment, but those who are inflicting it upon me." They only degrade *themselves* when they hate you. Straight up.

As a young person, it's easy to want to try and fit in with the crowd or the popular groups among us. Doing so can be a real confidence booster. But in trying too hard to fit in, we sometimes risk becoming something we're not. It's an age-old story, and it can happen unconsciously. Where I grew up, fitting in meant becoming as white as possible. And while I could gain favor through assimilating, the truth is, I never found my real confidence until I recognized the inherent value within myself and my own racial identity. How could I have? By putting on airs of whiteness, I was suppressing and therefore devaluing my own Blackness. And while the conformist gains a false confidence through seeking sameness, those who find pride in their own uniqueness earn a genuine appreciation for what sets them apart. Personally, I'd rather do that.

That genuine appreciation of self is untouchable and can never be stricken away. And that genuine understanding of self, the root of self-love, is so important for imagining and securing what is also a birthright for today's young racialized people: a bright future. That's what Muhammad Ali saw for himself before becoming the world heavyweight boxing champion, not to mention a household name. "I am the greatest," the great fighter frequently affirmed.

A bright future. That's what Assata Shakur's grandmother predicted for the young Black freedom fighter after dreaming that Shakur would soon get out of prison. "My grandmother has always had dreams and her dreams have always come true," Shakur stated following her escape from incarceration and her safe passage to Cuba.

A bright future. That's what Malcolm X predicted for himself years before his infamy as an orator. While he himself was a young man in prison, Malcolm would daydream inexplicably about speaking to large crowds, uncertain and confused as to why he had these visions, which would later be revealed as premonitions.

A bright future. That's what Harriet Tubman predicted for herself and the estimated 70+ enslaved Black people she helped liberate through the Underground Railroad, a network of abolitionists fighting enslavement in North America. Tubman was known to endure fainting spells during which she reported receiving visions and guidance from God, which she used to help navigate herself and others toward safety. Hell, even as she lay dying, Tubman quoted the Bible for her last words ever spoken. "I go to prepare a place for you," she uttered. I mean, that kinda confidence gives me chills! I can probably bet that when my time comes, there Harriet'll be, greetin' my ass up in the stars somewhere with a big smile on her face like, "Ha! I told you, son. You're free at last!"

As you can see, intuition played a huge role in establishing confidence in so many of our great Black icons from history, although few colonial history books will tell you so (likely for fear that you too will learn its benefits). But the confidence that intuition helped foster in these leaders was crucial to the success they experienced in their powerful endeavors. Systems of oppression are meant to be systems of despair, but having confidence in yourself and your ability to overcome adversity is a sure antidote for that despair—confidence is the basis of hope, and hope is itself a deeply intuitive feeling. Straight up, when you don't have confidence in yourself, in your value as a human being, or in your ability to overcome your oppression, hope goes out the window fast.

And we're gonna need that hope, family, if we're gonna win this fight.

While some of us might have lost sight of it along the way, we are all born with great confidence, which is strongly linked to our imagination and creativity. Picture yourself as a young child drawing, role-playing, or making up a whole storyline and a universe for your toys. You weren't only exercising your imagination and creativity, but also your confidence. Children have been doing improv since way before it was cool. Wait, improv *is* cool, right? Anyway, what I'm trying to say is, most of the time, little kids are simply not afraid to play. When did we older kids and grown-ups learn that fear? I mean, imagine sitting in biology class or in your cubicle at work, playin' with your dolls and your Play-Doh and your dinky cars and shit. I'm willing to bet that about 90 percent of us would be too self-conscious to do it, even though it *could* be fun. Even though it could add joy to our lives! Ironically, while we alter our lives out of fear that even one person might make fun of us, collectively, we could easily overpower that potential person, if only we came to know and understand the power that we have together! Well, as I intend to show in the next chapter, anti-racism is joy-positive, and through anti-racism, we have the potential to unlock power, too. The power to change and enrich not only our lives, but also the world in which we live.

We can get our confidence back. We can get our inner children back; we can let them breathe again and *dream* again. We need to; the youthful confidence that others have tried to drive out of us for so long is a legit homing device for success. Even "new age" spiritualists know this, and have developed language and teachings about positive thinking, vision boards, the laws of attraction, and manifesting to describe it. Hell, Muhammad Ali said it all before they did: "It's the repetition of affirmations that leads to belief. And once that belief becomes a deep conviction, things begin to happen." Don't get me wrong; I'm not suggesting that you can positive-think your way out of experiencing racism. On the contrary, I believe that positivity, especially when enforced by institutions and organizations, can often get out of hand, become toxic, and allow racism to thrive. But when we unlearn the awful *un*truths that racism has taught us about ourselves and replace them with the real and positive *truths* about who we are, we will not be able to hate ourselves any longer.

We must unlearn white supremacy, unlearn Black and racialized inferiority. We must unlearn the white supremacist standards of speech, attire, headwear, beauty, religion, spirituality, career choices, and ways of knowing, doing, and being that have been shoved down our throats for centuries. Only then will we begin to see the true beauty and the true value that is within our own selves and our own racial, cultural, and spiritual identities. Only then will we know our own greatness.

I never did quite believe it when they told me beauty was in the eye of the beholder. Partly because I knew all along, without being able to put words to it, that the true beholder (or standard-setter) where I lived was the white male gaze, an ever-surveilling and ever-judgmental eye. Our hard work comes in reclaiming our own gaze, our own eyes, and by unblurring them from the influences of colonialism, patriarchy, and other forms of oppression. That means slowly but surely arming ourselves with the knowledge to understand power structures and how they have warped society's view of us and our own view of ourselves. We've gotta raise our heads above those murky waters of oppression and gain what is sorely needed to combat internalized oppression: an *accurate* view of ourselves.

Spoiler alert—we are beautiful, powerful, and profound beings.

Realizing as much is what Brazilian educational philosopher Paulo Freire referred to as conscientization. In his work teaching literacy to people living in poverty in Brazil, he came to understand that one of the biggest roadblocks to the liberation of oppressed peoples was a lack of awareness of their own oppression. Knowing that oppressors would never willingly liberate the oppressed, Freire argued that only the oppressed could liberate themselves, and that they could only do so after fully understanding (conscientizing) that they were being actively oppressed. This understanding forms the root of what we think of as social consciousness today—the awareness of oppression, and of the fact that all human beings are worthy of dignity, respect, equality, and the true fullness of life on Earth. There's great wisdom in that awareness, and they say that wisdom only comes with age, but I guarantee you that with anti-racism, you can get it early.

resist.

The fact that becoming socially conscious can lead to liberation is precisely why oppressors like to keep the workings of oppression *secret* from the oppressed. As we know, institutions and organizations work to deliberately suppress and police conversations about overcoming oppression. For example, in 2020, then-U.S. president Donald Trump issued an executive order banning the federal government from sanctioning education about systemic racism and racial bias, or anything to do with critical race theory, the underlying framework for all authentic anti-racism education. The former president's comments on the matter showed that he, like many conservative politicians still in office, viewed critical race theory (CRT) or indeed any anti-racist teaching as divisive and "un-patriotic."

Thankfully, Trump's ban on so-called divisive concepts was rescinded by the next administration. But that didn't stop several states, like Oklahoma, from instituting similar bans on critical race theory in their school districts, aimed at ensuring that the concepts taught in schools make no student feel "discomfort, guilt, anguish or any other form of psychological distress on account of his or her race or sex. . . ." But instead of white students feeling discomfort or guilt from learning about their role in oppressive structures, students of color will continue to feel discomfort and anguish from suffering under those structures (which are bolstered by these policies). This is what some institutions think of as "safe space," but we must ask them, "safe for whom?"

In the words of scholar and author Dr. Bettina Love, critical race theory " . . . helps young people realize if you understand the systems, you can work to change the systems." But those in power, who *benefit* from oppression, don't want the systems to change—they've got too much to lose. And their unwillingness to allow anti-racism work to happen really messes things up for us freedom fighters. You see, every person among oppressor groups is a potential ally, and if only we could have a fair chance to share our perspectives with them, we might reach them. Undoubtedly, the people in power know this, and so restrict the sharing of anti-racist perspectives in the first place. They know that if we garner enough co-conspirators from within the oppressor group that we will begin to *win* the freedom fight and weaken oppression overall.

They know we can win. Do we?

I've talked a lot about confidence in this chapter, which I believe is crucial to our fight. Unfortunately, some people will interpret any amount of Black confidence as an affront to white supremacy, and perhaps it is. But it's also a simple expression of dignity to which every human being is entitled—to be comfortable in our own towns and communities, to be comfortable in our own skin. That sense of human dignity is innate, along with our right to experience it. All of that predates oppressive power structures. That means our confidence must not be viewed as a response to white supremacy, but rather as something that came well before it and that will outlive it too. Our confidence is a celebration of our humanness, and a signal to ourselves and others that we too deserve to be treated as human beings. Malcolm X said it *most* confidently in 1964: "We declare our right on this earth . . . to be a human being, to be respected as a human being, to be given the rights of a human being in this society, on this earth, in this day, which we intend to bring into existence by any means necessary." X's infectious and powerful confidence was so threatening to white supremacy that he was killed for it, only a few months after he spoke these words. See, they don't want us to know our own greatness; they'll even draft laws and policies to prevent us from knowing it. But we must know it still.

If you're just coming to feel and know your inner confidence today, get ready. Perhaps you're still shaking off some of the negative feelings about yourself or your race that you've been carrying around for so long, still identifying what your negative self-talk sounds like, or where it even comes from. It's okay to stop talking down to and feeling bad about yourself. Having a negative self-image is *never* your fault. It comes from believing what you've been wrongly taught about yourself. You may, like me, realize that you've done things you would never have done had it not been for racism or white supremacy. You may even come to understand that who you have *become* is not who your inner child truly wanted to become. Luckily, you can change all of this. Believing that change is possible will help guide you toward it, and as you go out into your communities and spread your messages of change to inspire others, the same change will become possible for them, too.

Taking a lesson from some of the greats, here is an affirmation for your consideration; a pledge to your own highness, if you will. Dr. Molefi Asante, known for his writings on **Afrocentricity**,[14] has argued that based on the ancient spiritual beliefs of some West African tribes, words have the power to create reality.

If you're so inclined, consider the words of this affirmation as having that same power. Practice the affirmation, memorize it, *believe* it.

---

[14] **Afrocentricity:** in scholarship, theory, or practice, Afrocentricity strives to center African and diasporic Black culture, Black history, Black ideas, and the overall Black experience, with a focus on promoting and protecting the social consciousness and the agency of Black people historically and today.

Know that you are valued, that you are important, and that you are sovereign—in charge of yourself, your beliefs, and your future. Know that *you* can make change happen—in your life, in your community, and in your world.

Oh, and one more thing: if it's needed, remember to forgive yourself . . . for anything they made you wrongly believe about yourself, about your race, or about others. Forgive yourself for what they may have done to you, or made you do to yourself. It's alright, family; you are *more* than *all* of those things. And you're so much more than your past may portray. In forgiving your past, trust that you also forgive whatever futures you may have neglected to imagine for yourself. Trust that those futures are still out there waiting for you, right now—available for the claiming. Today, you can love yourself, and be angry with anyone who stopped you from doing so in the first place. Today, you can dream bigger again. You can find your true passion, your true calling, and pursue it wholeheartedly. Love something? Go do it. Want something? Go get it! Today, you can do and be . . . anything. Reclaiming your *freedom* is the greatest resistance of all.

So go on, and *don't* apologize. Become yourself.

4

how to show love,
and rage, too

don't laugh, they tell me;
when you laugh it's too loud.
so i don't even smile
when they take their cameras out.
my lips lock shut
when their knuckles hit my mouth.
don't cry, they tell me.
you got nothin'
to cry about.

snuffing out Blackness

Back in my high school days, my friend Harper went through one of the most involved Eminem phases a person could go through. Harper, who's white, had the music, the style, the hair, the anger at the system, and the whole aura to boot. In his emulation of the white rapper and my emulation of Black rappers, we met up somewhere in that hip-hop middle ground. By the time we were old enough to go into bars and do karaoke, pickin' Eminem's songs was a no-brainer for Harper. But one fateful night at the "Rockin' Royal" in Moose Jaw, I had a bad feeling about his choice.

Before I go any further, I have to describe the Royal Hotel bar for any of you who mighta been lucky enough to have missed out on it— the whole building has since been demolished. For young partygoers in Moose Jaw, there was a time when the Royal was not just the best spot to hit up on a Friday night; it was the *only* spot, meaning it was the worst spot, too. Among the large numbers of young, mostly white people who went there, you had all kinds of cliques: skaters, jocks, goths, preppies, you name it. I had enough trouble trying to find my place within all *that*. But the Royal was also home to a significantly older, more country-and-western–style crowd. The place might as well have been segregated officially. On any given night, you could walk in and find a bunch of rowdy young people on the dancefloor on the left, and a sea of cowboy hats, handlebar mustaches, and tight Wrangler jeans on the right. From the dancefloor, there were a few different ways to get to the bathroom, which was right next to the country-and-western section. But I hardly *ever* walked *through* cowboy land; it gave me the willies.

I don't know whose bright idea it was to host a karaoke night at the Royal—they hardly ever did that, and social tensions there were volatile enough. In typical Moose Jaw fashion, there were usually at least two or three bar fights per night at the Royal, either inside the bar or outside on the street. Somehow, karaoke night drew the interest of both the younger and older crowds. From the time we got there, everyone was singing either country songs or pop songs—that was to be expected. To my memory, the Royal literally only ever played two hip-hop tracks: "Family Affair" by Mary J. Blige and "You Can Do It" by Ice Cube, Mack 10, and Ms. Toi. I swear they played them shits like clockwork, back-to-back, every weekend night around midnight for about 10 *years*. Since I was usually the only Black dude in there, the songs were my one cue to groove on the dancefloor, but boy, did they get old fast. I have no idea why the longstanding Royal Hotel DJ included these and *only* these songs. I can only assume it was due to the songs being at least semi-palatable to the largely conservative white crowd; in Moose Jaw in the early 2000s, even a song containing the word "ass" was risqué.

If you're getting the impression that Moose Jaw wasn't exactly hip to the whole rap thing or even a little bit edgy, you'd be right. *I* sure as hell wasn't planning on droppin' a rap song during karaoke night. And when Harper decided he was gonna rap Eminem's "The Real Slim Shady," I already *knew* it was a bad choice. My head was on a goddamn swivel lookin' at all them cowboy hats millin' about. My BSP was on code red, and that shit never lets me down.

I realized Harper had no idea that his song choice could possibly cause problems for me. I may have even asked him, "You sure 'bout this?" But I couldn't stop him. Dude was hyped on throwin' it down regardless. He took the mic like he was on *8 Mile* himself or some shit.

"May I have your attention please? May I have your attention please?" he started out in his best nasally Eminem voice. When I looked over at some of the cowboys at that point, it was just confusion on their faces, like "What the *hell* is this?" Then when Harper started actually rappin', their confusion turned to recognition, then to disgust and resentment. Harper was oblivious. I guess he was in the zone, doin' what he legit loved to do. It can be hard to pick up on a crowd's energy when you're in that state. I started to wish he would snap out of it and read the room. Then, someone decided that *they* were gonna snap him out of it. Somebody threw a goddamn cowboy boot at Harper. Straight up.

Harper was stunned. "What the hell was that?" he said into the microphone. "Did somebody just throw a *boot* at me? Are you fucking *serious*?!" He never did finish the song.

A middle-aged cowboy who I swear was eight feet tall stood up from a nearby table. "Enough of that nigger music!" he shouted. Even though I'd pretty much predicted such an outcome, it still caught me off guard. That word always does. The only Black man in the whole bar that night, I tried to stay incognito among the crowd.

"*What* did you just say?!" Harper yelled.

"You heard me."

Then it was on. Like I said, this cowboy was gigantic. Harper literally had to jump just to get at eye level with this guy, and jump he *did*. Harper took a running start and made a giant leap up onto the man, straddling his torso and trying to tackle him—a tough task without any leverage on the ground, which was about four feet of tight-jeaned cowboy leg below Harper, *one* of those legs being conspicuously bootless.

I sprang from my spot and tried to intervene verbally. "Harper, it's okay, man. Harper, don't worry about it." I knew Harper was, in a way, fighting on my behalf, and I didn't want him to. But there was no stopping him. The two made their way toward the front entrance, and the tussle, acting as one entity, was soon shoved out the door, where I found myself trying desperately to call it to an end. A crowd had of course gathered, egging the two brawlers on as they wrestled and punched and clawed at each other. Eventually, I think my voice got through to Harper, and he relented. I gotta hand it to him; once the shock wore off, I realized that he'd put up a good fight, having been outweighed by at least a hundred pounds.

When the dust settled, the irony of the whole incident began to sink in. The giant one-booted cowboy eventually clued in that *I*, a real live Black person, had been accompanying his white musical nemesis from the beginning. I doubt if that instigator ever did realize that Eminem is a white rapper himself. At any rate, this cowboy dude clearly hadn't noticed me before. But when you're Black and out in public, you can never truly be incognito, so eventually he did notice me. That's when he approached me, huffing, and with a softened disposition.

"Listen man, I didn't mean anything by that 'nigger' comment, not against you. That was intended for *him* and him only," he said, ironically indicating Harper. "I'm not racist by any means," he added. I nodded quietly. I just wanted the whole night to be over, and as usual, I was unsurprised by the man's fake-ass attempt to appear innocent of racism. I was a *little* surprised when a much shorter Indigenous man in a red windbreaker stepped forward then in a peace-making stance with his arms outstretched. He identified himself as the tall brawler's friend. I must have been looking a bit shook, 'cause this man put his hand on my shoulder.

"Hey buddy, look man, that guy's not racist," he said. "Trust me. I'm his best friend, and *I'm* a fuckin' Indian." The man was invoking the hard reality that in Saskatchewan, there was and is a special kind of racism reserved for Indigenous peoples. But I didn't respond. There was a lot to unpack with his comment and the complexity of the whole scenario, but at the time I just couldn't believe what the fun night we'd been hoping for had turned into.

The big cowboy stepped forward again. "We good, buddy? We good?" he asked, seeking my forgiveness so he could go home and get a good night's sleep, I guess.

"Sure, man," I said. My ass just wanted to go home, too. There was a lot that was weird about that night—the fact that my white friend was the one getting called the n-word, and that I was the one getting apologies after people noticed in surprise that I existed.

how they see us

Just as Black confidence and a whole spectrum of Black emotions have been suppressed historically, so too has our rage. It's safe to say that the suppression of our anger is related to the longstanding fear of Black people in general, and especially of Black men, that lies in the hearts of white North America. It's a terror that runs so deep that even a Black musical genre, performed by a *white* person covering the lyrics of *another* white person, is seen as a threat to the usual order of things. It's seen as a threat to the whiteness of space, of sound even, in the otherwise "peaceful" prairie landscape. If this white man had thrown a boot at my white friend for rapping, what would he have done had it been my *Black* body doing "Black things" on that stage? God forbid if I'd intoned anger in my voice while rapping, as Eminem is known to do.

The truth is, following the whole incident, I *was* deeply angry inside, but Harper was the one who'd been able to show his anger and to act on it. I've always worked hard to avoid street fights. For one, I don't believe in violence as a way to resolve interpersonal problems. Secondly, I was acutely aware that if I ever did enter a fight, I wouldn't just be one of those Moose Jaw men fighting another Moose Jaw man, but that I would be perceived as a Black man fighting a white man, and perhaps by extension, white*ness*. And facing a lynch mob was never on my bucket list. Besides, as angry as I was, I was not at all shocked by the incident. More so, I was disappointed in the way the whole thing had only reaffirmed my expectations of my home community. At the time, I was also left very confused. I didn't understand then that in fighting my white friend for singing a rap song, that older white man was actually fighting *Blackness*—in his mind, trying to snuff it out lest its supposed unruliness, lawlessness, and anger take hold in his beloved hometown, whose slogan at the time was "the friendly city."

Combine the worst white imaginings of Black rage with widely held fears about the mythically dangerous Black male body, and you may just conjure up a "super-predator." That's what John Dilulio did when he warned Americans in the 1990s of a new, harsher-than-ever breed of criminal, in the widely circulated article *The Coming of the Super-Predator*. "We're talking about kids who have absolutely no respect for human life and no sense of the future," he wrote, noting that Black, inner-city (often code for "poor") neighborhoods would see the "greatest trouble." Dilulio argued that these super-predators were "capable of committing the most heinous acts of physical violence for the most trivial reasons . . . for as long as their youthful energies hold out, they will do what comes 'naturally': murder, rape, rob, assault, burglarize, deal deadly drugs, and get high."

Then-president Bill Clinton was likely motivated by similar discourse in drafting one of America's most sweeping and socially detrimental anti-crime bills ever. The 1994 bill, emboldened by white America's fears of a growing population of kids who were young, Black, and poor, instituted harsher criminal sentences—including wider use of the death penalty—and encouraged states to pass similar laws, to build more prisons, and to try children as adults. All of this in a country whose mass incarceration rates had reached astronomical levels even before the law was passed, and whose incarcerated persons were and are disproportionately Black.

My BSP is tingling, family. And this time, I really do mean my Bull Shit Perception. Clinton wasn't the first politician, nor the last, to veil white supremacy in a "law and order" crusade. And it's narratives like these and that of the super-predator that make Black men hyperaware of our own presence as potentially fear-triggering or suspicious in white spaces. There are times when I feel I have to go out of my way to be extra friendly, flash a smile, or extend a greeting, even when I'd rather not, just to make sure white people feel comfortable and safe around me. Sometimes, it's to try and convince a storeowner or security guard that I'm not gonna steal anything. Sometimes, it's to convince white people I meet on the street that I'm not a threat. Other times it's to try and convince others that *they* shouldn't threaten *me*.

In 2018, 33% of people incarcerated in the U.S.A. were Black, while Black Americans represented only 12% of the total U.S. population that year.

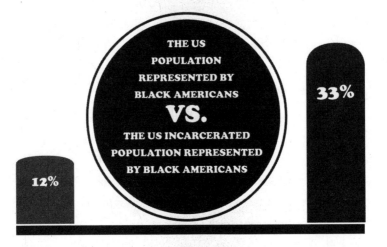

I have learned to read people and energies of rooms, and to keep my distance when necessary, in order to stay safe. Perhaps this hypervigilance is a vestige of the self-preservation strategies, such as shyness, that I was forced to learn in my childhood. But I'm not alone in my hypervigilance. As Black Canadian journalist and activist Desmond Cole pointed out in *The Skin We're In*, "... our safety depends on us anticipating racial violence." In social situations, my guard is up at all times, and I am ever ready to fight to protect myself or my family. Following high school, I began to study how to throw punches and tried to build up my body for just that reason. But I was never a super-predator, rather a kid trying to *avoid* confrontation. A kid trying to survive. It is easy for young Black men to want to alter their appearance or persona to *look* scary for the same reasons I've mentioned—making people think we can hurt them so that they won't even think about hurting us. Sadly, this may make some of those people, and even people among our own communities, even more afraid of us. And beneath all that forced masculine performance is often a tenderness, even a fear, that I wish we Black men could express more freely. Unfortunately, we often can't (and aren't welcome to). And regardless of whether we try and play the "I'm-a-threat" card or the "I'm-not-a-threat" card, it's people out here threatening *us*, and Blackness entirely. Because we have seen, felt, and internalized the reality of violence against us, we are often stuck in that state of hypervigilance, rarely able to relax. We are caught somewhere between pragmatics and anxiety, between PTSD and a sort of pre-TSD.

how they stifle us

James Baldwin said about America, "To be a Negro in this country and to be relatively conscious is to be in a rage almost all the time." Ms. Lauryn Hill powerfully explored the multilayered foundation of this anger in her song "Black Rage," which I mentioned earlier. The song's sobering lyrics are set in contrast to the bright tune of "My Favorite Things" from *The Sound of Music* film. As Hill laments in her mournful tone, Black rage is certainly not unfounded, but rooted in such things as rapes, beatings, suffering, denial, dog bites, spiritual treason, learned self-hatred, greed, and social control. As a Black woman, Lauryn Hill has likely experienced the social resistance to her anger even more palpably than many Black men. The intersection of white supremacy and patriarchy means that Black women who express anger often pay for it ten-fold. And as Dr. Brittney Cooper noted in her book *Eloquent Rage*, they are often labeled as "irrational, crazy, out of touch, entitled, disruptive, and not team players." "The story goes," wrote the author, "that Angry Black Women scare babies, old people, and grown men."

When I think about all the reasons to be mad about the treatment of Black people in North America, it's overwhelming. But heaven forbid I lose my cool in some bar, out on the street, or in a meeting. At work, I could be accused of verbal harassment and risk losing my job, and at a bar or in the street I could be mobbed, arrested, or worse. Chances are that what I would call expressing indignation, they would call intimidating, instigating, or if *they* are the police, maybe even resisting arrest—the tried-and-true legal justification for state-sanctioned murder. Black people are regularly prevented from or punished for expressing what is a normal human response to the atrocities over which Lauryn Hill sang her heart out in "Black Rage," with some people willing to go to unspeakable lengths to try to stifle our anger and silence us.

Thank God I found my art.

Hell, if I really wanted to scare somebody on the street, I could just whip out my slam poetry voice on 'em. I swear I'd have 'em runnin', family! When I am on the spoken word stage, I often hit the microphone on some Tupac energy for real. Most of my spoken word poetry comes out like hip-hop. I spit my bars a cappella, with a fast pace, sometimes yelling, and sometimes *growling* about the racism faced by Black people, Indigenous people, and people of color in our society. Lettin' all that anger out? It can feel pretty good, and it's necessary.

However, in my experience performing poetry at competitive poetry slams in particular, I've often felt like I'm just there to entertain the audience, often full of mostly white people who simply walked in to see a show. That can really complicate the otherwise powerful catharsis I might experience when sharing a poem, since, despite my desperate calls for justice, it's easy to expect that nothing will change outside the venue doors.

Few honors of mine can hold a candle to the opportunities I've had to perform poetry for predominantly racialized audiences *outside* of the slam circuit. When I share my work at predominantly Black or predominantly Indigenous events, I experience a completely different dynamic than what I've become accustomed to at mainstream slams within Canada. Instead of feeling removed from the audience and like part of a show, I can feel like part of an actual resistance. A synergy of purpose and meaning can emerge between me and the crowd; that feels a lot different than when the trauma and pain I share on stage are taken up as fleeting entertainment or as part of a fun competition. And when Black, Indigenous, and other racialized poets share their work on stage, and *I'm* in the audience, I often feel the exact same affirming dynamic. As these poets cry out for social justice, their words, their energy, it all reaches out to me and touches me. Those artists are *seeing* me while I am seeing them. They too fight every day against colonization and white supremacy. Many of them are fed up, too. They too are angry and broiling inside. And something about discovering in others this same sort of discontent that I hold, perhaps counterintuitively, fills me with hope and love.

See, in our shared righteous anger, there is actually deep compassion. There is empathy, which I believe is the very root of anti-racism work and is crucial in the work of allyship. The reason racialized poets are angry about racism is that we *love* ourselves and our communities. We *love* our children and our elders. We want us all to experience the fullness of life and the freedom that today is only experienced by some. And so, when we are angry and expressing that, however indignantly or angrily, we are actually loving. My experiences performing and sharing poetry within Indigenous and Black communities helped me come to understand that, sometimes, rage is love too.

That realization led me to see how the same righteous anger, that same resounding *demand* for justice, that use of *voice*, is a thread that connects all people who've become aware of their oppression in any of its forms, including working-class white folks, women, members of the 2SLGBTQ+ community, all racialized people, and people with disabilities. And we'd all be a lot stronger if we joined forces, as many of the same social forces organize against us.

In Regina, where I lived as a young child, I would often hear grim tales about the violence and danger lurking in the north central end of the city. While some skirted around mentioning race, others would allude to the area's large Indigenous population as the reason for the neighborhood's perceived problems. These deficit-based narratives were seldom challenged by the grown folks around me. Nobody intervened to say that the problems of poverty and crime were not inherent to any racial groups, but that some within these groups were *faced* with these problems due to our social design.

When I finally woke up and learned that poverty and its related issues are enforced mechanisms of oppression, and realized that the same **class racism**[15] faced by so many Black communities across North America was also orchestrated against Indigenous people where I lived, my desire to try and support Indigenous liberation efforts was automatic.

After all, Indigenous peoples are my neighbors, and the original inhabitants of the land we all call home (and land that is often exploited in spite of treaty promises made by white colonizers). If I want anyone outside of the Black community to support Black people in our struggle for liberation, then I should try and support other social groups in their quests for liberation as well. That's just basic ethics, and shouldn't require much contemplation.

When it comes to Black–Indigenous solidarity, one thing has become clear to me: colonialism orchestrates the oppression of both Black people and Indigenous people simultaneously, and on a global scale. Remember, a lot of us Black folks are coming to terms with reclaiming our own Indigeneity to the African continent, from which so many of our ancestors were forcibly displaced. In lots of ways, though not all, the Black fight and the Indigenous fight against colonization are one and the same. That makes our solidarity with each other not only sensible, but in fact critical to our collective liberation.

Solidarity work, or allyship, is a complicated and often circular process,

---

[15] **class racism:** the intersection of classism and racism, where the adverse effects of unrestricted capitalism, such as poverty, disproportionately impact racialized groups in various complex ways.

full of many opportunities to learn and do better. I have had many such opportunities, following various missteps, and I've done my best to grow with a humble eye toward moving forward still. I know a lot of people are nervous about practicing allyship, especially today when you may worry about getting cancelled for saying the wrong thing. But no matter how intimidating it is, I feel that speaking out is always preferrable to silence. Depending on your identity and your own social positioning, knowing how, when, and where to speak out may vary. Your allyship must include a whole lot of listening and taking cues from people in the communities you wish to support. That takes time and it takes work, but it's worth it. Be ready to apologize and make amends if necessary, but don't worry about getting cancelled—just worry about cancelling any problematic mindsets or behaviors you may have as you learn to recognize them. Just worry about cancelling oppression, wherever you see it (hint: it's everywhere).

While we often glorify freedom fighters of the past, including those whom I've quoted in this book, every one of them was far from perfect, especially when it came to understanding how racism intersects with other forms of oppression. No doubt, many of them benefited from these other forms of oppression obliviously. Instead of trying to sanctify these individuals, we would do well to remember their imperfections, not only to allow ourselves some room for imperfection, but also so that we can critically perceive *their* mistakes and misunderstandings, further learning from them. So that we can allow ourselves some room for growth. To me, critiquing some of the attitudes or behaviors of great historical figures does not diminish their accomplishments or their legacies, but it can certainly enrich our own.

We are going to make mistakes. But with the right collective attitude, we can win this fight. I believe that our love and our rage, which are often one and the same, can get us there. Some may try to paint us as angry activists, but the one inarguable fact about anti-racism work is that, at its core, it centers compassion. When we are angry, it is only in reaction to a *lack* of compassion. We social justice fighters choose compassion, and we have a right to be angry and a right to fight for it when it's denied.

We need to carve out places in our society where we can effectively express our anger and our other emotions so that they are heard and not silenced or ignored. We need to speak truth to power, and make power *listen*, whether it hurts or not. I get the impression that a lot of people don't fully understand what it's like for some Black folks to live a lie by going around smiling all the time, which is what is routinely expected of us. There is a special type of exhaustion reserved for those who are required to put on such a forced performance for so long, when our true feelings are often wrapped up in pain and rage. Sometimes, all that pretending wears us thin. The injustice of it can have a way of catching up to us.

the results of repression

The cost of having no outlet for our true emotions is grave. Within both Canada and the U.S.A., Black people and other racialized communities face higher rates of mental health problems and other health inequities than white people do. As I've alluded to, many of these inequities are, according to a Canadian government report, "linked to processes of discrimination at multiple levels of society," and "the impact of these experiences [with discrimination] throughout a lifetime can lead to chronic stress and trauma." As for the U.S.A., the situation is much the same. These clear side effects of colonialism are exactly why, in anti-racism work, we refer to all forms and degrees of racism as violence. Whether the trauma we experience due to racism is physical or emotional, it causes real injuries and health problems—just as violence is meant to do. Let's peep some stats, bearing in mind that they reflect social injustices, and not faults or deficits inherent to any particular group.

Indigenous people in Canada experience mental health problems at disproportionate rates, and are two to three times more likely to be hospitalized for mental illness. When it comes to suicide, Indigenous people are also put at much greater risk than non-Indigenous people who live in this country.

While the government of Canada has admitted that these issues are a result of colonialism, they have failed to recognize that colonialism is ongoing, that it is a part of the very structure in which we continue to live. If this were not the case, there would be no such inequity to report on; only racism makes it so. That means statistics like these need not represent nor predetermine anyone's future. Remember, as we work to curb racism and decolonize our society, we will improve these numbers.

Here in Saskatchewan, 28 percent of all people who died by suicide

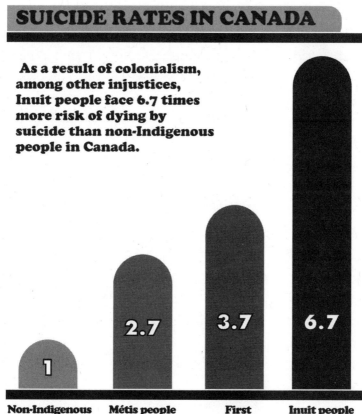

SUICIDE RATES IN CANADA

As a result of colonialism, among other injustices, Inuit people face 6.7 times more risk of dying by suicide than non-Indigenous people in Canada.

2.7   3.7   6.7

1

Non-Indigenous people   Métis people   First Nations people   Inuit people from 2005–2019 were Indigenous, despite the fact that Indigenous people make up only about 16 percent of the population in this province. And while some will argue that Black people, Indigenous people, and people of color need only to make better use of existing mental health resources, research also points to discrimination within the health care system and inequitable access to extended health care insurance as major barriers. Besides, would treating the mental health problems of so many North Americans without addressing the root cause of their problems—that is, their oppression—really work?

A report from Columbia University states that "exposure to violence, incarceration, and involvement in the foster care system can increase the chances of developing a mental illness." Certainly, Black and Indigenous populations are especially implicated in such "exposure," along with the forced family separation that often comes with it. I would argue, as others have, that it's best to look at the mental health problems facing some among these groups in context, and perhaps as symptoms of a much bigger social issue: racism. I mean, think of it this way: if you go and get a dog and that dog keeps biting your family, you wouldn't be treating too many dog bites before the dog just had to get the hell on out. Is it even possible to treat stress that is trauma-related without removing the source of the trauma? For many racialized people, to find trauma, all we have to do is go on social media, check the news, or be otherwise alive in North America. That's why decolonizing mental health and addiction care is so important.

Trust that understanding and fighting racism should be a part of the mental health care plan for any racialized person dealing with the chronic stress of living in North America, or working on recovering from racially based trauma, which may be ongoing in our lives. I know that medications and therapy can work wonders, but again—if you're only treating the wound from the dog bite and not re-training or removing the dog, trust that you're 'bout to be in treatment mode forever. The onus of this work can't fall solely on those seeking treatment either. Doctors, psychologists, therapists, and other mental health professionals everywhere need to understand that many of the mental health or addictions problems they may see in clients who are from racialized communities are direct results of the hostile social design of the society in which we live. However, few people among the so-called helping professions have enough—if any—training in this area.

Undoubtedly, we're gonna need a lot more Black and racialized doctors and therapists in the field. Personally, my comfort level in discussing racism with a therapist who's never experienced it is limited. And the potential for them to gaslight me about my problems is *un*limited. So, for you young racialized people out there with dreams of entering school to become mental health helpers, you know what to do. Take your lived experience and your socially conscious perspectives with you and go get it. Your presence is not just welcome, but necessary. Others within health care systems have begun the fight but cannot go it alone. Through your collaborative efforts, *you* will help to change people's lives, by helping to change the systems, and our world, for the better.

Unfortunately, there remains a stigma around mental health and addictions issues—both in the broader society and within Black and other racialized communities. Though the taboos around mental health have lifted somewhat in North American society in recent years, the stigma around substance use and addiction (which are often connected to mental health issues) holds strong. People in our society remain very judgmental of racialized and working-class people who use drugs, and are especially judgmental of the street drugs that people within these communities are most likely to be able to access. The so-called justice system plays a key role in that. See, its ongoing criminalization of only certain drugs is simultaneously the criminalization of only certain people. Many racialized folks who turn to these substances as a way to cope with colonially imposed violence are jailed for doing so, rather than offered help. Meanwhile, people among the white middle class who develop a dependency on prescription drugs outside of the advice of doctors are commonly viewed with compassion and care, and are often offered health care–based resolutions from which racialized communities have generally been excluded.

Unfortunately, the stigma around these issues also extends to some Black Christian communities, where there is fear that seeking help for mental health problems may be perceived by others as a weakness, or even a fault in one's faith. The reach of colonization is long, deep, and broad. It goes without saying that the historical suppression and prohibition of traditional Black and Indigenous spiritualities in North America has had a grave impact on the holistic well-being of countless human beings. And when we take the colonial religion that was forced upon our people (or indeed any religion) and wield it like a weapon against our own communities, our own happiness, our own well-being, and our own prosperity and health? Then we are no longer in the business of saving souls, but rather suffocating them, including our own.

It ain't a weakness to experience depression, anxiety, or other mental health problems. Often, it's a normal human response to trauma. We mustn't let anything get in the way of us recognizing that trauma, accepting the reality of it, and working to resolve it. Not even religion. My stance here is not meant as an affront to Christianity. No doubt, many Christian churches have joined the fight for the liberation of oppressed peoples everywhere. If you're a part of a religious community, just try and make sure that your own liberation is valued there. If it's not, trust that you'll be able to find a community where it is, religious or not. Both your health and your freedom depend on it.

The stigmas attached to mental health problems make the hard work of recovery even harder. While the word stigma today generally refers to a *metaphorical* "mark of disgrace," the term's original meaning was more literal, referring to the wound left by a branding iron on the skin of a criminal or a slave. The cruel practice of hot-iron branding was commonplace during the transatlantic slave trade. Today's stigmas hurt us no less than those historical ones. To take them on *willingly*, or condemn others within our communities to bear them, is an offense to our own humanity, one orchestrated by colonialism. There is much to reclaim here: our cultures, our spiritualities, our rituals and traditions, our languages, our ways of knowing, doing, and being, our pride in ourselves and our communities, and in some cases, our ability to be happy, healthy, and alive. I'll pray to *any* god that we can all get there one day.

the cost of composure

There are plenty of reasons why Black folks feel compelled to hide our mental and emotional states. Since the days of the transatlantic slave trade, Black joy has been suppressed nearly as much as Black rage. Due to the perceived connections between joy and confidence, any Black people who were happy were often viewed by white people as *too* happy, too big for their britches, and, most fear-inducing of all, potentially insubordinate. As Desmond Cole has documented, "negro frolics" such as parties and dances were once legally barred in certain cities within what is now called Canada. They couldn't just let us go around having fun, after all. Nah, for centuries, the only happy Black people acceptable to society were those Black people who were "happy to serve," which is why James Baldwin once remarked on the burden of Black people having to wear a pretentious perma-grin around their bosses at work. It's why Malcolm X, in his early days of shining white people's shoes, perfected his bright smile and cheerful but fake enthusiasm, which his white customers would lap right up. For Black folks, any diversions from the happy execution of our service toward white folks (be it in labor, entertainment, athletics, or otherwise) have been and *continue* to be actively suppressed. See: commenting on social issues, taking a stand, or even taking a knee.

As it would appear, any Black joy that isn't a result of our servitude to white folks is a threat to white supremacy that must be stamped out. Black people enjoying themselves at a restaurant, or in a theater, or worse yet at school are often perceived as being too loud or raucous, and as potential troublemakers. Eternity Martis recalled encountering such perceptions during her days at university in London, Ontario. In *They Said This Would Be Fun: Race, Campus Life, and Growing Up*, the author wrote, "Some of the white girls stopped talking to us because our noise made them mad, totally oblivious to their own rowdy squealing on weekends." The truth is, it can be hard for young Black people to gather at all without raising suspicion, or even drawing unwarranted police attention, because, if you're Black and enjoying yourselves, you must be up to no good! Hell, you may even be a gang of super-predators planning a riot. For decades upon decades, many wrongful beatings, arrests, convictions, and unduly harsh sentences in the courtroom have been based on white fears about Black people expressing too much joy.

For this reason, many Black thinkers have argued that our authentic joy is resistance in itself. As writer Dr. Hadiya Roderique explained, our joy is not only deserved and essential, but also an important counter to the ways in which "mainstream media fetishizes Black pain." When you think about our representation in the media, whether through works of fiction or through the news, it's a whole lotta struggle out there. Hell, our struggle is all some people see of us. And it's entirely reasonable to assume that for some seriously sheltered folks, even witnessing pure Black joy at all could come as a surprise and be taken as an affront to their expectations. Straight up, Black pain is not just something a lot of folks are accustomed to—some people *want* us to feel it. "So," Roderique argued, "when Black people express joy, we're not just happy; we're also signalling our strength and humanity in the face of a history and culture that sought to keep us down."

A full range of Black emotions has been suppressed and regulated since slavery and early colonization. It has been a long road of forced repression, y'all. But if Black folks ain't allowed grief and we ain't allowed joy and we ain't allowed anger, what else is there? Certainly, the record shows that stoicism—a complete lack of outward emotional display—is normally welcome for Black folks in North America. United States president Barack Obama was literally *famous* for his even keel and cool demeanor. People everywhere would praise him for his composure, shown even in the face of extreme criticism, conflict, or overt racism. His unflinching cool was key to his approval by Americans. A lot of other factors likely weighed into this approval: Obama's cis masculinity, his mastery of the English language, his relative wealth, and his light-skinned complexion, to name a few. But white presidents elected before and especially after Obama's stint have shown that, for them, composure was far from a requirement for their political success.

Composure—read: stifling our emotions and biting our tongues—is a social prerequisite that every Black person knows about, even if it's rarely spoken of. To maintain this composure in the face of indignity requires great personal strength, but as indignities pile up and become more common and more egregious, that composure becomes increasingly difficult to maintain. For how often we could scream. How often we could lash out. How often we could lose control and take back by force the dignities routinely clawed away from us. How good it would feel. But a Black person who uses violence either gets killed or goes to jail, and we know it. Thus, we are stifled, and left without even a healthy outlet through which to share our righteous indignation.

In public, we Black folks often feel like we can't show either too much anger *or* too much joy. The reasons for this sort of self-regulation (which is not really *self*-regulation, but rather social regulation) are obvious to *us*, but many still struggle to understand. You ever heard the stereotype that Black men don't smile in pictures? Well, I had bought into this goddamn trope myself as a younger man, refusing photographers' requests to "say cheese" whenever I could muster the resolve. And nobody had to teach me not to smile, family; I just did what I saw other Black folks and especially Black men within my frame of reference doing. I did what felt right. Employing this sort of "resting Black face," both in and out of pictures, was like a protective beacon that said: "Don't mess with me."

Unfortunately, there is a grave side effect to looking so guarded all the time: alienation. Some may call it self-imposed, yet we often can't help it. We are coerced into carving out these corners of solitude. Within predominantly white public spaces where we often can't feel assured of our safety, we may refuse to smile or laugh for fear of attracting too much attention, putting off even would-be friends with our "standoffish" and "unfriendly" demeanors. Ian Williams, writer of *Disorientation: Being Black in the World*, alluded to this phenomenon when he wrote ". . . I would like to have the privilege of a neutral face." The aspiration is a relatable one for me and, I'm sure, for most other Black people. Sadly, it just doesn't feel attainable at present.

the liberation joyride

Unfortunately, people often assume that the stoicism we tend to show is actually inherent to Black culture and bodies, which couldn't be further from the truth. This is a widely held racist assumption, which ignores racism itself as the root cause of Black emotional suppression. Black people can laugh, cry, and sometimes do both at the same time just as well as anyone else—although the *freedom* to do so often comes more easily in private company, and away from the critical white gaze. Recently, social media hashtags like #BlackMenSmiling as well as viral videos of Black people laughing have become welcome tools in the resistance against misconceptions and erasures of Black emotion.

Perhaps our joy *is* an act of social justice. That might be why author Eternity Martis said that she and her friends didn't give a you-know-what about the white girls thinking they were too loud back in university, and just kept goin' on being Black and having fun. A joyful resistance. That's what groups like Upset Homegirls of California have brought to

126

the social justice table. Donning shirts that read "BLK JOY," the Black women leading this activism group have provided both inspiration and exuberance in Black Lives Matter protests, which have been widely misrepresented and misunderstood as being violent (*TIME* reported that in the three months following George Floyd's murder, 93% of the protests had been entirely peaceful). In the company of Upset Homegirls, Black protestors have been invited to do what you might least expect—dance. As founding member Brandy Factory stated, the presence of happiness at a social justice protest is important "because you can't fight anything without love and I think there's a lot of love that's rooted in Black joy." When it comes to anti-racism, remember, rage can be love, and love can be joy. And we oughta let that joy ride.

Decolonial feminist scholar Erica Violet Lee, who is Cree, also promoted the importance of joy and love, which she cited as crucial in the struggle against racism, patriarchy, homophobia, transphobia, and colonialism: "Being in love is not a distraction from our revolution, but a constant pulsing reminder that if we truly love, love deeply enough and honestly enough, we put ourselves on the line to take down the greedy few who want to steal the places, things, and people we love." It's simple; if we love ourselves and each other, we will fight for ourselves and each other too.

That decolonial and anti-oppressive love Lee speaks about shines through in her brilliant essays and poetry. For Upset Homegirls, it comes about through dance. My own favorite outlets are spoken word poetry and hip-hop. You see a common thread here? Because our feelings are so regulated in everyday public spaces, art can become a very important avenue for us to express the emotions we experience due to racism. And not only that, art and social change go hand in hand. As legendary Black activist, author, and philosopher Dr. Angela Davis has told us, "Art and activism can transform . . . tragic confrontations into catalysts for greater collective consciousness and more effective resistance." The good news is, we can all participate in this resistance.

In creating art, such as writing, we soothe our own souls first. That's my experience, and it's no coincidence that people have used art as therapy for ages, even if it's only recently earned recognition as useful in that regard. When I pick up a pen and start writing rhymes, I go somewhere else mentally. The same is even truer when I step into a freestyle cypher session.

rhyme-sense

Freestyle rap circles, or cyphers, as we call them, can be nerve-racking at first. If you're a newbie rapper, it's hard to even conceive of coming up with coherent words, let alone rhymes, off the top of your head. But when you step into a circle of rappers who are super dope *and* super supportive, something happens, something verging on spiritual. I remember this one time, early on in my experience of cyphers, I was nervous as hell. But I got on this wave about what I felt it took for me just to keep on fighting sometimes. I wasn't in control of my words at all; to this day, I'm not sure who was. But I dropped this fierce couplet like, "It takes everything you *got*, and everything a*round* you! / the *sweat*, the *tears*, and the *ditch* where they *found* you!"

I ain't even realized what I'd said until the other rappers started mouth-gapin' and goin' "Oooooooh!" like they usually do when someone spits fire. When I snapped out of my trance-like state, I realized that somehow, without thinking about it, I'd vocalized a conviction that I'd been holding deep within me, and did it all in a dope rhyme to boot. In that moment, that conviction struck *me* and everyone who was with me profoundly: I was—until then, unconsciously—willing to die for the fight that I found myself in. This fight, for Black liberation.

I was shook for a minute after that. But I feel like I needed rap to help me come to that understanding, needed the cypher. I had no place else to go to help me work through my feelings about racism. That night, with those other rappers around me, I felt like a huge weight had been lifted off my shoulders, and it took me a while to even process it. But hip-hop demands this important sort of introspection. As emcees challenge themselves to come up with dope bars, they are at the very least forced to reflect on their lives and their surroundings, often critically so. Our society affords people so few opportunities to do as much, whether in schools, in the world of work, or in other public spaces. Therefore, for rappers, hip-hop becomes a refuge. Like all art forms, it's a place where we can contemplate and try to make sense of our identities, our living conditions, our problems, and our gifts. And when we say something that helps to make sense of these things *and* that rhymes and sounds amazing? Well, damn. We call straight fire.

To come back to my own freestyled epiphany, I should qualify: it's not that I *want* to die. It's just that some days, I don't want to live . . . like this. Like less-than. Like a second-class citizen. Like somebody whose life is viewed as dispensable, disposable, worthless. I have a beautiful life. It's worth cherishing. But the weight of thinking about generations beyond my own still living without equality is legitimately unbearable at times. For Black and Indigenous kids and kids of color coming up, I want the world to know that their lives—*your* lives—are beautiful! I want the world to understand and to safeguard this truth. Regrettably, we just aren't there yet. How can I sleep at night while it's still this way? How can I live on without fighting? And how can I fight without risking something? History has shown that those who stand up do so at great risk to themselves. But the risk to humanity itself is far greater if we remain silent and inactive about racism. The art of rap music taught me that.

no hip-hop allowed

Unfortunately, society has long demonized Black art forms like rap music, meaning many kids don't even have access to the cultural phenomenon that is hip-hop. Through the '80s and '90s, Black artists living in hostile and systemically racist environments began to rap about their lives, describing with righteous anger the challenges and obstacles they faced as young Black people. They described, sometimes imperfectly, their encounters with police brutality, with drugs, with violence, with crime—in other words, their experiences of class racism. The grown folks among the largely white middle and upper classes, who reap much of the benefits of this social design, didn't want to hear about life on the other side of it, and often still don't. To them, these real-life stories of poverty and oppression were just a bunch of foul language and deplorable behavior, a "bad influence" on young people of any racial group, so they censored not only the individual lyrics which they considered foul (likely because of their association with a "lower class" vocabulary), but also the artists and the whole genre itself.

This is only one of the ways that experiences of oppression have been silenced over the years. It's one of the ways through which oppression has been allowed to persist as an invisible specter, haunting all the time. As rap was suppressed for fear of a few four-letter words, young Black people were blocked from accessing potentially life-changing messages of resistance and empowerment. Misogyny was often pointed to as an inherent flaw of the entire rap genre, despite the prevalence of this form of oppression across other musical styles. Meanwhile, talented women artists like MC Lyte, Queen Latifah, Ms. Lauryn Hill, Missy Elliot, and Eve had their music barred from radio play. These artists' perspectives on the world, their communities, and the rights and power of Black women have been crucial to shaping the entire music industry, and to fighting various forms of oppression, including misogyny, within that industry and in our society as a whole. But their perspectives were unduly blocked from reaching a wider audience.

Collectively, rap has its problems, sure. But as a youngin', it was the only musical genre I could find that incorporated racial justice as a prominent theme, and that celebrated Blackness to any degree. As I alluded to earlier, despite its ongoing suppression, rap has some seriously rich history behind it. For ages, throughout West Africa, people known as griots, or djelis, have held highly respected roles within their communities. These poets, musicians, and storytellers have been the keepers of their people's histories and ways of knowing, and the teachers of them too. Here in North America, rappers have been like the griots of our own displaced Black communities, documenting our lives, our struggles, and our culture, reclaiming and continuing a tradition that enslaved African people brought with them across the Atlantic Ocean against all odds. The suppression of rap music from popular platforms is akin to the suppression of our collective voices, of our culture, and of our history as it unfolds. The fact that this suppression is ongoing today and not something that only occurred a hundred years ago doesn't mean it's not still cultural erasure. So, do we gotta wait a hundred years for people to see that? Or can we start fixin' this problem right now?

While rappers like Eve, Missy, Tupac Shakur, Nas, DMX, and yes, even Eminem were being restricted from the airwaves in the '90s, white musicians like Garth Brooks enjoyed widespread exposure with songs like "Friends in Low Places," which arguably glorifies alcoholism. There are countless examples of problematic content in country and rock music, though few people today are seeking to ban these forms of music. No doubt, all popular musical genres have long histories of substance use, violence, sexism, misogyny, and homophobia in their lyrics. Listen for yourself, but listen closely; oppressive attitudes in genres outside of hip-hop are often written in coded ways that can be easy to miss, often precisely because the attitudes are so normalized. There's no doubt that misogyny and homophobia are stark problems within hip-hop, but singling out only that genre for having these problems is hypocritical and racist, too.

The reason that oppressive social narratives exist in all forms of music and art is because art reflects life, and oppression exists in our lives and is promoted within our society. And that's where our criticism needs to be pointed first—at our society and ourselves, not only at Black musicians who dared to become commercially successful. The longstanding suppression of hip-hop music and musicians was the original cancel culture, brought to us by the same conservative North Americans who are banning critical race theory and its proponents today. Ironically, these same people are often outraged at the very thought of being de-platformed by anyone.

As white singers in other genres were widely embraced in spite of their questionable content, U.S. Congress was holding hearings on whether to ban so-called gangsta rap out of existence. They didn't need laws against hip-hop in Moose Jaw, Saskatchewan, though. It was effectively banned by community consensus, except for those two songs they played at the

Royal. Remember, not even Harper's attempt to bring Eminem to the masses was welcome. For me, the struggle to find good, up-to-date rap music in my youth was really real; since this was pre-YouTube and pre-high-speed Internet even, my access to *any* Black music forms was highly restricted. Thankfully, my friend Rotha was always good for burnin' a CD. For you youngin's, that's what we used to call it when we made a compact disc with illegally downloaded music. I would always have to put in my order early, though; with Internet speeds back then, it could take Rotha a couple days to download an album. But that shit was well worth the wait, lemme tell you. See, art and music don't just help *artists* work through their emotions. As I mentioned about my own experience as a listener of spoken word poetry, the positive impact of art on those hearing and viewing it can be immense too.

the glow-up

My first experience of really listening to Black music wasn't even rap. It was RnB. My mom used to order these CDs from a mail-order music subscription service, and half the time, those discs wouldn't even make it out the package at our house. I think you had to sign up to buy a certain amount regularly, so at some point, my mom was probably just winging her selections. As fate would have it, she ordered an album that changed my life. It was still in the package, just like I said. It caught my eye because the cover was this black-and-white photo of probably the coolest Black man I had ever seen. He was standin' with his arms crossed and his head down, just kinda brooding like that. His pants were low enough that his underwear was showing—a distinctly hip-hop trend that a lot of white people *still* don't understand. But it wasn't just any old underwear either; them shits was *Versace!* Thirteen-year-old me was like, "What's *this*?"

The CD was Ginuwine's 1996 album *The Bachelor*. When I opened it,

KHODI'S ESSENTIAL STAY UP PLAYLIST

Ginuwine
Ginuwine 4 Ur Mind

Mary J. Blige
Family Affair

Queen Latifah
Unity

Common
Be (Intro)

KRS-One
Sound of da Police

Nas
If I Ruled the World
(Imagine That) ft. Lauryn Hill

Tupac
Changes ft. Talent

Noname
Reality Check ft.
Eryn Allen Kane & Akenya

Lauryn Hill
Lost Ones

DMX
Who We Be

Sa-Roc
Forever

Rapsody
Power ft. Kendrick
Lance Skiiiwalker

J. Cole
Be Free

I saw Ginuwine's face printed right on the disc itself. It was sorta purposely pixelated and angled off to one side, so you could see one of his sideburns. That thing looked like it had been painted on with a thin little paintbrush, or a Sharpie, but it was his real hair. The sideburn swirled and zigzagged like a perfectly stylized letter E or somethin', groomed with surgical precision. Again, I was like, "What's *this*?" When I finally got to listening to the album though, my world was changed.

The Bachelor was produced by Timbaland, and the release was probably a main launching pad for his career. Listening to Timbaland's synthy bass lines blow the hell out of my mom's speakers, I knew it wasn't just me; *nobody* had ever heard sounds like those before. That shit sounded like the *opposite* of the tinny-ass music I'd become used to hearin' on the car radio. Timbaland's heavily synthesized beats were that new-new; the rhythms *he* made would reverberate all throughout your body, and make your chest vibrate. Somehow, Ginuwine's silky slick vocals were the perfect pairing for those revolutionary bass lines on that album. For the first time in my life, I had found music that spoke to me deeply, that really made me feel something. Once I started researching the often fedora-clad Ginuwine and saw more of his Michael Jackson–inspired dance moves and his unmatchable cool, a whole new realm of experience opened up for me. I found what I didn't even know I needed—a dope-ass example of Black swagger.

I probably went out and bought a fedora the next week, and started exercising my singing voice (much to the dismay of others). As it would turn out, singing like Ginuwine just wasn't in the cards for me, but I modeled my young persona after him in many other ways. See, where sprinter Donovan Bailey had taught me how to have confidence in my athletic abilities, Ginuwine taught me how to own my Blackness on the daily, and not just own it, but flaunt it. That was an important lesson. Before then, I was used to wearing my Blackness like a bad haircut, nervously aware of my difference from others. Some days I wore it like a suit of armor, knowing I'd better always be ready to fight. But after being introduced to Ginuwine, I started to wear that shit like a crown.

I'm not saying the bad haircut days and the fight-ready days went away completely, only that I could finally have some days that weren't entirely governed by the sense of Black inferiority that society had forced upon me. Finally, I could resist the urge to feel downtrodden. My confidence became even greater as I began to search for more Black music and discovered the world of Black RnB and hip-hop that was exploding as a cultural renaissance in the '90s and early 2000s. Black music, including rap, lifted me up out of self-doubt and despair. It helped get me through the racism I experienced, and it still does. Thank God I found it in spite of how hard some people worked to keep it from me. Black music saved my life. Yet to this day, there are people out there working to quash that music, quash our culture, and quash our lives, too.

resist.

Black music is rebellion out here. Simply being Black and not feeling *bad* about it is rebellion. Black confidence is rebellion. And the Black-positive self-image I was developing in my youth would become crucial as I began to participate more actively in the struggle for equity. Armed with the blazing confidence of an emcee or an Olympic sprinter, I *know* that Black lives are worth fighting for, and that the fight for Black liberation can be won. And in fighting against oppression (and knowing the prize), I simultaneously fight any *de*pression I may be experiencing. Remember, happiness is part of the fight. And the complete and unfettered joy or spiritual awakening that one can feel while making anti-oppressive art ain't bad therapy either.

If you find yourself feeling depressed, know that you can fight that feeling. What has worked for me may not work for you, but trust that between western medicine, traditional holistic medicine, spirituality, counselling, the arts, and anti-racism, you're gonna find something that helps. You'll find that healing often starts with sharing your feelings. Our racial liberation must also be an *emotional* liberation, since freedom from oppression and depression must mean freedom from *re*pression too. Healing starts with showing love, rage, and everything in between. Just try and point your love, and your rage, in the right directions.

One of the main reasons I'm writing this book is because I remember what it felt like to have my rage, but no place to put it. I remember the absolute futility of that, the mind-numbing confusion, the searing pain. Without identifying what we are truly up against, we become like anxious fighters who are all alone in the ring, ready to attack but seeing nothing; we are desperate shadowboxers striking out in turmoil and disorientation, punching dramatically but hitting nothing and changing nothing, while an invisible opponent batters us relentlessly.

But then, when you learn how racism works, and how the system is much more to blame for your station than individuals, you come to understand that the system . . . the *system* must be our target in fighting back. And we can land our devastating punches there. We must. To do that effectively, though, we will need to get ready first. That means learning and unlearning a whole lot. And for some of us, it means we gotta get well.

Around the time of writing this book, I started to notice a recurring pain in my chest. I began experiencing heart palpitations intermittently, and noticed that, at times, I couldn't seem to take a full or satisfying breath. Like a good parent, I went to the doctor to get my heart and my lungs checked out. After a gamut of tests, I was initially shocked to hear the doctor tell me there was nothing wrong with my body. "It could be stress," he suggested.

Until then, I hadn't considered that my mental and emotional state could manifest physical symptoms within my body. Plus, I had styled myself as mentally invincible and emotionally sound, perhaps from years of telling myself that I wouldn't let racism get to me. I left the doctor's office and returned to my full-time teaching job and my heavy writing work a little bit confused but resolved to persevere. I should never have been so dismissive of the possibility that I may have been taking on too much. Plus, in writing this book, I have needed to recall and no doubt relive decades' worth of racist trauma.

I spent a long time staring teary-eyed into a laptop screen that began to tell the story of my suffering. Previously, I had intentionally tried not to think about many of the painful memories I've shared here. I had pushed them away, pretended that they'd never happened. I'd been gaslit so much about my experiences that even *I* hardly believed some of them had happened, or happened as I'd thought—that is, until they appeared here again, on these pages, in this book, catching me soberingly by surprise.

Suddenly, when my wife Carly would ask me how I was doing, at times I couldn't respond without bursting into tears. That's when I realized that I was doing myself and my family a disservice by continuing to try and fight forward with no help, and continuing to ignore the mental health problems I was obviously wrestling with. Just because I hadn't noticed them doesn't mean these problems hadn't started long before writing these pages. Every racist incident and microaggression and each moment spent simmering in the hot stew of white supremacy all around me had put a crack in my identity, my esteem, and my self-image, which I'd convinced myself were bulletproof—partly because I'd convinced myself, or society had convinced *me*, that I was doing all the right things in order to succeed. And although I wasn't consciously feeling broken, inwardly, I was tearing apart, and my writing only helped to illuminate that fact. My true self, my very identity, had been eroded. You see, it's entirely possible to erode so much of your true self that you start to become accustomed to the feeling of emptiness. You begin to believe it's normal. For me, it took me some time to understand that as my Blackness was consistently denied and demeaned, and as I too began to deny and demean it so as to shelter myself from racism, I made my true self invisible, almost irretrievable. A ghost.

From this solitary place of erosion, I'd been trying to continue my full-time work as a teacher, keep up with my anti-racism speaking engagements, promote my debut picture book, and create this book, all while trying to still be a good father and partner. Putting aside the immense pressure of all these responsibilities, writing this work and critically examining every subtle nuance of my relationship with racism was, however slowly and deliberately, re-traumatizing. I knew that something had to give, or else that something would be me.

Upon this realization, I took a much-needed leave from my work as a teacher. I acknowledge that being in a position to do so is a privilege not available to all, another aspect of our society that needs to change if we are at all serious about achieving equity here. Leaving work was difficult for me, because I love my students at my alternative high school in Saskatoon almost as much as I love my own family. In many ways, those young people became catalysts for me to do the hard work of making this book a reality. I want the social justice work that I know *they're* going to do to be just a little bit easier than it is today. For me, I know the work has been easier than it was for my ancestors, and I know that they'd have wanted us to pay that forward.

I couldn't help but cry when I told my students I would be leaving work, in the middle of the term, unexpectedly. With some students, I'd established such a strong relationship that I feared I would be letting them down, disappointing them, making them feel abandoned. I should have known they would defy and exceed my expectations as they so routinely did. They knew what I'd been going through; I had been an open book in that classroom, as they were with me. We had reached the pinnacle in student–teacher relationships—ours was one of trust, reciprocal respect, understanding, and empathy. On my last day, my brilliant students surrounded me in a circle at my desk after the final bell rang and humbled me. "You need to do what is best for you, Khodi." "We understand." "Take care of yourself." "You have been amazing." "You're more than our teacher; you're our mentor." I had never felt so loved or so appreciated as a teacher in my life. Dear students, if y'all are reading this, thank you. You inspire me, and the promise of what all of you can achieve in this world helps keep me going.

As legendary Black American writer Audre Lorde argued, caring for ourselves is both necessary and important to our continued quest for social justice. So I'm still working on myself, caring for myself. I have to. In many ways, I feel torn apart; dismembered emotionally and spread into pieces that need to be put back together. But the thing is, I'd rather feel this way—all torn apart—than all put together but not really me, not really free. Assimilated, repressed, brainwashed into uncaring, or otherwise. When I allowed myself to be repressed, I was *de*pressed. I see that now. And upon breaking things open, beginning to express myself fully, I can begin to climb out of that depression. I know I can. When you don't recognize that you're at the bottom, it's hard to tell which way is up. That's the disorienting stage of things. But once you can truly see the bottom for what it is, you can at least start looking up and knowing that it's the right direction. It's the direction I feel I am moving in now, however slowly. And there is such optimism in that. Now, in some ways, I feel very happy and hopeful, knowing that I'm moving back toward myself, back toward wholeness, and back toward Blackness.

To help me keep moving in this direction, I am accessing counselling. The rest that my leave from work affords me is helping, too. Far too often, we have been trained to think that we don't deserve such rest, or even self-care of any kind. I have to admit that I struggled with the idea that seeking rest or seeking help might be taken as a sign of weakness. But that is a colonized, patriarchal, and self-damaging way of thinking that I am trying to unlearn. In other words, I am trying to break free from my suffering, from *racism*. And I can't begin to help anyone else do that unless I start helping myself, too. I encourage anyone out there who is feeling pain to do the same. Trust that that pain is not your fault. Nor have my mental health problems been my fault. Racism is to blame.

Since I'm still busy learning my opponent, I'm not willing to throw in the towel. I want to be here. I want to participate. I want to be free. And I want all my people, and all people, in fact, to be free as well. In order to make that happen, though, we all need to be well enough to band together and fight the racism that is every day working against us. If we can agree to get ourselves well, and we can agree to fight together, then with every battle we fight, we will lessen the pang of oppression on ourselves, our communities, and our future society. It's a ripple effect like no other. For each time you stand up for yourself or your fellow human beings, you lessen someone else's chances of suffering trauma and mental health problems in the future. Every time you teach your friends or your family to unlearn the racism they've been taught to believe in for years, you prevent the enforced poverty of class racism from deepening and spreading. You help a politician strike down racist legislation that keeps racialized communities hungry; you help a young parent feed and house their child. Every time you challenge a racist policy in the institutions that are meant to serve you, you don't just serve yourself, you serve your whole community and you *better* it too. Generations after yours shall reap the same benefit of equity that *you've* helped to create. If that sounds like a worthwhile life goal for you, I can't overstate the importance of finding yourself, finding your *joy* and your true confidence and wellness, before fighting forward.

Family, you gotta know—every time you help yourself, you help me too. We are in this together. So be well, and if you're not, then put in the work to get well. When I say that, I don't mean that you should try and fix yourself. Far from it. As a dear friend once told me in one of my lowest moments, you're not broken. However, our society may be steady trying to break you. We should all be angry about that. Why? Because human beings deserve better. We all do. And healing starts with the awareness of that fact. We deserve freedom. We deserve joy! So get angry. And get movin'. Put in the work to change our society and its unjust ways. *This* is the work of healing. This is the work that will help make you well and will make others well too, in quelling the source of so much pain. Encourage your friends and your family to join in your efforts. Help each other. Lean on each other. Laugh with each other. Lift each other up. Smile in your pictures.

And keep fightin'.

It's how we show love. And rage, too.

5

Black like you

Black like him? nah, never that.
Black like them? damn, take it back.
Black like her? shoot, that'll never do.
then Black like who?
fam, Black like you!

all Black people can dance, right?

I was in ninth grade when I realized that I had no clue how to dance to Black music. I was at my school's first ever MuchMusic video dance party, which was actually fire. Growing up in Canada, I always thought MuchMusic was dope. It was like our YouTube for music videos. It was a TV channel, kind of like MTV, but based out of Toronto. They had this one show called *RapCity* (not to be confused with BET's show of the same name) where, if you were lucky enough to tune in at the right time, usually late at night, you could catch five or so random rap songs—a goldmine in the rap desert of my upbringing. So having MuchMusic VJs come out to our little high school in Moose Jaw to put on a dance party was a trip.

My classmates and I were all a bit starstruck, even though the VJs coulda been anybody, maybe even some local dudes that Much had farmed the job out to. The VJs were white too, but much to my astonishment, they played a couple rap songs at our dance. It woulda been hard not to, despite the disapproval of school leaders. Like I mentioned, in the late '90s, hip-hop and RnB music were *exploding* in innovation and popularity. In fact, that very year of 1997 had a top 100 list *full* of artists like Puff Daddy, Mase, the Notorious B.I.G., Allure, 112, Usher, Monica, En Vogue, Tupac, Lil' Kim, Jay-Z, Foxy Brown, Dru Hill, and others. I mean, the charts were definitely gettin' Blackified that year. It's a wonder I had to work so hard to ever hear any Black music back then.

I remember them VJs at the dance played "Hypnotize" by the Notorious B.I.G. What was so cool about these video dances was they didn't just play the music but they also played the music videos on this giant screen. It was somethin' we'd never seen before in those days. And trust it woulda been tough for these VJs to pull off. It wasn't no digital projectors or even digital videos back then. Nah, the VJs were in the booth steady changing VHS cassette tapes like there was no tomorrow, handlin' them things like hot potatoes! Anyways, so Biggie came on. I almost didn't know what to do. It felt like my worlds were colliding. I mean, by then I already knew about Biggie, Tupac, and all kinds of hip-hop music; my buddy Rotha had helped make sure o' that. But all of the sudden I was in a very white space listening to very Black music, something I'd previously enjoyed only in private or in the comfort of my close-knit friend group. The whole experience was brand-new, and straight-up odd. Plus, I had one serious problem.

I couldn't dance worth *nothin'*.

For real. Years of acculturation into the pop and country music dances of my childhood had me knowing how to shuffle my feet side-to-side a little bit like everybody else, but nothing more. And I mean, that's my *dad's* signature move, you know what I mean? No offense to him; that move got me through a lot, but it was no way I could be doin' that to them bassy hip-hop beats on a *Biggie* track.

I had to do *somethin'*, so I started awkwardly bobbing my upper body back and forth, kinda like how a giraffe moves its neck when it walks—trust it was not pretty. If anybody looked at me it woulda been a sight, even in the dark of the dancefloor. I mean I know for sure my eyes woulda looked shifty as hell as I darted them around in a mad panic trying to find somebody who knew what they were doing, so I could copy them. By that time, there was one or two other Black kids at my high school, and I couldn't spot 'em. Damn. I even looked for the white kids who I knew liked rap music, but I couldn't find *anybody* who could actually groove.

Then came a light from heaven, fam, for real. I caught sight of Leang, Rotha's older brother. He wasn't Black; he was Cambodian, of course, but I'll tell you one thing—he *danced* Black fosho. I'd hit the jackpot. I mean, I shoulda known he'd know what to do. One time when he was driving us younger cats around in his drop-top Suzuki Samurai, he played the song "Pony" by Ginuwine, and loud, too. Dude had that Timbaland bass pumpin' so heavy through his subs that I felt my *heart* vibrating in my ribcage, right along with the music. I don't even know if that was healthy, but I'll *never* forget *that* day. I thought Leang was cooler than a cucumber on ice.

But yeah, at the dance? Leang looked like he musta studied a lot of Usher videos or something. He moved so smooth, and most importantly, so *differently* from everybody else, as if his body had become one with the music. He was leanin' back, gettin' his shoulders moving; he had the stank face goin' on. I mean his *whole* expression was hip-hop. So while *he* mighta studied Usher, *I* studied *him*. I musta copied every single move his ass made, I swear. And since I did it on the low, nobody knew any different! I felt like an authentic-ass Black person that night! It was a dream, for real.

Thing is, that feeling of authenticity didn't last long. Let's face it, it's hard to feel authentically Black when you're secretly copying the Cambodian guy's moves, right? To say I was feeling insecure about being Black in a predominantly white school, town, province, and *country* is an understatement. And it didn't help when people challenged me. See, as hip-hop began to get more and more popular, people began to ask me about my connection to it. Since most white people where I grew up only ever saw Black people on TV, usually in hip-hop videos, a lot of them assumed all Black people must be involved in hip-hop in some sort of way.

As I mentioned in Chapter 2, random people started to come up to me on the street and ask me, "Hey, can you breakdance?" Somewhere along the line, all those questions did lead me down the path of trying to breakdance. I spent many nights in my bro Rotha's basement with the cardboard laid out and everything. Even some of our white friends was out there tryin' to get down. It was fun, but I swear to God I messed up my wrists for *life* trying to do them power moves, family. I ain't feel like I could breakdance; I felt like I could break myself dancing! Shit is hard on the joints. In the end, I found out that doing power moves wasn't for me. I wasn't half as good as Rotha to begin with, and I just didn't have the patience for all that. I *like* my wrists.

It's weird though. I mean, if I *could* breakdance, like if I'd perfected it, and the answer to people's questions had been yes, I know for sure they

146

would've asked me to prove it to them, as if my Blackness existed solely for their entertainment, just as the storied history of minstrel shows would seem to suggest.

Black ways / white gaze

I honestly don't know if the love I did eventually develop for hip-hop music was partly based on trying to fulfill white people's expectations of me. But it's a complex scenario. While a lot of white people wanted me to fit the stereotype of a hip-hop-loving, breakdancing Black person, others wanted me to be the opposite, and wanted me to assimilate forcefully. I don't know how, but in a weird way, I think I did both. I studied hard both in my subjects in school and in hip-hop at home. I became a dual-identity person, both white and Black, just like my racial makeup, with the ability to navigate both sides as needed for survival. I still feel that way sometimes, like not just one person inside, but two. It's a daily struggle just to feel like an indivisible individual, like one whole self, when it seems that people never want you to be too Black in white spaces or too white in Black spaces. I know I'm not alone in this sentiment. It was in 1903 when W.E.B. Du Bois wrote about feeling his own "two-ness" as a Black person in America. ". . . two souls," he wrote, "two thoughts, two unreconciled strivings; two warring ideals in one dark body, whose dogged strength alone keeps it from being torn asunder."

Back in my youth, when I did decide to "go Black," I went hard. I'd rock bandanas daily, and I eventually got me some Lugz boots, baggy-ass jeans, jerseys, a New York Yankees hat, and an *obnoxiously* large silver chain—the whole early 2000s hip-hop head starter pack right there. Decked out like that, I stuck out like a sore thumb in my communities. One time, a white person even mistook me for a performer at the 50 Cent concert in Saskatoon! A question I still wrestle with, though, is this: is the "Black me" even really me? Or is it just an impersonation of other Black folks? People who are "more Black," or more "truly Black," if those are even real things. I mean, where does a little biracial kid from Moose Jaw get his Black swagger from anyways? At lots of times in my life, when I wasn't scrutinizing my*self* in this way, others would question my Blackness for me, which happened a lot when it came to my writing.

By the time I got to university, I'd started to develop a fairly Ebonic writing style.

Though I'd never felt welcome to try using Ebonics in academic assignments in high school, I *had* included a dope 12-bar rap at the end of my valedictory address, when I knew they couldn't stop me. It was a real surprise for that Moose Jaw crowd, and unusual enough in that city to make the newspaper the next day. The moment had been well received, and it brought me extreme confidence in embodying a rap cadence in more of the poetry I wrote later on. Entering university, I was emboldened to lean into my burgeoning identity, and become "more Black" than ever. It may seem strange to talk about this transition as if it was a conscious decision, and perhaps it wasn't. After all, my intensifying racial consciousness was more so something I was experiencing than something I was being deliberate about. But it's true that I did have to try out certain activities, dispositions, and ways of doing things before I could understand that they felt comfortable and right to me. This sort of awkward self-discovery process may well be a part of the quintessential diasporic Black experience, in which we're often removed from the very elements of culture from which our people stem. Moving toward these elements consciously may feel oddly foreign at first, but in truth many of those elements were taken from us, and so are rightfully ours to reclaim.

When I signed up for a creative writing class in university, I was hyped about it, feeling like I had finally found my (Black) voice and that it was a great time to start taking my writing practice more seriously.

Only, once I started attending that class, something happened—the *prof* didn't take my (Black) writing seriously. Our class format was simple. We'd get a prompt, write on it, and the next day we'd share what we wrote, opening it up for critiques and feedback from our classmates and the professor. As usual, I was one of the only Black people in the class.

One day, I wrote a very hip-hop-esque response to the prompt. In my poem, I said something about how "I got my peeps behind me," "peeps" referring to people, obviously.

The next day, I proudly distributed the copies and read my poem to the class. I loved having the opportunity to speak my poems out loud, since I could spin the rhythm and accentuate the rhymes and cadence how I wanted. I had a few positive remarks from some of my classmates, then the prof spoke up. Now, I could tell he wasn't meaning any harm by what he said; he was just plain ignorant. It was like he'd never heard of or read any Ebonics before in his life. With the whole class watching, he asked me if I thought it was suitable to intentionally misspell a bunch of words. For example, I wrote "your" as "ur" and he was like, "If I didn't know any better, I might pronounce that "er." And the word *peeps*? That was too much for him. "Well, how am I to know you're not talking about your eyeballs or something?" he asked. And the thing is, he was serious! I mean, it took me a straight-up minute to realize he wasn't joking, for real. He didn't understand that I was writing in a traditionally oral form, or that my use of Ebonics on paper was an expression of cultural voice, sure to be understood by the intended audience.

Anyway, I kept writing like I did, and eventually that prof figured out my writing style. But if I hadn't been as confident or as determined as I was, he could have changed the path of my writing forever, diminishing and then assimilating it—and me—the way much of my schooling leading up to that point had tried to do. But the hip-hop writing style I'd developed in my poetry was the only poetic style that ever truly felt comfortable to me, in spite of the fact that the odds were stacked against my relationship with the art form.

Later in my life, and even once I was well established in the spoken word poetry community, I would be questioned on my style. I remember I felt like I had absolutely *kilt* it one night on stage. When I got back to my table, though, this new cat who'd had a few too many drinks accosted me. Like most people in the spoken word community in Canada, he wasn't Black. He started asking me, "Why you gotta sound all hip-hop in your poetry? Just because you're Black? That's exactly why you *shouldn't* sound hip-hop." He said, "You got up there and I was so hoping you would sound more *literary* and stuff, like at least then it would be a *surprise*, you know?"

But nah, I didn't know.

This race stuff is so complex. At the time, I was the only Black spoken word artist performing regularly at slams at that venue. And this dude wanted me to sound more *white*, like most of the other attendees and competitors. The suggestion was absurd, but it also didn't stop my insecurities from setting in. Within the next two years, I started experimenting with a more literary cadence and blank verse style, leaving a cappella hip-hop bars behind. The thing is, I felt like I could do blank verse okay, but based on the reactions of audiences, I could also tell it wasn't what they wanted from me. Plus, I felt like an impostor—*this* time for trying to act white, something my society both demands of me and yet will never give me full license to do.

I had to learn the hard way that Blackness doesn't ever have to be only one thing. That it can be expressed in a variety of ways, carried and embodied by individuals with their own uniqueness. Expressing it means following your inner voice and your inner compass to help you navigate your Blackness; its impact on who you are means both everything and nothing at the same time. It means having and *rocking* your own interests, without fear of judgment, and without self-judgment, which is rooted in others' judgments anyways. For years, I downplayed my own love for the outdoors for fear that it wasn't something I should be interested in as a Black person. After all, in North America, Black folks have been so stylized as "urban" that that term itself has become synonymous in many ways with "Black," and is often used as code for Black when people are scared to name our race outright (suspiciously, that's often).

Black man of the woods

I'll never forget the first time I heard coyotes howling in the night. I was camping with my dad at Lake Diefenbaker in Saskatchewan, in a remote campsite, surrounded by tall trembling aspen trees. My dad is the one who got me into the outdoors, taking me on camping trips from a young age. Finding the tranquility of a secluded spot in nature in which to cook, eat, chill, and sleep was game-changing for me. To this day, it's a form of respite that nourishes my soul.

On the first night of that trip, it was pitch-black out except for the fire, and my Dad and I were sippin' hot chocolate. We were quiet, not really talking, just watching the flames and listening to the crackle of the wood as it burned. Then came a shrill howl in the distant night. Then came a response. My dad and I looked at each other and our eyes got big. Then came a raucous frenzy of yelps and howls from the surrounding trees, reverberating through the forest like pinballs bouncing around in a machine. It sounded like there could have been hundreds of those wild dogs just on the other side of those aspens, surrounding us. Chills took over my spine, and despite the fright it gave me, I fell in love with that feeling.

I had always loved dogs, but that was when I fell in love with *wild* dogs—foxes, coyotes, and especially wolves. I began to study them voraciously, signing out every book on 'em I could from the library— dinosaurs be gone! (No pun intended.) Soon enough, I forced my fifth-grade classmates to sign a petition to save the wolves in Yellowstone. A few years later, my Canadian grandmother took me to a talk by Candace Savage, a Canadian author who was launching a non-fiction book about wolves at the Royal Saskatchewan Museum in Regina—this was *huge* for me. Savage spoke eloquently about her book, *The Nature of Wolves*, which contained facts about the animals, philosophical reflections, beautiful photography, and a passionate call for conservation. During the Q and A portion of Savage's talk, I raised my hand to ask her a question about the book. Of course, I felt the audience's collective side-eye shifting all around me like "Who's *this* kid?" but Savage was

152

gracious as she answered, and she treated me with the same respect as any adult in that room—she made me feel like I mattered and signed my book, endearingly, "To a wolf person." My passion for wolves endured, and the caption below my eighth-grade school photo clearly states my future plans: to become a wolf biologist.

While my love for wolves and the great outdoors never died, the ways in which I flaunted it waned. I had been a Boy Scout for a minute too, and loved almost every minute of it, but by the time I hit high school, and started to come of race, I began to shy away from my association with the outdoors. See, what I realized without realizing it was that I didn't really see any Black people represented in relationship to outdoor lifestyles, wilderness survival, or a love of animals (let alone biology careers). The message I'd internalized was that the great outdoors was not for us, not for me. I even used to try and hide the fact that I'd once been a Boy Scout. And if people somehow found out about it, I would laugh it off like, "Yeah that was on some weird shit. I'm more into hip-hop now."

If you read much at all about wolves, you will discover that they are among the most misunderstood, wrongfully feared, and widely hated animals in the Western world. Through the ages, their image has been drastically tainted by Euro-Western misconceptions and narratives that overexaggerate the threat they pose to humans—everybody knows the Big Bad Wolf, right? I mean, in the storybooks, he was on some super-predator energy for real. Although, maybe he was just fed up with colonialism, the destruction of natural environments, and everybody hasslin' his ass all the time.

I guess I could relate.

But even as I grew older, I never realized that I could love hip-hop *and* wolves *and* nature all at the same time. And I sometimes wonder how that affected my life path overall. I never did become a wolf biologist. Some of y'all reading this may be thinking, what's all this got to do with racism? Dude made his own bed, right? But you have to view a person's life choices in context, as they relate to the person's environment, their system, and the racial hostilities within it. Oftentimes, the decisions of racialized people are based unconsciously on socially imposed compulsions not felt by others, and that really complicates the whole concept of free will as it applies to us.

Why are Black people, Indigenous people, and people of color still so underrepresented in biology and conservation careers, outdoor lifestyle communities, or promotional materials about outdoor adventure? How is it that when you think about outdoor activity, you think mostly about affluent white folks with brand-name down-filled jackets, carbon-fiber hiking poles, and techy camping gear? These questions are

especially poignant when you think about how all of the land being used by white folks for outdoor activities in North America is Indigenous land. Going back hundreds of years, European colonizers used church-backed legal concepts such as the doctrine of discovery and terra nullius, a Latin phrase meaning "land belonging to no one" (within this concept, non-Christians didn't count as people who could lay claim to land) to justify the forceful takeover of these lands, and the removal of Indigenous people from their traditional territories and ways of life. In much of North America, governments established small reservations, which they set up with the aim of containing Indigenous populations. As I mentioned earlier in this book, for decades, the Canadian government employed a pass system requiring any Indigenous person wanting to leave their home reserve for any reason to obtain the prior written consent of a government official called an Indian agent. The practice was entirely unconstitutional, but it lasted decades.

This illegal pass system, in conjunction with residential schools and strict immigration policies, ensured that colonization could flourish here, free from interference by non-white peoples. This was part of how the concept of "the great outdoors" was conceived to begin with. For many white people, the thought of land that was "untouched" by humans has always been compelling, often because they've wanted to be the first to touch it, or even "settle" it. Scholars like Dr. Sheelah McLean have troubled these "white-settler fantasies of the Canadian landscape as empty and wild," noting that their basis is inherently false. Without colonization and the ongoing dispossession of Indigenous peoples from their lands, these lands would by no means be empty. Only ongoing violence makes them appear as such.

That makes camping complicated. We campers who are not Indigenous to North America pay fees to enjoy a loose approximation of some of the ways of life that colonization has worked to extinguish here, and the world over. I *love* camping. It fills the soul. But I think it's important that when we're spending time on land that has been "preserved" for our enjoyment, we also think about whose land it is that we're enjoying, who is being excluded from that land, and the processes that led to its preservation (alongside the mass destruction of countless other North American landscapes). It's easy to forget about these realities when most campgrounds use various social gatekeeping mechanisms to keep Indigenous and racialized people out of sight and out of mind.

With this level of erasure, it's easy to see why some Indigenous people here may feel like strangers in their own land, as the late Innu leader Daniel Ashini described. For Black people, since many of our ancestors were stolen from Africa and brought to the Americas by force, it's easy to feel like strangers in someone else's. The lack of diversity among outdoor communities here creates a subtle (and sometimes not so subtle) hostility for racialized peoples that ignores any prior connections to land that we may hold. Other communities yet appropriate those connections completely. Sadly, as a result, Black and Indigenous people in outdoor environments are more likely to be viewed as criminals than enthusiasts, like that birdwatcher I mentioned in Chapter 2.

the rise of the wannabes

While I'm busy trying to figure out how to stay true to my Blackness and still enjoy my own interests, some white folks have had no problem just going ahead and pretending to be Black themselves, something that's been going on for decades. You're likely aware of some of the contemporary examples, so let's take it back for a minute. Even outside of the **minstrel show** circuits, some people went all in on pretending to be us. John Howard Griffin was a white American impostor who, in the U.S.A., took on the persona and appearance of a Black man. Having used drugs and UV rays to darken his skin beginning in 1959, the man journeyed in blackface throughout

America's Deep South, known for its virulent racism. His aim was supposedly to understand the plight of American Black people and expose the country's racism for what it truly was. He was the target of tremendous individualized racism, and kept a diary of his experiences. In 1961, he published a book chronicling what he had heard and seen. The book was titled *Black Like Me*, a line likely stolen from Black poet Langston Hughes's 1926 poem "Dream Variations." Griffin's writing captured the hearts and minds of white people everywhere, who felt changed by it, made more compassionate and understanding. When I was 12 or so, an adult family friend, who was white, told me I should read this supposedly eye-opening book. People still read and recommend this book by one of the most prominent white people ever to pose as a Black person (for so very many have done the same).

This ultimate form of appropriative cosplay extends to Indigeneity as well as Blackness. In my province, outdoor enthusiasts will often trek to a historic cabin site in Prince Albert National Park. There, they pay their respects to "Grey Owl," a man whose real name was Archibald Stansfeld Belaney. Belaney was a white, British-born impostor who, in Canada, took on the persona and appearance of an Indigenous man. In the early 1900s, the impostor grew his hair long, began regularly dressing

minstrel shows

Wildly popular with the general (white) public during the mid-to-late 1800s, these shows usually featured white people in blackface singing and dancing and portraying racist stereotypes about Black people. They often depicted Black people as happy-go-lucky, subservient, lazy, and especially unintelligent. When the American civil rights movement began to gain momentum into the 1950s, the popularity of minstrel shows finally began to dwindle, but their various aftershocks still resonate today.

in garb reminiscent of North American Indigenous attire, and advocated for nature conservation in his many writings and public appearances. In Canada, the national parks service adopted "Grey Owl" as something of a spokesperson, and even created a film about him and his conservation ideas. Many in North America fell in love with the persona of "Grey Owl," his lifestyle, and his beliefs, and never fell out of love, even after he was revealed as a fraud following his death in 1938. He was one of the world's most prominent Indigenous impostors and is still revered by many today. Countless impostors would follow, reaping rewards and praise for Indigenous excellence, all without a shred of true Indigenous identity.

What's most troubling about Griffin and Belaney is that both of them were heralded for sharing appropriated, watered-down, and disingenuous versions of teachings that real Black and Indigenous people had been living by and trying to tell about for years. These impostors ignored the fact of their own privilege, and yet leveraged it to achieve public acclaim. The same dynamic persists today. While racialized people are afforded little, if any, credibility, even regarding their own lived experiences, white people are regularly afforded too much credibility for supposedly knowing *other* people's lived experiences, even without any real-life experience with systemic racism.

reclaiming Blackness

The takeaway for me in all this is that I don't need anybody to tell me how to be Black. And no racialized person should need anybody to tell them how to embody their race. That's as personal a thing as how someone embodies their personality, their gender, their unique memories and experiences, their interests and goals

I remember when my good friend Jordan, who's Black, told me he was about to get his horticulture diploma, his hunting license, and a gun. Dude ended up doing every one of them things too. I shouldn't have been surprised about the horticulture thing. Jordan had always loved plants. I once saw him walking barefoot down the sidewalk in the north end of my city. I was driving by and had to do a double take, fam, for real. Dude looked like Black Jesus as he glided down the sidewalk in some loose-flowin' linens. I checked in my rear-view mirror and by that time he had knelt down to smell somebody's front-yard flowers like they were part of God's beautiful creation or something. To him, I'm sure they were, and I envied the way he moved so freely out in public like that, guided by his will and not by the fears and projections of others. But I had to wonder what the home's occupants woulda thought if they'd looked out the window and seen him lost in reverie among their begonias. In my city, police have been called over similar scenarios, at times with violent outcomes.

Jordan's interest in hunting seemed cool to me at first too, but it didn't take long for me to worry. Generally speaking, white people, and especially cops, don't like to see Black people with guns. As much as North America tends to fiercely support its gun culture, it's truly a white gun culture, one that excludes non-white people from participation, demonizes us even, ironically using our perceived violent tendencies as a rationale for *more* guns and looser controls. In this culture, the freedom of white people to carry a gun is more protected than the freedom of racialized people and even schoolchildren to remain alive. All along, gun advocates dismiss a disturbing number of white-perpetrated mass shootings as isolated incidents, often pointing distractingly and problematically to mental illness as the enemy, rather than a society that perpetually fosters this sort of senseless destruction through a lack of empathy, compassion, and solidarity. Without a shred of doubt, anti-racism can help curb that destructiveness too.

Speaking personally, I hardly feel comfortable walking around my own property with a pellet gun; even Black *children* have been killed for as much. This sort of trepidation hovers over almost every aspect of my life, as I'm often too busy worrying about what white people (or police) will think of me to just be myself and enjoy my life. Living on the prairies,

159

I have all too often seen myself through white people's eyes rather than my own, impacting so much of what I have thought and done. Others, like Ibram X. Kendi, have commented on this same phenomenon. It is through the white gaze that I see my own reflection; it's through this gaze that I see my past, my present, and my future. It often affects my day-to-day decisions and the goals I set for myself, usually subconsciously. These days, I can interrupt it sometimes, transcend the white gaze and see myself for who I truly am, and my world for what it is.

People like my brotha Jordan, who is truly a role model for me, remind me of my own dreams, once forgotten—the ones that exist in spite of anti-Blackness. They remind me of my own memories, of listening to coyotes howling in the night, and feeling alive. They remind me of my own history, of how my own mother was raised on a homestead in the wilderness of Cat Island, in The Bahamas. Of how my people have always been of the land, even before being stolen from Africa. They remind me of my right to participate fully in my society. They remind me of my right to be free.

When Jordan bought himself an acreage in 2021, a life I'd always dreamt of but could never imagine for myself, it gave me pause. But a few months later, I secured my own plot of land, and found the inspiration to write this book on it; here, in the expanse of the prairie, under the vastness of the living skies, where the coyotes howl vividly in the night, in a place of endless horizons where I can breathe and dance, too.

troubling manhood

I mentioned that John Howard Griffin probably stole the title for *Black Like Me* from a poem by Black American poet Langston Hughes. In the source poem, "Dream Variations," Hughes wrote poignantly about yearning for the freedom to dance under the sun, until night came ". . . tenderly/ Black like me." I marvel at the gentleness and softness that Hughes relays in this poem, not only of the night, but also of Blackness itself, and, presumably, of Black masculinity, a theme Hughes examined and problematized often in his work. If there's one thing that the commercial music artists I listened to did me dirty on, it was in presenting me with a rigid and one-dimensional portrayal of Black masculinity. And just as I was struggling in my youth to embody and embrace my racial identity, I was also becoming desperate to be seen as a man instead of as a boy. Only I was like wait . . . a man? What's that?

Ha, I remember getting my first goatee hair around seventh grade. I thought I had hit the *lottery*. I started rockin' that single hair like a badge of honor. When I eventually had like five of them? Well, I felt like I was 'bout to join ZZ Top or somethin'! Nobody could stop me! Looking back, the whole situation was gross. Boys, please don't do this.

But I had way bigger problems than my goatee hairs, family. There's no question that both misogyny and homophobia were rampant and even glorified by some high-profile hip-hop artists in the '90s. As I mentioned in Chapter 4, rap certainly wasn't the only music genre peddling misogyny. Indeed, others promote(d) white supremacy on top of that—commercial artists in all genres often reproduce the values of the capitalistic, patriarchal, misogynistic, ableist, racist, homophobic, and classist society that pays them to do so. In rap music by men, tropes around gettin' both money and women took a stronghold, as they did in more coded ways in rock music at the time. Across genres and racial identities, the message from many cis male artists was that the more power and control a man had over women, money, and other men, the better—that was the dream North America sold, and still sells; it's called patriarchy. And when people buy into it, they start selling it to others, too, like clockwork.

Unfortunately, I bought in. Subconsciously, I let these skewed representations of Black masculinity as aggressive, sexist, and homophobic seep into how I thought of myself and how I carried myself in this world. When I was a kid, a lot of my friends and I would use the word "gay" to describe anything we didn't like. "Gay" in the '90s, in my circles, was practically a synonym for "stupid" or "wack." We didn't even think twice about it, and if anybody did anything stupid or wack, well then *they* were gay too, and we'd let 'em know, like publicly. Usually, the response came right back at us, that no, actually, *we* were gay. However horrifying, this is legit how a lot of boys and young men talked to each other back then, and even the most responsible adults seldom called us on it. It was so normalized. Even some teachers I had back then, or that I have worked with even *recently*, used the word "gay" as well as homophobic slurs to tease their colleagues *and* their students. Today it's easy for me to recognize the hostility that this rampant culture of homophobia, ongoing in many ways, must have presented to people who were part of 2SLGBTQ+ communities, and I'm deeply sorry to have contributed to it in the past.

My guy friends and I used to always make fun of and antagonize each other; as is unfortunately true for a lot of young men, it was like the only way we knew how to bond. We constantly threatened to hurt each other and occasionally even did so, to the point that I hardly questioned the role of violence in our lives. Then one day at my house, my friend Craig threatened to eat my chocolate bar. I looked at him and asked him coldly, "You wanna *die*?" My dad happened to be walking past at that moment. "Khodi?!" he said incredulously. He looked like he didn't even recognize his own son. "That's a terrible thing to say," he finished. *Oh,* I thought. *Yeah, jeez, I guess it is.* But I'm not sure the practice of threatening my friends' lives left my repertoire anytime after that. Because we all did it to each other, we had to keep it up in order to fit in, or perhaps, in order to not feel beaten down. Big-ups to my dad though. He's a real man, one who uses his mind, rather than violence, to solve his problems. I shoulda just listened to him back then.

Regrettably, using derogatory words to refer to women and girls became a thing in my youth as well. The sexist terms were so commonplace in the hip-hop I was listening to, and the hip-hop was so commonplace in my life, that the words felt normal and harmless, like they couldn't hurt anybody. Misogynistic slurs were never as common in my vocabulary as "gay" was, but I still used them, often to mimic the male rappers I loved. When I was including those words in the rap lyrics I would freestyle and write, I did so because I mistakenly thought that that's how rap was supposed to be. Not once did I realize the true harmfulness of my words, nor how phony it was to use words in my rap bars that were at odds with my own beliefs. I mean, that's the very definition of a *fake* emcee.

I imagine that the giddiness I felt in using these terms back then was something like the giddiness some white people feel in using the n-word today. And what might feel giddy for them, feels rotten for me. For people who experience oppression, this sort of awareness of how it affects *us* should help us form empathy for other groups experiencing oppression. But if the discovery that you may be demeaning *others* just as *you* have been demeaned doesn't change you, well, they might just need your photo next to "hypocrite" in the dictionary.

In my youth, I thought that using slurs to refer to women and gay people was no big deal, because I didn't understand the true consequences of using them. But slurs work alongside discourses. And just as slurs and dominant discourses position Black folks as unwelcome campers, natural breakdancers, dangerous super-predators, and worse, they also position women and people among the 2SLGBTQ+ community in problematic ways. When you use a slur against these groups, or any groups, whether in a song lyric or in a heated confrontation, or, yes, even in a joke, you invoke these discourses and further embolden the systemic oppression of the targeted groups.

Reclaiming and using a slur that's been used to target your own community is certainly different, depending on how it's used. Reclamation happens when we take something—such as a word—that was once used against us and claim ownership over it in an effort to diminish or remove its harmfulness. It's a powerful process, and it's one of the reasons why variations of the n-word are so ubiquitous in hip-hop and among some Black communities. Few white people have understood the social and historical complexity of this trend, often either condemning the practice or feeling entitled to try and participate in it. If you are a part of a racialized community, don't go rushing off reclaiming slurs to everybody you meet. Even racialized people's comfort level with this sort of thing varies tremendously.

Today, I understand that Black masculinity is a lot more complex and nuanced than rappers like DMX, Tupac, and Biggie may have led us to believe through the music they made in their own youth. I mean, I thought DMX was the scariest person alive after I watched the video for "What's My Name?" But shortly after the iconic rapper passed away, I was surprised to learn that he was a huge fan of *The Golden Girls,* a 1980s sitcom about a bunch of elderly white women living together in Florida. Actress Gabrielle Union recalled sipping Heinekens with DMX and watching the show while he busted a gut laughing. This image of DMX was a far cry from his musical promises to murder your whole family except your grandma. Wait a minute. Grandma? Damn, it just clicked; maybe he always *did* have a soft spot for elderly women.

Thinking about it too, I remember DMX had this one track called "A'Yo Kato," about missing a homeboy of his who'd passed away. The emotional song was one of few in that era of hip-hop to celebrate platonic love between men, and to feature a flute track front-and-center on the instrumental, and I remember imagining this hardcore gangsta rapper who often talked about his opponents being "homo" and "pussy" listening to the instrumental and thinking, "Hell yeah, I love the *flute* on that shit! I'ma write about my bromance with Kato to this." I wish we coulda seen that side of DMX more often, but he very likely felt compelled to shelter it.

Back then, I was young and impressionable; I was trying to form an identity as a Black man, and looked to some of the only Black men in my field of vision—rappers—as models. But what I couldn't see behind the commercialized smokescreens of the hip-hop industry was that these

rappers were all poets and artists at heart, truly complex and emotionally intelligent human beings. Due to the self-reproducing power of
patriarchy, these rappers were hiding their complexity in plain sight, or
being forced to. They were downplaying their affinities for flutes and bro
love with aggressive dog-growling impressions, misogyny, homophobia,
money brags, and machine gun sound effects, likely for fear of becoming targets of homophobia themselves. It makes me wonder who *they*
styled themselves after, and if this cycle of problematic homophobia,
misogyny, capitalism, and violence in rap music has been a big copy-
cat show all along—one with grave consequences for countless human
beings. No doubt these forms of oppression lie at the heart of the North
American social structure. These artists often came from impoverished

Black neighborhoods in the U.S.A. If they'd had better access to education, especially anti-oppressive education, I wonder if they would've seen how these misguided values have actually been used to keep Black and other marginalized communities down and "in check" for centuries. I wonder how many would have changed their perspectives and their songwriting for the better.

resist.

Today, when I listen to "A'Yo Kato," I know and understand that there is nothing inherently masculine or feminine about a flute, nor anything wrong with expressions of love between two men. Rap doesn't have to be a hypermasculine hyperhetero genre that is constantly recycling misogyny and homophobia. But these problematic elements often showed up in the music I was raised on, likely polluting how I saw myself and the world I lived in. Still, I have to acknowledge that the Black music I struggled to access was the only avenue for me to see Blackness and Black masculinity represented with any vividness or consistency. Witnessing the talent and the literary acrobatics of Black artists spinning lyrical webs with unmatchable imagery, metaphors, puns, and even triple entendres (to which most school English teachers still refuse to pay any attention) took me on a journey of self-discovery. It instilled me with confidence and gave me a much-needed emotional outlet for the discontent I felt due to racism. I believe that hip-hop, which is itself born of protest, can be a weapon of mass inspiration, and that it can save lives. It has surely helped preserve my own. That's partly why restricting young Black people's access to the art form is so complicated. What I could have used to pair with my early listening habits was some serious anti-oppressive education. But I had no place to access that either; institutions and the people who run them made sure of it. And they still do.

If you're a young student of hip-hop, or any other musical genre, I believe what's most important is educating *yourself* about oppression: how it works, how it's reproduced, even within music. You've gotta learn about how oppression can be intersectional, how it may parallel your own experiences if you have them. You've gotta learn how to recognize it, resist it, and, if you wanna *make* music, how to replace oppressive ideas and discourses with more equitable and compassionate vibrations. Promoting homophobia, misogyny, or other forms of oppression in your music can poison the well that our whole culture drinks from, and there's enough people out here poisoning it already. In making rap music, it's easy to want to emulate the greats of hip-hop history, but you don't gotta emulate every aspect of them. Humans are complex. We've all got good things about us and not-so-good things about us, or as I like to believe, things we have yet to learn. Maybe you try and emulate somebody's style but leave their problematic content behind.

Besides, it's a lot of hip-hop greats out here to choose from. While nobody's perfect, as I said before, dope women rappers like Queen Latifah, Ms. Lauryn Hill, and others have artfully resisted the misogyny within hip-hop culture for decades. Other emcees like Common, Yasiin Bey (aka Mos Def), and Talib Kweli have stayed killin' it on some woke vibes, for real. And today, a new generation of artists like Rapsody, Noname, Kendrick Lamar, J. Cole, and Sa-Roc have released volumes of socially conscious bangers for us to choose from. Look for the independent artists in your town or your hood, too. The best independent artists have a way of transcending the tropes that the commercial music industry can restrict artists to. They're good at keepin' it *real* most of the time. If you wanna be a successful rapper, you gotta do you, and rap what *you* believe in. Hip-hop is about self-expression, not the expression of tired-out problematic foolishness that every other wannabe emcee is pushin'. Like I said, if rappers like DMX or even Pac and Biggie had been allowed to live longer, learn and unlearn a little more, we might have seen a lot more growth and awakening in their art too. And wouldn't that have been something? We don't gotta wait to show that we already know better. We can listen to what the late, great Black poet Maya Angelou taught us and *do* better . . . today. Angelou was a dope emcee in her own right, steady bringing the messages we *needed* to hear.

Rap is a traditionally Black art form, but that doesn't mean there's only one way to do it or create it. Today's rap music oughta represent the diversity within us all—from our gender identities to our sexualities to our cultures, our interests, our dreams and belief systems. After all, Blackness itself is not a monolith either. We Black people are a diaspora, a people with a remembered homeland, but spread out far and wide, from Africa to the Arctic Circle, and in many manifestations, with all manner of personalities, interests, and passions. Today, I often try and remind myself that I can be Black and be *myself* at the same time. It's true; I can *do* that. Like rapper Blackthought of the Roots taught me, it's actually more ideal for me to *never* do "What They Do," but rather just do what *I* do. Have my own dreams. Be who I am. Believe what I believe. Talk how I talk. Rap how I rap.

And dance how I dance, too. Not by copying others, but by feeling the music intuitively. By moving and being moved by it, becoming one with the beat and the energy of the song—getting lost in it. Truly going in. Having the courage to let go and just dance . . . like white people aren't watching.

The enlightened Black author, scholar, and activist bell hooks once declared, "I will not have my life narrowed down." And that's my hope for you, family. That whoever you are, wherever you are, you'll find the courage and the resolve and the *resistance* to just do you, dance like you, and dream like you, without being swayed or feeling blocked by society's problematic ideas or depictions of your race, class, gender, sexuality, or ability. Just go on and be you! Be masculine. Be feminine. Be neither. Be *both*. Redefine those very terms if you want. Just be somebody. Be a *person*. Be angry. Be sad. Be happy. Be loving. Be loved, and know that you deserve it. Be beautiful. Be brown. Be Black. Be.

Like you.

SECTION III
social transformation

6

make the
old school new

one-hundred dollars
for the skinny white boy,
two-hundred dollars
for the girl.
three-hundred dollars
for some little white kids.
for you,
all the trauma in the world.

people on sale

I was in seventh grade, just a little Black kid, sitting in my elementary school gym, watching my white teachers auctioning off my white school-mates in a mock slave auction. Apparently, the other seventh-grade homeroom had been learning about the transatlantic slave trade in class, which I guess is a good thing? Their teacher had the bright idea to give them the "real-life" experience of being enslaved African people for a day, including getting auctioned off to their fellow students in front of everybody at a school assembly. This one tall and lanky white kid, Neil, stood there in front us as his number was called and people started bid-ding on him. He looked embarrassed as hell. The thing is, everybody was taking the whole exercise as a joke, and somewhere along the line, the bunch of horny middle-grade kids even took it sexual. Kids in the audi-ence started wolf-whistling and getting suggestive with their outbursts as teachers looked on disapprovingly but stayed silent. I could feel Neil's discomfort, but it was competing with my own.

At the time, I didn't know why I was uncomfortable, only that some-thing wasn't feeling right. Call it a throwback to the BSP-type stuff I was on about earlier. I knew enough to know that my family on my moth-er's side were descended from enslaved African people. I also knew enough to know that a lot of my classmates at that school in Moose Jaw were probably descended from North American or European slave owners. But even though I was one of the only Black people around, probably for miles, it felt like nobody even looked at me that day in the gym. My white classmates and teachers were just entirely enraptured with the spectacle before them, watching Neil shrug in embarrassment and all that. They were laughing, whooping, and throwing their hands up in excitement. As they made an absolute mockery of what would have been for my ancestors one of the most inhuman and inhumane, most fatal and fateful, most evil events of their lives, it was almost as if my peers and educators didn't even realize that I existed—or that my Blackness existed, anyway.

And that pretty much sums up a good portion of my school experience.

Back then, in the thick of the '90s, Canada and its institutions had jumped wholeheartedly into the good old we-are-all-the-same multiculturalism BS. What that meant for schools was that they strove to deliver a completely colorblind education to their students. No matter who you were, and no matter what race or color, the goal was that you'd all be learning the same thing, and you'd all be treated the same way, ignoring social barriers for certain groups and enforcing conformity at the same time. Many school systems still run on this very same model. This, education leaders say, is equality.

One of the major problems with this approach is that someone somewhere is always deciding just what it is that students will be learning. Usually, it's a *group* of people deciding, and most often, they're predominantly white, no matter the racial demographics of the students. My K through 8 school, which did have its share of merits and great teachers, also did me dirty on a lot of things. One of them was my education about Indigenous peoples in North America. Indigenous students at my school were, like me, not completely invisible, but in many ways *made* invisible by the school and the community. Together, our racial identities were both obvious and taboo, not to be spoken of. I was friends with some Indigenous kids growing up, except their Indigeneity wasn't something I truly knew or understood, similar to how I didn't know or understand my own Blackness.

It's unclear how much of our racial identities were made invisible by their being unwelcome at school, or how much we and our families downplayed our racial identities out of fear that that they were *likely* to be unwelcome. Then again, perhaps those scenarios are one and the same, both stemming from the conditions of white supremacy. Regardless, the compulsion to hide or downplay one's racial identity is very real in education settings, especially when representations of racialized identities can be so skewed or non-existent there.

Authentic racial and cultural representation can be a form of validation for students. Through the Euro-Western curricular materials that schools tend to promote, white students experience this validation all the time, an immense privilege. But this privilege is easy to deny since, for them, it's not called cultural representation—it's just called school, and the disadvantages it creates for racialized students are rarely noticed or questioned by others.

colorblind?

Somehow, my school even made some groups of people invisible while simultaneously presenting their cultures as objects of study. One time in fourth grade, we did a whole weeks-long unit on First Nations people and culture. We learned all about the "Plains Indians" and their way of life. We learned about everything from their hunting and fishing techniques to their transportation methods and shelters. For one project, I made a mini tipi out of rawhide and twigs, and painted it with tribal-looking designs I'd made up out of thin air. I put a little moss at the base of the tipi, to look like a bush or something. I was proud of it. My friend Josh made a pretty impressive bow and arrow. His dad even tracked down real sinew for the string, to make it look more authentic. That thing actually worked, too. My classmates and I all fought to take turns using it in the schoolyard. Another time, I made a mini travois out of sticks, and later, my dad and I made pemmican at home. Well, I shouldn't say we made pemmican. I don't know what the hell we made, to be honest. Pemmican is supposed to be a dried meat product, but the meat in mine was raw and wet, like a paste almost. Oops. My poor teacher had to taste that moist, raw slop in front of everybody, and she could hardly bring herself to. It was a tense moment, no lie. She did lick it once, though, so I'll take the win on it. She was a brave-ass teacher, family, for real.

Looking back, it's clear that the curriculum focusing on Indigenous ways of life was inauthentic, appropriative, and itself a mockery, just like the slave auction I mentioned. In both cases, we were studying only imitations and skewed representations of historical objects, ideas, and events related to groups of people who were actually still alive and thriving in modern society—and fighting contemporary oppression to boot. Only, you'd never know all that based on what we were learning. Policies of multiculturalism, and the schools that promote them, have a way of constantly situating Indigenous people within the past, which allows these institutions and our whole society to continue to ignore and silence contemporary Indigenous issues. As Dr. Verna St. Denis has argued, this is not a mere side effect of multiculturalism policy, but one of its aims.

I can't remember what my old classmate, Chaz, who *is* Indigenous, made for a project, or what he thought of the whole unit. Just as my classmates weren't looking at me during the slave auction, I wasn't looking at him in those classes either. My brain didn't even come close to connecting what we were learning with my classmate's real-life modern-day Indigenous identity. My school was somehow both upholding and enforcing colorblindness while directly teaching about Indigenous people. I don't know how they pulled that off, but I'm pretty sure I know why.

Separating ideas about color and inequality from what we were taught about Indigenous people ensured that whiteness could not be scrutinized in relation to that content. In school, I never learned about the awful truth of colonization; I never learned about residential schools, the pass system, or the forced starvation and relocation of Indigenous peoples by the Canadian government. I never learned about treaties, broken or not. I never learned about contemporary land claims, Indigenous title, or ongoing Indigenous resistance to resource extraction and environmental destruction. When it came to Indigenous people and issues, I never really learned *shit* in school. And that's a lot more than I learned about Black people and issues. Trust me.

The way that so-called colorblindness supports white supremacy is clear. In North America, when color is not recognized, there can only *be* whiteness, the color so prevalent that it need not be named, bringing with it white ways of knowing, doing, and being. White education. White history.

White standards. White excellence. White *Indigenous studies*. Only they'll never call it that, because that could be perceived as racist! It's much more effective to pretend to ignore race altogether; if they pretend they can't see us, they can pretend we aren't even here. The whole colorblindness thing is a false ideal at any rate. While there are approximately 300 million people in the world today who are actually colorblind, ain't *nobody* out here race-blind. There's no such thing, only race ignorance—a less ableist term anyway. For me, this race ignorance came out at school in a variety of ways.

un*believ*ably excellent

I've talked in previous chapters about how I took wholeheartedly to studying the English language from an early age. As I increased my command of sentence structure and my vocabulary, I impressed some teachers with what I was able to do in both English *and* French. But for other teachers, my written assignments were less well received. There was this one English paper I wrote at the beginning of eighth grade. All my classmates got their papers back with grades on 'em. But the teacher gave me mine without a grade and in front of everybody said, "Here, Khodi. I highlighted some words in your paper for you to define for me." I was like, "Now?" "Yes," she told me. "Right now, please." The pleasantness in her voice was masking something, and I knew it. I just wasn't totally sure what it was. Everyone was looking at me, and I was confused as hell. I pretty much panicked, then I did my level best to define words like "Victorian" and "knack" for my teacher.

I wasn't sure how she wanted the definitions worded, nor directly why she wanted them at all, but I gave it my best shot and returned my paper to the teacher. The truth is, I don't even remember getting that paper back, nor ever being openly accused of cheating. All I remember was the feeling of being disavowed of my intelligence. My teacher had made me feel and look like a cheat, even though I had never cheated.

Eventually, she got to know me and my writing baseline, but I could never shake the feeling of needing to prove myself as *actually* intelligent, which likely set me down the path of putting way too much pressure on myself to exceed others' expectations of me in school.

No matter how hard I worked in my English classes, it felt like there was always disbelief over my English skills. Still, I doubled down on my language studies through university, eventually deciding to pursue an English major and French minor. And while I am thankful for my language education overall, today I understand that some of the praise I've received for it has been marked by the same incredulity that haunted my youth. What I mean is, I see now that oftentimes I don't just impress people with my use of language, but rather impress them by surprise. And while surprise often brings with it a big reaction that can sometimes feel flattering, it doesn't exactly make a person feel worthy or impressive at all. Not deep down. Impressive is one thing. Impressive "for a Black person" is another, and there ain't no colorblindness in that thinking.

Often, people see us and automatically believe we aren't capable. I mentioned educational streaming practices in Chapter 2. If your school uses these practices (which sometimes go by other names) to sort and group students based on their perceived academic ability, you might have noticed more Black and Indigenous students ending up in the less academic programs. If you haven't seen this happening first-hand, know that it's a real, often targeted practice in schools across North America that can limit students' opportunities after graduation. Because streaming is largely unregulated, at times, students are streamed even without any prior skill-testing. Straight up, everything from family names, to skin color, to irrelevant behavior concerns, to flat-out stereotypes can factor into how students are streamed in our schools. Unfortunately, our teachers and school leaders often make the wrongful assumption that we don't have what it takes to excel in academic programming.

Blackwords

In her illuminating TEDx Talk "Why English Class is Silencing Students of Color," Dr. Jamila Lyiscott recalled being part of a speaking panel. During Lyiscott's panel presentation, an audience member interrupted her to announce that she found Lyiscott "so articulate." Lyiscott of course acknowledged that it was offensive to have someone deem her mastery of standard English exceptional, but she went further. The Black spoken word poet and social justice education scholar scrutinized how the mastery of dialects like African American Vernacular English (Ebonics) or the Caribbean dialect spoken by her Trinidadian family would be unlikely to receive similar praise from white commenters. If the same audience member had heard her speaking one of these dialects, Lyiscott asks, "would she have determined something else about my intellectual capacity? . . . would she have determined something different about my worth?" I expect that some people would judge my own family's Bahamian dialect in much the same fashion.

There's irony in all this too. As Lyiscott pointed out in her TED Talk, Black language forms are often denigrated in our society while at the same time being co-opted by successful companies for profit's sake. In Canada, the Kraft Heinz Company sold more than a few mac 'n' cheese dinners off its Ebonic-sounding slogan "It's gotta be KD" (short for Kraft Dinner). As another example, Lyiscott pointed to the common slogan of the billion-dollar corporation McDonald's: "I'm lovin' it." The scholar rightly questioned how dropping the *g* on the verb, a variation of standard English practice that is common to Ebonics, is a move that could be corrected or penalized in a school setting but is used by the fast-food giant to make millions. Commercials for McDonald's have featured the pop star Justin Timberlake singing the popular slogan and scatting, a practice which also has strong roots in Black music. George M. Johnson, author of *All Boys Aren't Blue*, lamented a similar situation while talking about how language expressions found in the 2SLGBTQ+ community are co-opted by people outside that community. This form of appropriation is especially common for language coined by Black trans women. Think: "Yaaas, queen!" As the memoir author explained, such appropriation of language is often being used for profit, "while the community that created it is being oppressed or harmed for using it." Real talk.

One of the places where Black language gets appropriated the most is the Internet. I know my news feed is full of reaction gifs featuring Black people making exaggerated faces or gestures. On some social media platforms, people of all races make videos in which they lip-synch over real Black voices, presumably amused by the inflection or perceived expressiveness of common Black accents. Where blackface is restricted, blackvoice takes its place. Proof, perhaps, that most people don't understand or care at all about the *reasons* why blackface is wrong, but merely understand the social consequences of wearing blackface publicly today. So, while Black people remain restricted from expressing themselves and their emotions in real life, white people often use us online as stand-ins for their own voices, feelings, and reactions. In this sphere, we become bite-sized entertainment, ripe for consumption. The minstrel show repackaged, **commodified**[16] for the new age.

If traditionally Black forms of expression and language use are so effective at capturing human emotions and encapsulating human experiences, as most memes are meant to do, then why are Black language forms not honored, upheld, or even studied in our schools? If they are so popular that they keep going viral in the world outside of school, what world are schools preparing students for by omitting Black language forms even from mention? No doubt, Black students often face academic repercussions for using their authentic dialects, grammar systems, or spelling variations in school assignments, a consequence of what Felicia Rose Chavez, author of *The Anti-Racist Writing Workshop*, called "the implicit imperative for people of color . . . to write, but not to exercise voice." Race ignorance strikes again.

same old standards

You may not be learning exactly what your parents or grandparents learned in school, or learning it in exactly the same way. But chances are the "teach everyone the same thing" philosophy behind your education hasn't changed a whole lot. In the United States, standardization is commonplace in school systems. Take the classic Scholastic Aptitude

---

[16] **commodification:** reducing something, such as Blackness, to a commodity, something to be traded or bought and sold, exploited or consumed for entertainment value.

Test, no stranger to some of y'all, I'm sure. In existence since the 1920s after its development by known eugenics supporter Carl C. Brigham, the world-famous standardized test is still widely used for post-secondary acceptance, though it has gone through some name changes in that time. The SAT today is aimed partly at measuring American high school graduates' aptitude with the Common Core standards, which are nationally set standards for learning in English Language Arts and Mathematics. What this means is that in most states in the U.S.A., a racially diverse country of 330 million people, all K through 12 students are expected to learn generally the same content, mostly reflecting Euro-Western values. Those who master that content and can prove it through standardized testing gain the easiest access to their preferred colleges and universities. This systemic practice, historically embraced by almost all U.S. schools and colleges, favors white students predominantly. But it doesn't have to be this way. In fact, with equity in mind, the University of California announced that they would no longer be relying on the SAT nor any other standardized test for admission to their institution, a bold move in the right direction.

Here in Canada, educators with idealistic multiculturalism in mind have tried to shy away from the *term* standardization. But what are called learning standards in the U.S.A. simply have other names within Canada: learning objectives, learning expectations, learning targets, and here in Saskatchewan, learning outcomes. Within almost every province in Canada, regardless of population diversity, these "outcomes" are pre-determined, and are the same for every student in each grade-level course. As you can see, the standardization in this country is thinly veiled. While there have been efforts to reduce the number of standardized *tests* that students are subjected to within Canada, those efforts don't add up to much if what you're forced to learn in school is standardized anyways. Am I right?

Standardized tests become only *some* of the racist barriers imposed upon us in North America's schools. As I discussed in Chapter 2, through racist dress code policies, our institutions even try to standardize what we wear. But even in the absence of formal dress codes, you're bound to see conformity. In fact, the reason strict policies of assimilation no longer exist in many of North America's institutions is because they are no longer needed; our broad culture does the work of these now unwritten policies and we tend to adhere to them without any need for formal enforcement. This is why we often refer to institutional racism as a well-oiled system—because it practically runs itself. By our forced participation in a system of schooling that erases us, we are compelled to erase ourselves and conform, to *become* standardized, or face consequences such as exclusion from school altogether. Well, the time has come for our redrawing.

A lot of North American schools are working on inclusivity, no doubt. But if this inclusivity just means including students of color in preexisting institutional processes, then inclusivity is actually a diversity *killer*. It may sound counterintuitive, but true equity in schools does not come from treating everyone the same. Nor does it come from lowering our expectations. It comes from diversifying them. It comes from diversifying the ways we serve students, responding to their individual needs, interests, and readiness to learn. All of these factors can be impacted by various forms of identity, including gender and sexual identity, class, race, and ability, and the forms of oppression to which these are tied. This approach strives to ensure that all students, though they may need not be treated equally, will *benefit* equally from their education. But few school systems are taking this approach. For racialized students, contemporary school inclusivity efforts usually mean that you either assimilate fully, or you exist as a token, a cultural artifact, "limited to the decorative," as Dr. Verna St. Denis once wrote. In this way, you become witness to but not a true part of the standardized values system that your curriculum is built upon—and maintains. Other students still are blocked entirely from participating in schools, where their unwillingness or inability to conform may be viewed as grounds for expulsion or other means of school removal. At times, this removal is accomplished easily enough through the sheer unbearability of school environments, meaning that what we often think of as school drop-out rates are better conceived of as *push-out* rates. And that's facts.

School-based standardization is connected to something Brazilian education philosopher Paulo Freire called the "banking" model of education, in which teachers simply deposit predetermined information into students' heads for storing and, maybe later, repeating. Sound like your third period History class? Freire, author of the groundbreaking anti-oppressive work *Pedagogy of the Oppressed,* stated that the students themselves within this education model become ". . . filed away through the lack of creativity, transformation, and knowledge in this (at best) misguided system." The change-making theorist, once jailed for his liberation efforts, also advocated for a more dialogue-based, inquiry-based, critical-thinking–based system of education in which both students and teachers "become jointly responsible for a process in which all grow." He called this *liberating* education, something we've yet to fully realize in our schools, but that we've gotta keep fighting for.

It's no coincidence that the harder I studied in my K–12 schools, the more distant I began to feel from my own racial identity and community. The core standards, learning objectives, outcomes, expectations, *whatever* it was I was learning, were built to prepare students for entry into the predominantly white and capitalist society in which we all live in North America. Today, I am embarking on a career path of authorship that allows me to critique such a system of education. But my ability to do that comes partly in *spite* of the learning objectives I was forced to meet in my years of public education. I can thank a few great K–12 teachers who, at times, flouted the government-sanctioned standards and leaned into teaching my classmates and me to be compassionate, critical, and independent thinkers. And I can thank a good number of openly anti-racist university professors, most of them Indigenous, who inspired us students as they worked to decolonize and dismantle the institutions that hired and paid them—pretty baller if you ask me. The role these teachers played in my own life and liberation was invaluable. But the fact that these educators were outliers among their peers is troubling.

Somewhere during my long, hard run toward mastery of the white educational standards my schools had set out for me, these fiercely resolved educators stepped in and helped me realize that for all my efforts to adopt and perfect white standards, especially around language, I wasn't just perceived as smarter by those around me, but also as less Black. Without realizing it, I fell in love with my increasing proximity to whiteness, that is, to the honorary white status that my English proficiency gave me. How could I not? That proximity to whiteness helped me to dodge individualized racism at times. But my anti-racism education helped me understand that you can never be fully running toward something without also running *away* from something else. In my case, I realized that I had been running away from my own Blackness. I'd been running from who I was.

And I mean, if I have to alter aspects of who I am in order to escape racism, am I really escaping it?

Perhaps it's more accurate to say that I was being drawn away from my Blackness rather than running from it. After all, schools are often nothing more than arenas of competitive whiteness. There, we are all encouraged to conform, and to fight for the elusive high grades that will provide us better access to the privileges that capitalism, white supremacy, and other systems of oppression have to offer a select portion of adult society. In these arenas, racialized and other marginalized students are the ultimate gladiators—unwilling perhaps, but forced to risk everything in the fight for our lives and futures.

the war on knowledge

While policymakers work hard to control what you learn in school, they often work just as hard to control what you *don't* learn. They're often aiming to suppress critical thinking. In my home province, the Saskatchewan Party government has worked to discourage teachers from using the federally funded Canadian Anti-Hate Network toolkit in classrooms, a resource which the federal government describes as a "comprehensive anti-racism education program." As we discussed in Chapter 3, Republican lawmakers in several U.S. states have been waging war against the teaching of anti-racist concepts, especially critical race theory, in schools and other institutions. Even a "Stop WOKE Act" has popped up in Florida.

Critical race theory, or CRT, revolves mainly around the ways in which race is socially constructed and connected to power structures such as white supremacy that produce inequity in our society. As a concept, it forms the basis for all effective anti-racism education, and in this book I rely heavily on its foundational theories. For those willing to look, the truth behind these theories is easy to see in our society. But in the minds of many educational decision-makers, the realities that CRT illuminates are not worthy of inclusion in the hallowed learning standards of our institutions. In fact, many misunderstand critical race theory entirely, and see it as an attack on patriotism, a word which, by the way, is usually code in North American countries for **white nationalism**.[17]

For Black people, Indigenous people, and people of color everywhere, educating society at large about critical race concepts is one of the few hopes we have for our schools to play a part in racial liberation, a scenario that both Paulo Freire and bell hooks championed, calling it "education as the practice of freedom."

Education can look a lot like oppression when you don't have

---

[17] **white nationalism:** a racist ideology supporting the belief that the white race is the most superior of all races and that white people should have full control of countries in which they make up a majority. White nationalists tend to feel threatened by non-white immigration, cultural diversity, and, certainly, the resistance efforts of racialized people.

the freedom to think critically in school. During the days of "legal" slavery in the U.S.A., many American states made it *illegal* for Black people, free or not, to even learn how to read; any who did could be fined or imprisoned, along with any white people who taught them. One such anti-literacy law from Missouri in 1847 was titled "An act respecting slaves, free negroes, and mulattoes," and prohibited people from even meeting or assembling for the purpose of teaching reading or writing to Black folks. Lawmakers have never been ignorant to the fact that knowledge is power, and the contrived lack of resources in schools serving racialized communities is ongoing proof of that.

For racialized people, becoming literate in critical race theory empowers us to know and understand our own oppression, and achieve the conscientization, or awareness of it, that critical philosopher Freire understood as essential for us to liberate ourselves. To that end, I must urge all of you readers out there to educate and thus liberate yourselves. There is no shortage of resources for doing so. There have been and there still are so many brilliant thinkers, speakers, and writers to choose from, whose work on issues of race, racism, and social justice have improved the lives and conditions of marginalized people everywhere. Many of their works, including some that I've highlighted in this book, have been banned by schools and institutions across North America. As I've already stated, these bans are aimed entirely at keeping you in the dark about the sort of personal and social transformation that's required to bring about true equality where we live. My own writing here has been very much informed and inspired by these powerful books and their visionary authors. Some have given me knowledge that has absolutely changed my life. If you really wanna decolonize your mind, and your school policymakers won't allow you to do it, then do it yourself. Peep the unlearning library at the back of this book (see page 256). It might just change your life too.

Self-education may just set us free from the brainwashing grips of white supremacy and its frequent side effect for racialized people—internalized racism, complete with its arsenal of hopelessness, self-blame, and low self-image. White supremacy is meant to keep us insecure. However, it is the anger, defensiveness, and denial of book-banning lawmakers over any ideas that even begin to highlight the existence of white supremacy that speak to a true insecurity. I mean, if systemic white supremacy didn't exist, would we really need laws to stop people from saying that it does?

It's when we *know* that we deserve better that we will *demand* better. And we must demand better. To this day, on average, white students continue to enjoy academic advantages, graduate high school at higher rates, and leave high school with higher grades than their racialized counterparts. These privileges further set them up for better and easier access to post-secondary education and the job market later in life. In the state of New York in 2019, the graduation rate for white students was 15% higher than for Black and Latinx students. In Wisconsin in 2020, the rate for white students was over 22% higher than for Black students. In my own province of Saskatchewan in the same year, the three-year high school graduation rate, which reflects those students who graduate high school within the expected number of years, was 42.5% higher for non-Indigenous students than it was for Indigenous students. Many would attempt to explain these disparities through racist assertions that grad rates simply reflect the academic merit of individual high school students (here we go again with meritocracy and deficit thinking). But when you look at how non-Indigenous students—particularly white middle-class students—are so much better set up for success in public schools than their Indigenous and Black peers, you begin to see the holes in these mythologies. For white students, going to school is kind of like a sports team having homefield advantage, knowing the playing surface and feeling the whole crowd cheering you on, even reflecting your colors back at you from the stands. For racialized students, we steady play away games, even when we're at home.

That's why we've gotta look at disparities in grad rates through a critical lens. Largely, social barriers and institutional policies are to blame for the so-called achievement gap between racial groups. Everything from how curriculums are designed, to how students are graded, to who's hired to do that grading, to the day-to-day operations of schools generally favors white students and disadvantages non-white students. The gap these policies create is based on systemic racism more so than any true measurement of academic ability; it's better termed a *power* gap than an achievement gap. Think about it: if Black

2020 SASKATCHEWAN HIGH SCHOOL GRADUATION RATE

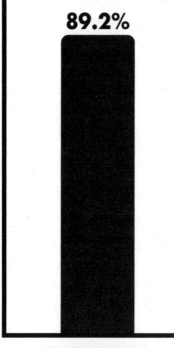

89.2%

46.7%

Non-Indigenous students

Indigenous students

and Indigenous students in North American schools are consistently failing at higher rates than white students, doesn't that mean, rather, that the schools are failing *them*?

prison high

What's worse, for many students who are failed by schools, future prospects can be grim. In fact, enough young racialized people end up in carceral systems like jails and juvenile detention centers that education critics have coined the term "school-to-prison pipeline" to refer to the trend, which the American Civil Liberties Union described as common enough to be "disturbing." And it's not just low academic achievement funneling young racialized people toward incarceration. Across the continent, school policymakers are reducing the number of academic and social supports available to students, such as tutors, counselors, social workers, nutrition coordinators, and transportation personnel. Other social barriers can make it hard for some racialized students to even get to school, let alone focus on their studies. And those who do miss class usually face consequences *at* school, including the aforementioned removal. If you've ever been frustrated enough to feel like the system is rigged against racialized students, you wouldn't be wrong. After all, "uneducated" ain't a personal characteristic; it's a socially orchestrated process. They don't want a whole bunch of us out here spreading *woke* ideas, after all. The anti-woke movement is enough proof of that. But I'd rather be awake to my oppression than asleep to it any day.

Stacked with Euro-Western values, ideas, and learning standards, schools have a long way to go before offering equitable learning opportunities for racialized students. A lot of times, they have no way of truly measuring your brilliance—they weren't designed to. However, even if the knowledge and wisdom that you carry can't be validated with good

HALIFAX STUDENT BODY SUSPENSION RATES

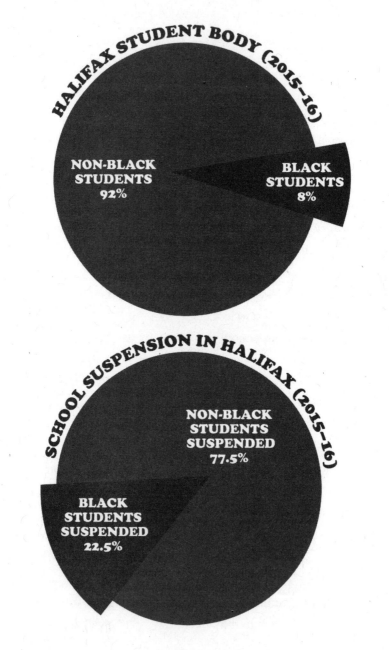

HALIFAX STUDENT BODY (2015-16)

NON-BLACK
STUDENTS
92%

BLACK
STUDENTS
8%

SCHOOL SUSPENSION IN HALIFAX (2015-16)

NON-BLACK
STUDENTS
SUSPENDED
77.5%

BLACK
STUDENTS
SUSPENDED
22.5%

grades in school, they may still be powerful tools in the fight against racism. And prison ain't a foregone conclusion for anyone who doesn't toe the line in school. If we all join forces and voices, instead of them always throwin' *us* out or lockin' *us* up, we may just be able to get these outdated policies and inequitable practices thrown out and locked away forever.

Right now, they steady *be* throwin' us out. *Policing Black Lives* author Robyn Maynard found compelling evidence that school districts across Canada routinely apply disciplinary action in discriminatory ways in their schools. Her report states that "in Halifax, during the 2015–2016 school year, Black students made up 8 percent of the student body but 22.5 percent of total suspensions." In Toronto, she found that from "2015 to 2016, almost half of the students expelled from the Toronto District School Board were Black, and only 10 percent of those expelled were white students." Maynard pointed as well to problems associated with police involvement in schools across the country. That problematic involvement is also deeply felt in the U.S.A. and plays a key role in the school-to-prison pipeline.

While schools and police departments may try to play off increasing police presence in schools as good public relations, Black students often feel and understand it as surveillance. History also points to ulterior motives underlying programs that place police in schools. Desmond Cole shared evidence that the school resource officer program in Toronto was formed in response to concerns around violence within the schools, and specifically targeted schools in neighborhoods with a higher population of Black residents. Shockingly, the broad-scale program was instituted without community consultation, and without a school board vote. The reality is that SRO programs are not about community building or school safety at all, but rather about racist perceptions of racialized youth as criminals, or at least potential ones. Ironically though, considering the disproportionate abuse of force and disproportionate killings of Black people *by* police, it is actually the presence of police in schools that may pose the most danger of all. Lurking there, they make schools look and feel more like prisons than they already do, especially for Black and other racialized students, and they create an effective means of funneling students straight into that condemning pipeline mentioned above.

According to research, the Edmonton, Alberta, school resource officer program labeled almost 21,000 students as "offenders" from 2011 to 2017. Why they would need a list of these "offenders" is unclear, unless it was to maintain surveillance on them. But over the span of a decade through 2021, police charged more than 2,000 people with offenses as a part of the SRO program. Alarmingly, researchers Bashir Mohamed and Alexandre Da Costa also uncovered evidence of a "bait phone program" employed by school police, where an officer would leave a cellphone equipped with a tracking device unattended. If the phone was stolen, police could then lay charges against the suspect(s) involved. The Edmonton SRO's own standard operating procedure states the goals of the bait phone program: to "identify the suspect(s) and seek appropriate consequences through the judiciary system." That doesn't sound like it's about safety to me. More like trickery, suggesting that police in Edmonton didn't just come into schools to *find* criminals; they came in to make them.

This trend of surveillance and removal of racialized youth is terrifying for those targeted, but often comforting to white people, including school staff members. This situation perfectly illustrates how racial privilege and disadvantage are relative; when it comes to police in schools, white comfort is rigidly secured, but only in correlation to the terror felt by kids of color. But that terror need not be everlasting. In Toronto, for example, social activists championed tirelessly for the cancellation of the School Resource Officer program in the city's public schools, and through their efforts, it came to a righteous end in 2017, following a landslide school board vote. Because resistance gets results.

schools reimagined

Creating better schools means securing better resources for students. In place of police resource officers, let's urge school officials to bring back the *actual* resources, the ones that will make all our lives better. Let's write letters and organize, stage walk-outs and demonstrations advocating for more tutors, more counselors and social workers; more mental health and addictions support; more housing coordinators. These are real human resources who will *actually* make schools safer and more just. Let's demand more differentiation of teaching and learning; more independent study programs; more inquiry-based, project-based, and student-centered learning. Let's demand newer, better, and more diverse books by diverse authors on subjects more relevant to young and diverse lives. Let's get the whole curriculum changed— transformed—to better reflect the lives of all people and cultures.

Truly, culturally responsive change in schools is possible. All over North America, students have called for and secured positive changes in everything from curriculum to dress codes to pronoun preference policies in our schools; they've achieved all this by staging strikes, circulating petitions, and organizing demonstrations to advance their cause. Some may argue that there simply isn't enough public money to fund the sorts of changes that activists are advocating for. But just *think* of all the money we can divert from police budgets by removing police from schools. In Ontario, Peel Regional Police alone spend over 9 million dollars per year on their SRO program. That ain't no chump change, and it could be useful to students. As a shining example of what is possible, students with the Black Lives Matter Youth Vanguard effectively ended random searches of students in the Los Angeles Unified School District, and secured 25 million USD in police funds to be reallocated to high need schools in the district. I'm here for all o' that.

To truly reimagine schools, we must think outside the box that we have built ourselves into. One element of culture that plays a crucial role in education is language, something I've pointed to often in this book. And many school districts could learn from the Oakland, California, example of reimagining language education. In 1996, the school district there moved publicly to recognize the validity of African American Vernacular English, elevating Ebonics far beyond its perceived status as lazy or "broken" English, and aimed to welcome the use of Ebonics within the classroom alongside the continued teaching of "Standard" English. Oakland educators faced enormous public criticism over this move, but big-ups to them. In the '90s, this method was well ahead of its time. Today, it's known as translanguaging pedagogy. Nowadays scholars are recognizing the effectiveness of translanguaging strategies in the classroom. As scholars Jasone Cenoz and Dirk Gorter said of translanguaging, learning a target language is much more effective if students "are allowed to use resources from their whole linguistic repertoire." For many Black students, this linguistic repertoire may include Ebonics or Caribbean English or various African English dialects, among other languages. Learning to see these speech patterns as advantageous to learning Standard English rather than interfering with it is not only brilliant, but also anti-racist.

A lot of us switch back and forth between different language forms spoken in our homes, communities, and schools or workplaces. It's a normal part of daily life. But if you're accustomed to speaking mainly one dialect from birth, learning how and when to "code-switch," as it's called, can be a difficult adjustment to make. Schools like some of those in Oakland as well as Los Angeles, and now beyond, assist Black students in learning to navigate these language dynamics, teaching about equivalent structures and vocabularies in both Ebonics and Standard English—an important and useful subject of study.

The need to code-switch is not power-neutral. Usually, young Black people are required to switch out of more familiar language forms when confronted by white people in positions of increased social power, like bosses, teachers or other school authorities, or the police. Personally, I'd like to see code-*blending* welcomed more often into schools. Unlike switching, blending allows students to blend the various dialects within their repertoire at will, depending on which dialect will be most effective for the specific voice, content, audience, and purpose of the writing or speaking assignment. Determining how to use language based on these conditions is a core principle of English Language Arts education, but one that's routinely ignored by school policymakers when it comes to Ebonics, which they will often dismiss—due to racial bias—as useless slang.

But what if the community you wish to reach with some of your writing or your speaking is your own cultural community? Whether it's for a school assignment or personal communication, in these cases you oughta ask yourself: is the language that you're speaking a language that speaks to *you*? And even when you're communicating with speakers of Standard English, you may ask yourself, why should I constantly be required to change my use of language? Why should I always be the one to acquiesce? When schools restrict students' use of language to Standard English, they go against their own learning principles, and cut out our very tongues.

As I hope to have shown in this book, droppin' the occasional *g* at the end of a word doesn't mean you're stupid. And people shouldn't perceive it as such either. Sometimes, doing so helps you get your point across in just the right voice for the occasion. I mean, seriously, teachers? You 'bout to let the folks at McDonald's get rich off o' that move and reduce students' grades for doin' the same thing in school? Please! Ha, I used to have teachers who would joke that if we didn't properly learn what they were teaching, we'd end up working for McDonald's for the rest of our lives. I guess the joke's on *their* asses now. Somebody's up on them golden arches laughin' their head off as we speak, just for ignoring what they were taught in school. One of the biggest arguments my teachers used to have in favor of Standard English spelling and grammar was that it was a *requirement* in order for any written work to be published.

Well, ahem, I guess that idea be out the window too.

Cultural dialects aside, a lot of the writing that you young folks out there do probably happens on electronic devices. Are your knowledge and skills in texting, using emojis, and posting on various social media

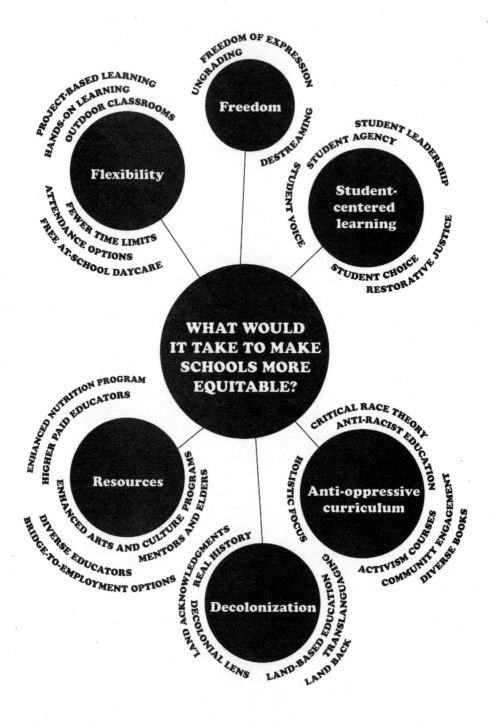

platforms recognized in school? You think most school officials could keep up with you on those fronts? Hell nah. And why *is* that? When westernized schooling first began, there was no such thing as texting or social media. But today, these are among the most relevant, widely used forms of communication. Why won't schools get relevant, too? Many jobs in marketing, tourism, journalism, and beyond require social media savviness. Not to mention the many influencers and YouTube personalities who make their whole living through how they express themselves online. Any policymakers who claim to be preparing young people for the "real world" oughta be welcoming digital forms of communication into the classroom, not omitting or criticizing them on some holier-than-thou type shit.

smh.

The truth is that the strict standards and rigidity of the old-school education model are completely tired out. Despite efforts to rename and reshape them, these standards have been used for so long and have caused so much inequity for racialized groups that we need a complete and radical reform of schooling across the continent. Such a reform should recognize and validate every student as an individual and a human being, acknowledging their racial, gender, class, and sexual identities, as well as their varying abilities. These factors should be taken into consideration along with learning styles and student interests when planning the learning and *un*learning program. And this program ought to be student-led primarily. Our new schools should be *un*schools in all honesty.

In your schools and colleges, you shouldn't need to conform to pre-set molds that predominantly wealthy white people have created for you. Instead, you should be able to experience intellectual freedom, learn critical thinking, and pursue learning that best reflects who you are and the fullness of what you imagine for your future. This means that all the people involved in planning a curriculum need to give up and give over their rigidly maintained power. They must start embodying humility and act in service to students, to you. *You* should be able to help to shape your own education. Surely some teachers and school leaders already strive to share their power with students, but often they face bureaucratic roadblocks in trying to break free of the established norms and rigidity of school and curriculum. Many fine educators feel compelled to leave the often hostile environments of school systems entirely, and end up taking their invaluable gifts with them.

I personally trust that, if given the freedom, y'all young people out there can actually produce and *create* knowledge that will be more valuable to society than the knowledge that has been set out for you to learn by your government. So what are we doing with these played out standards in our K−12 curriculums? *You* all have so much to offer the world of education with your own unique perspectives, input, ideas, and discoveries. It is foolish, dismissive, out-of-date, and straight-up oppressive for school systems to ignore that.

unmentionable history 101

I often wonder who I would have become if I'd had the opportunity to pursue a more culturally, racially, and personally responsive curriculum. My passionate interests in spoken word poetry and rap music were never validated within my K−12 experience. I could rap at the occasional school talent show, but my performances and writing in this area were, like my Blackness, unacknowledged in my classes. Black activist Assata Shakur referred to the proverbial cold shoulder that schools give us as "hostile indifference." I *feel* that. I remember preparing a poem to perform for my grad talent show in 2001, before I even knew what spoken word poetry was. The piece was pretty dope; it was a responsive thing that my friend Dave and I co-wrote and were gonna perform together. At the audition, my teachers liked it, but they had no idea what it was, or what to call it in the printed program. I didn't either, and much to-do was made about what the hell to call our performance. This was way before YouTube and

Wikipedia, and I was just doing what felt right, like an a cappella rap kinda thing. Nothing in my education had provided me with a model of the genre; I came upon it independently while seeking a style of my own, possibly because I knew that my writing voice didn't fit within any of the poetic genres I'd been taught in school. Anyway, in the end, we settled on calling the piece a "vocal presentation." A few classmates who'd read the program before grad asked me if we were planning on singing—most of them shoulda known from my earlier attempts at emulating Ginuwine that I couldn't sing worth nothin'.

My school never taught me that spoken word/slam poetry emerged in the '80s in the U.S.A., in close tandem with the radical rise of hip-hop music and culture. They never taught me that it was popular among modern Black communities, that it could be interpreted as an extension of the ancient African oral tradition, a means of reclaiming the culture that was stripped away from our ancestors—and consequently, from us. They never told me about griots and djelis and the ancient legacies of Black oral histories, far predating the beat poetry movement of the 1950s. I had to learn these things on my own, with some help from Black Canadian writer Lawrence Hill and his novel *The Book of Negroes*, a gripping realistic account of slavery, which the author published six years after I'd graduated high school. Its title, based on the name of an actual government document, was somehow too unmentionable for the market in the U.S.A.; there the book is sold under the title *Someone Knows My Name*.

The thing is, beyond watching my classmates partake in a painful reenactment of a slave auction, I hardly learned anything about Black history in my prairie school experience. It's too bad, and not just for me. As scholar Dr. Karina Vernon wrote about Black prairie history in particular, "It is not only Black students who are robbed when the richness of their histories is excised from the history books. All of us are deprived when the full complexity of our collective history is denied. It cheats us of a full understanding of our own present moment." In 2020, Vernon released an anthology titled *The Black Prairie Archives*, compiling the works of over 60 Black prairie writers from the 1800s to the present day. The book is an overdue gift to Black students and indeed all students of history, language, and literature. In it, Vernon returns to Black prairie people much of the writing that our institutions withheld from our eyes, tried to erase from our memories, and that some governments have worked to criminalize. She returns to us our forebears too, documenting the Black fur traders and translators of Canada's pre-confederation days, the previously undocumented, unmentioned, and unmentionable of our history books.

The list of unmentionables in the story of Canada is long. Our history books are rife with omissions that work to glorify colonialism and colonizers, and that deny, diminish, and degrade the existence of Black, Indigenous, and other racialized peoples here. It ain't by accident either, family. In 2020, curriculum advisors for Alberta's provincial government suggested removing references to Indian residential schools from the K–4 social studies curriculum, for fear that the topic wasn't age appropriate. Not long afterward, as I mentioned in Chapter 2, Indigenous groups within Canada began finding evidence of the unmarked graves of children at former residential school sites. I wonder if those curriculum advisors from Alberta ever questioned the "age appropriateness" of the deaths of these children, who, just like those advisors, were human beings.

While stories of these grisly discoveries reached mainstream media, non-Indigenous people and the government of Canada itself have failed to sustain attention on this important issue or to offer a meaningful response in the way of action or amends. Telling the truth about it all in today's schools would be a good place to start. Calls to action for truth and "reconciliation" with Indigenous peoples in Canada predate the discoveries of child graves by far, but still, here we are, ignoring and silencing these issues both in schools and in our broader society, though they should be alarming. How can we ever reconcile a truth that many are barred from knowing in the first place?

Growing up without the full knowledge of our histories hurts all people, but it can actively disengage racialized youth from their school communities. The erasure of our peoples' histories from textbooks can leave today's young students of color feeling rather "placeless" here; an unjust reality for young Indigenous folks especially, whose ancestors have called these lands home from time immemorial. But we *have* histories, y'all.

When I was growing up, I did know and feel that Moose Jaw was my home, but I always struggled to find my place there. I wouldn't learn much about the long and intriguing Black history of the prairies until I had graduated university and become a teacher myself. At my first teaching job, I was stationed at a school in Moose Jaw's South Hill neighborhood. In that town, a railyard separates the north and south sides of the city, and you'd be right to assume that, just like the river in Saskatoon, the railyard creates some division. The north side has always been viewed as wealthier, while the south side was seen as home to more working-class families and recent immigrants than the north. Moose Jaw's South Hill had once been given the nickname Garlic Heights by North Hill residents, used to refer derogatorily to the sizeable population of Ukrainian immigrants who called the city's south side home. As I alluded to in Chapter 2, at the time, even whiteness itself was once defined more narrowly within North America, and as an identity, during some historical periods, it was available to born English-speaking and Protestant white people primarily. Even white-skinned immigrants to Canada who fell outside of these identity markers often faced serious prejudice. Today, whiteness is still malleable like all socially constructed concepts, but it tends to encompass most white-skinned cultural groups, making it more powerful than ever, and distinguishing it definitively from racialized identities.

The trainyard that separates Moose Jaw's two sides could be thought of as a no-man's-land, frequented only by the town's rail workers. Otherwise, a few bridges carry Moose Jaw residents over top of the wide, shallow valley so they can get back and forth across town. One of the city's hidden gems is the ghost under the 4th Avenue bridge. When I was a teenager, you could access the underside of the bridge via a dirt road. If you parked your car under the bridge on a dark night and stared long enough at its distant piers above the railyard, eventually, through half-optical illusion and *maybe* half-paranormal activity, you'd see a dead man spinning at the end of a noose—a serious thrill that my friends and I sought out often and did in fact witness, sending shivers up our spines on every occasion.

During my time teaching at the school on South Hill, I made friends with a colleague named Jan who was also a trusted local historian. Occasionally we would go for walks, and he'd point out little-known landmarks and quirky facts about Moose Jaw's history. One time, Jan's impromptu history lesson left me breathless. "See that building there?" he asked as we passed near the train tracks. "It's been repurposed now," he said, "but at one time it was the residence for the Black rail workers here in town." I think I stopped walking and just stared at the building. It was brick, bland, unassuming, and right near the edge of the no-man's-land I mentioned. Until that moment, in my twenties, I had never known two things that became immediately apparent. Number one: Black people had been posted up in Moose Jaw at least a handful of *decades* before my family and some of our friends had shown up. Number two: they'd been segregated, forced to be alone, right near the noise and the danger of the tracks. I was discombobulated and struggled to place myself on this previously hidden timeline of inhumanity.

Today, my own research shows that the building in question was indeed a Canadian Pacific Railway rooming house, built around 1912 for the workers of the rail line's sleeping car division, the **Black porters**.

Nobody taught me that in school. I've long known that Moose Jaw has racist white ghosts—in the 1920s, the small town was a known and vibrant hotbed for the **Ku Klux Klan**. But now when I look at that brick building, which to date has no heritage designation, I know that Moose Jaw has Black ghosts, too.

Black porters

These workers were integral to passenger train travel in North America from the late 1800s through the 1950s. In charge of hospitality in the overnight stay cars especially, these porters were, almost without exception, Black men. Frustrated by their terrible working conditions and meager pay, the porters rose up, resisted, unionized, and demanded better treatment from both their companies and train passengers alike. Their efforts created a ripple effect on racial and class justice that still reverberates today.

Wait a minute, could the ghost under the 4th Avenue bridge be Black?

It was the teaching degree I'd earned at university in Regina that had led me to the job in Moose Jaw in the first place. That higher learning institution had been the place of my awakening to anti-racism education, as well as Black history. A white English professor there even offered a revelatory course in "African Slave Literature," which surprised me and had a big impact. But nobody there told me that in 1969,

Ku Klux Klan

Also known as the KKK, the Ku Klux Klan is a historically white North American hate group with a history dating back to the mid-1800s. Existing throughout several iterations across time and across various landscapes, the racist group has been known to use terrorism, such as lynching, to instill fear in Black and other racialized populations and to uphold white supremacy, one of its primary and most long-standing base ideologies.

Fred Hampton, the chairman of the Illinois chapter of the Black Panther Party, had visited that very campus to give an address on "topics including the oppression of African Americans in the United States and the treatment of Indigenous peoples in Canada." Between 600 to 700 students gathered eagerly to see the revolutionary speaker.

When I was in university, my only understanding of the Black Panthers was a misled belief that they were some sort of militant Black gang engaged in illegal activities in the U.S.A. Public fear had long spun narratives of the group perpetrating senseless violence in that country. But in truth their violence was retaliatory. For nothing is more senselessly violent than the colonialism they worked to resist. In reality, the Black Panther Party was a grassroots political organization with a truly righteous quest to educate people, provide Black children with proper nutrition, protect their communities against police brutality, and achieve equity for all in America. As shown in the description of his talk, Hampton himself promoted unity among many separate social factions, including working-class white people, themselves oppressed by classism and capitalism, in the fight against oppression. Perhaps unusual by today's standards, Hampton, along with several other past social justice advocates, was undeterred from associating with groups who may have harbored oppressive attitudes toward his own group, understanding keenly that if you can't reach them, you can't change them.

A few months after Hampton's widely attended but somehow forgotten visit to Regina, police in Chicago raided his apartment in the early morning hours of December 4th, 1969, and shot him dead as he slept. In the bed next to him was his partner, activist Akua Njeri, who was nine months pregnant at the time of Hampton's assassination by police.

They never taught me that part in school either.

Let me make it clear: I still got love for most of my schoolteachers who taught me over the years. A lot of them did the best they could with what they knew at the time, and some of them fought hard against the system that imposed itself on all of us. In doing so, these teachers showed a lot of love for us students, and inspired me to become a teacher myself. But today I understand that in many ways, the schoolboy they loved in me wasn't really me at all. Rather, he was who my race-effacing school experience made me be—the person I was *compelled* to become—a walking white boy impersonation, eagerly chasing down white accolades in brown skin. My criticism today isn't about anything my good teachers did intentionally. It's about the impact of the conditions my schools operated under—conditions that I was subjected to and that are still prevalent in schools today. The conditions of white supremacy.

holy*istic*

As racialized people, our ability to see ourselves represented as fully human in our schools is crucial to our self-image. We have always been excellent. We have always been innovating, game-changing, intelligent, and powerful—we need to affirm that. There is so much to change about schools here in North America—from how they look and feel, to who runs them, to what is taught and what is not taught within their walls. Our histories, knowledges, and art forms, so long erased from school curriculums, are calling out for us. The same goes for our spiritualities. But that's a gaping hole in our school systems, too—ain't *nobody* talkin' about, or especially *to*, the ancestors around here. Personally, I feel there's so much for us to learn and gain in doing so. For me, reclaiming pre-colonial forms of spirituality helped me to learn and *love* my Blackness.

While some see the erasure of spiritual education from K–12 schooling as an appropriate observance of church and state separation, I don't see it that way. See, the predominantly Christian values remain in K–12 public education, despite the separation on paper. My own high school graduation ceremony featured an oral prayer to Jesus Christ from one of our teachers. That came as a surprise to many of us students, and to one Muslim family in the audience in particular, whose synchronized side-eye I happened to catch from my seat on the grad stage. In my primary school years, we were forced to say the Lord's Prayer every morning. While most Christian prayers are gone from public education now, our own Canadian national anthem contains a prayer within it, and students in schools across the country are forced to sing this Christian prayer, sometimes daily, without a thought given to religious or spiritual diversity. In the U.S.A., schools in most states are legally required to make time daily for the pledge of allegiance, which contains the words "one nation under God." While American students are supposed to now be legally able to opt out of reciting the pledge, many have faced consequences for doing so, such as with the actual arrest of an 11-year-old Black boy in Florida in 2019.

Christian values form part of the reason why Black and Indigenous spiritualities and ways of knowing have been historically excluded from school curriculums. Socially powerful practitioners of Christianity have long worked to demonize all non-Christian spiritualities, as seen in the ongoing removal of certain fantasy books from some schools over fears about the books supposedly promoting witchcraft. I mean, really? The reason our diverse spiritualities aren't welcome in schools is not because we've separated the church and state. It's because the Christian church never left. The ongoing Christianization of schools is at once the Christianization of students. And removing Black and Indigenous spiritualities from schools separates Black and Indigenous people from knowledge of ourselves. Despite any religious affiliations I may have personally, I don't *want* that. But I also don't want us to erase spirituality altogether; it's an important part of any truly holistic education. We oughta look at it *all* in schools, in affirming and non-judgmental ways. We should stop pretending that spiritual well-being isn't an important part of the overall well-being of all people. Personally, spirituality changed my life.

My mother never talked much about ghosts in my childhood,

only sometimes in passing. Her occasional stories from "back home" in The Bahamas made me raise my eyebrows but I also knew better than to probe further. Though folk stories of "sperrits" and tricksters abound throughout The Bahamas, along with a now taboo form of West African–derived spirituality known as Obeah, I could tell that my mom's own conservative Black Christian upbringing there had made such topics uncomfortable to talk about. Due to European colonization, Christianity is widespread throughout the Caribbean, as it is here. Because of its prevalence, I can't count the number of times I've been warned that believing in ghosts, calling on spirits, or even practicing meditation were dangerous or *evil* pursuits. But crusaders of white evangelical Christianity have used these condemnations in order to advance their religion at the cost of demonizing other, mostly Indigenous spiritual belief systems. Belief systems whose validity and inherent worth are frankly untouchable, regardless of the arrogant judgments of others.

Straight up, a few years ago, the spirits began to call me. And before long, I was compelled to try calling them back. In doing so, I felt I was walking into unchartered and even dangerous territory. I had no road-map and no role model to help me with my efforts; there certainly wasn't no app for reaching people on the other side. I simply felt moved, like it was right for me to try and connect with them, and I followed my own intuition, against all guidance from my schools and churches. It wasn't until 2021 that I had a very eye-opening spiritual experience, and learned about some of my Black ancestors who'd followed the same path of intuition before me. But more on that hidden history later.

resist.

Without knowledge of ourselves, of our ancestors, or of each other, who are we? *What* are we, truly, as a community? This lack of true knowledge of ourselves can lead to self-doubt and self-loathing. For we are brilliant and powerful people. Maybe they don't want us to know that. But I want you to know who you are, and where you came from. I want you to understand that there are other ways of knowing, being, and doing, family. Like I said, we have histories. We have art, creativity. We have intuition. We have spirituality. Individuality. We have culture. We've got dignity and demands that we've yet to see fulfilled. *All* of these, I dream about for our schools, *your* schools. All of these, I dream about in color.

In 2006, the year after I taught in Moose Jaw, I was posted at a high school in a small town in Saskatchewan. There, my Blackness was a novelty all over again. When the school began laying plans for its own annual slave auction fundraiser (roughly ten years after my troubling experience in seventh grade), they weren't banking on any opposition from *anybody*. To tell the truth, despite my BSP reading off the charts, it took me a while to muster up any vocal opposition at all. I was the new person on staff, and I found myself—as usual—in a white-dominated environment in the school and its staffroom. I wanted to maintain my dignity too, and thought about doing it the way racialized people often do, by acting ". . . like it didn't mean a thing," as Lawrence Hill once wrote in his short story "Meet You at the Door." I know this dignity preservation strategy well and have used it often—for much of my upbringing, in fact. The "it-doesn't-both-er-me" approach is a proven way to avoid conflict, but only because it excuses racist people from feeling any discomfort for their actions and beliefs. Meanwhile, the approach maintains our own *dis*comfort, which can pressurize beyond measure over years and years of giving out these free passes.

Luckily, there is another path toward dignity, family. It comes in recognizing your own discomfort after an offense, noting the cause and then *saying* something, speaking out. You don't have to do it right away though, especially if you're feeling too shaken in the moment of the offense. The truth is, this school's fundraising plans were giving me painful flashbacks of my painful elementary school experience, then put in perspective by the beginnings of my formal anti-racist education in university—my awakening. But after hours of tormenting myself by ruminating on the issue, I was finally compelled to intervene. "Hey," I eventually said to my vice principal, one of my bosses, in 2006. "Mind if we talk about the auction?"

I only taught at that school for one year. Overall, I had a fine expe-rience, and I made a couple of good friends on staff. I have some fond memories of my time there, but more than that, I have an optimism for the school's future; if it stays the course, any Black students or staff may at least suffer one less indignity around fundraising season than they would have in the past.

I want tomorrow's schools, colleges, and universities, the *new-school* ones, to strive for this enduring dignity by practicing active anti-racist and anti-oppressive education. I want them to have an anti-racism coordinator in every building and every school district office, helping guide and shape every move and policy decision that's made. I want teaching positions and other school staff positions to be filled by people who are racially representative of their student bodies. I want all educators to believe in anti-racism, to be trained in anti-racism, and to help train students in it too. I want discriminatory dress codes and hat policies *gone*, yesterday.

I want to see holistic, diversified, decolonized, student-led curriculum planning, with learning areas like rap music, social media, global spiritualities, and spoken word poetry. I want to see schools fully embrace experiential and land-based education. And I want all of these learning areas to be just as available and just as well-resourced as conventional math and science programs are today. I wanna see our histories taught, all of them, so that we can *all* see our futures too.

Schools can be so much more than they are today. My suggestions are but a few of the ways they can be reformed for the better. If you're down with any of these proposed changes, or if you have your *own* suggestions, then let's all of us get together and start demanding that they happen. Let's compel our peers, parents, caregivers, teachers, neighbors, and communities to get involved. We can write letters to school districts and city and state or provincial education offices to urge action on these changes and then some. We can stage teach-ins and die-ins and flash mobs and walk-outs and social media campaigns. We can raise a little hell, or at the very *least* raise our voices.

I want the schools of tomorrow to be what y'all students out there never dreamed of. And I want you students of today *and* tomorrow to have the freedom to become what your schools never dreamed *you* could be . . . glorious, powerful, brilliant, influential, revolutionary, and free, in your *own* way.

And in your own skin.

Surely, these changes to our schools, the institutions that help to mold us and mold our society, if they do come to pass, will help change that society too. But if we're ever gonna get there, we'd better talk strategy first.

7

pick your battles
and your team

they were lookin' at me sideways,
twisted, upside-down.
i was lookin' up at em, up to em, all around.
it's when i got the nod
that i thought i coulda died.
dude was hangin' from the rafters . . .
but very much alive.

the power and the poison

Back when I was in seventh grade, a few things stopped me from speaking out against the injustice of the mock slave auction at my school. One, I didn't fully understand what was wrong about the situation, only experienced the confusion and distress that it caused me. Two, as a shy racialized tween, I didn't have the confidence to raise concerns with school officials, especially about something I struggled to understand in the first place. And three, in that assembly, I was heavily outnumbered. In that moment, I was embarrassed of what was happening, and felt like I ought to have been ashamed of my own Blackness. While all of these elements of my experience—my ignorance, my lack of self-confidence due to internalized racism, and my sense of isolation—may seem only natural or perhaps unalterable, I can assure you they are not. I wasn't born with them; rather they were borne out of my social environment. And these disadvantages all contributed to my social powerlessness, something that the beast of racism both feeds on and breeds.

It's worth unpacking this experience of powerlessness, which is again partly the result of a theft of agency. Social powerlessness is often hard to pin down or point to, and conveniently impossible to prove by Euro-Western standards of science. Because of its seeming inexplicability, feeling powerless can often present itself as feeling less than worthy, less than fully free. No one should ever feel that way, especially young people, who have all the worth and potential in the world and who should have all the freedom in the world, to explore and grow and experiment and change. It's important for us to understand that social powerlessness is always *relative*. It only exists in relation to social power, and to people who use their social power to take that of others away—intentionally or not.

In my childhood, the white teachers and students in that gymnasium held all of the power over me in the moment of the slave auction, in their great numbers. In their relative distance from the true traumas of slavery. In their relative proximity to the ownership of enslaved human beings. In their collective glee. In their laughter and exuberance in the midst of my turmoil. The thing about their power in that room was that, even if I didn't fully understand it, I could feel it, shrinking me down. Consequently, the whole situation felt like a battle I *couldn't* pick, even if I'd wanted to. It wasn't me versus my schoolmates and teachers. It was me versus white supremacy—a powerful but often intangible specter. Under its weight, I was effectively silenced, erased.

The good news is that there are ways to help curb each of these disadvantages (ignorance, lack of confidence, and isolation) that I felt in seventh grade, kinda like antidotes or anti*venom* for white supremacy. There are ways of reclaiming your power.

antivenom 1 – **fighting ignorance**

If you're not careful with how you go about things after experiencing racism, you might end up seeking out the wrong remedies. There's no telling how much damage I inflicted upon myself and others in trying to cover up the pain I felt from racism in my youth. I had no way of understanding the racism I felt, the power dynamics at play, nor my own power to fight against my oppression. So back then, instead of trying to break down my oppression, I tried to break down other people. I'm ashamed to say that, unconsciously, I embodied an attitude of superiority over anyone whom I perceived myself to have power over: notably, guys whom I perceived as feminine or gay, young women and girls, and other racialized people, including other Black people. This was my unhealthy way of trying to build back my sense of power and self-worth.

As I mentioned earlier, I was largely oblivious to the oppressive attitudes I held at the time—they were partly the product of me playing wannabe gangsta rapper—but that didn't stop these attitudes from having real-life consequences. I'd been properly conditioned by my homophobic, transphobic, sexist, classist, ableist, and racist society, and

wielded my own perceived superiority over others as a salve for the inferiority that mostly older or more socially powerful white men made *me*
feel. This phenomenon of misdirected anger is regrettably not uncommon. At any rate, experiencing the hurt that oppression causes should
be no excuse for hurting others—especially once you've woken up to it
all. We ought to take that energy and that anger and direct it back at the
source of our pain, where it will make a more righteous impact, one that
restores equity, rather than further destroying it.

216

People will often tell you that prejudice is learned. Whenever I heard that, I thought it meant that somebody's parents were sitting there teaching them to hate others. In some cases, that may well be true. But in the case of *my* youth, nobody ever sat me down and taught me to be homophobic, sexist, racist, ableist, or classist—quite the opposite, as my parents have always been believers in the equality and inherent worth of all human beings. Nobody taught me that to be poor was bad and that to be Black and poor was worse. Nobody taught me that showing any signs of affection toward another young man would mean I was gay, or that there might be something wrong with being gay to begin with. Nobody sat me down and taught me any of those things. Yet I arrived at these conclusions still, well-armed with problematic attitudes and beliefs that I'd learned through osmosis, just by growing up in Anywhere, North America, and by bearing witness to the common conversations, social dynamics, media, and other influences that I consumed along the way.

Unfortunately, I myself may have become the most dangerous type of oppressor there is—the oppressor who doesn't even know he is one. The type who would probably get defensive if you'd told him he was responsible for causing harm to others. We see this so often among those who not only don't *understand* oppression, but who refuse to try, likely out of fear that their own sense of superiority will crumble in the wake of their unlearning.

It's actually quite normal for young people to be conditioned as I was, especially young boys—the most powerful of social forces work hard every day to mold us into toxic, and problematically "masculine," men. For real though, without intervention, how could we expect any young people brought up in our oppressive society to ever go against the only norms they've known? Any adult role models who might intervene with anti-oppressive teachings are often the ones being silenced, excluded, banned, or disengaged from educational spaces and institutions, although they may stay fighting for change in other avenues. Meanwhile, those white schoolboys from my generation who never got to experience anti-oppressive ideas are out here fully grown, dispro-portionately running schools, school districts, corporations, and gov-ernments to boot. But I got hope for them yet too. Within all young people, there lies almost infinite potential to do more good than harm in our lifetimes—a worthwhile goal for any of us. If only we could fight against our ignorance. People today think of being called ignorant as an insult. But the truth is that all of us are ignorant until we start to unlearn the lies we've been taught about who and what really matters in this world. And undoubtedly, racism itself works to *keep* us ignorant. Therefore, ignorance is never our own fault, unless we acknowledge that better ways of thinking are out there but remain stagnant in our colonized mindsets.

There's a reason we call the work of anti-racist, anti-oppressive edu-cation unlearning. Our very worldviews and many of our deeply held principles are often learned unconsciously. That means that, while we often don't know what we don't know, we also sometimes don't know what we *do* know, what we really do believe and have learned and internalized through conditioning. This is a damaging and damning unknowing. It can lead to folks walking through life with no knowledge or consideration of the harm they may cause others, just by them doing them, in ways that are socially acceptable and socially supported even. If you ever find yourself watching a bunch of white people laugh it up while putting on a mock slave auction, you'll have seen firsthand the social support that oppression so often enjoys in our society, even with-out intentional malice. Remember, racism is often served with a smile, not because those who perpetrate it are inherently evil, but because many of them don't fully understand the harm they are causing (sadly, others yet do understand the harm but cause it anyway). Their racist words and actions may have been completely normalized throughout the course of their lives.

For anyone who's willing, there is a direct path toward unlearning. A lifelong study of anti-racism and anti-oppression that uses critical race theory as a foundation is a good start. As I mentioned earlier, opponents of anti-racist education will often call this field of learning "divisive." I cannot overstate the absurdity of suggesting anti-racism is to blame for social division. Without anti-racism, the chasm between social groups can only continue to grow. It is racism that is divisive. It is inequity that is divisive inherently. And by seeking to repair that inequity, anti-racism is actually a *unifier*, aimed at bringing all groups of people together on a level playing field, so that each may benefit equally from the society in which we live.

Of course, if our society is to foster equal benefit for all people, we will first need to change it *radically*.

There is something beautiful about unlearning. Like removing a blindfold or a pair of dirty sunglasses, it revitalizes your perspective on the world around you, making everything, especially injustice, clearer. For me, learning about the historical and ongoing oppression of Black and racialized people in the world opened my eyes not only to my own experiences of oppression, but also to how oppression is experienced by people of other identities. Becoming awake to the systemic workings of oppression doesn't just make you want to help yourself, or "get a piece of the pie," as detractors will snidely suggest; rather, it will likely make of you an ally to other groups experiencing oppression. For the very same systems that may hold you down hold others down too. Once you see that, you're likely to feel a magnetic compulsion toward change. You're likely to understand how you have actually played a part in that machine with your own words, actions, and inactions. I know I did. And there is a ripple effect to all this change, family.

If you do experience racism or other forms of systemic oppression, your own lived experience is a wealth of knowledge. The perspective that anti-racist education affords racialized people is priceless, because it helps you understand that you already *know* much more about racism than you may have previously thought. After all, we live it. Sharing *your* experiences and your own narratives with others helps *them* to see the world before them with new eyes. When, as an adult, I finally approached my vice principal about stopping the school slave auction in 2006, I was very nervous. But she ended up being receptive. Her apologetic explanation that she and the other white fundraiser organizers had "never thought of it that way before" was one that I expected. It demonstrated the unknowing that is often at the root of how privilege works. But in sharing my perspective with the VP, she learned something new, and unlearned something harmful. Meanwhile, the whole school population benefitted greatly from the change, myself included. In this small act of restorative justice, I truly reclaimed my power. There ain't much that feels better than that.

As you unlearn, and as you acquire new knowledge in anti-racism then share that with others, your knowledge may become a cure for their ignorance too. Not every experience will go as smoothly as the one I've just described. I've had lots of experiences dealing with pushback from people too. You may get anger, you may get tears, you may get "how-dare-you!" You may be made to feel like the bad person for making allegations or disrupting the "positive atmosphere" in this place or that. Do not be swayed out of your convictions, though; when faced with scrutiny, people will often try to preserve their power as well as their perceived innocence in all manner of ways. And when the dust settles, you'll find that it's always better to have said something when you saw something that was harmful. When you do speak up, which can happen in the moment or any time afterward, you lessen the chances of that harm continuing, and embolden others to speak out also. *These* are the times when our unlearning becomes, importantly, un*doing*.

Anti-racist and anti-oppressive education is an ever-evolving field of study. What you learn about it today might be different from what you learn about it tomorrow. That's a good thing. As our society evolves, oppression continues to reinvent itself in astounding and sometimes stealthy ways. It's our job to keep up with that, and to not be caught slippin'. That means understanding that you can never go from full ignorance to full knowledge of how oppression works, only always somewhere in between.

My jump from understanding anti-Black racism to trying to practice allyship with communities facing other forms of oppression has by no means been a straight-and-narrow journey. We call allyship a *practice* for a reason; it's often full of mistakes, and my own practice is no different. At times, I will get on a roll with my activism, slip up, get humbled, and start trying to unlearn and learn anew all over again. That cycle is a healthy one, so long as it helps you trend upward in your progress. In this fight against oppression, and against ignorance, we must remain forever humble, and aware not only of the oppression working all around us, but also of our own ignorance to the lived experiences of others. I guess that makes the cure for ignorance two-fold: acquiring new knowledge and humbling ourselves in our lifelong *un*learning process. As Ojibway author Richard Wagamese once wrote, ". . . humility . . . is the foundation of all learning." I'm elated to say that, even as I've been writing and researching for this book, I've been humbled by the amount of learning that I've been doing. However, I don't feel badly about that at all—I'm growing. And growth is empowering.

With that, I hope it's clear that you need not wait until you "know it all" to go out and start the work of activism or allyship. If that's a part of your plan, then you may as well turn in your protest sign and your megaphone right now, because you will never know it all. Just keep learning and unlearning. And if you've been on your proverbial ass for too long, then get off your ass and go *do* something! Anything.

antivenom 2 – **boosting confidence**

I hope my little pep talk there fired you up a bit and gave you some *confidence* that you have everything you need to get started in this fight. To some, it may seem strange for me to go from promoting humility to promoting confidence, but that's exactly what I'm about to do. Because I don't think the two ideas are at odds with each other. While there may be a *false* confidence in thinking you know everything, true confidence comes in being absolutely sure that you *don't* know everything. It's a cold hard fact that you'd just *better* be confident about. It's from this strong base of humility that real confidence can begin to germinate. As a teacher, I had to learn to have the confidence to tell my students "I don't know" when they asked me a question that I wasn't sure how to answer. Many failed attempts at trying to make something up taught me better. "Actually, vermillion is a color, Khodi, not a rodent." "Got it."

The intellectual and emotional humility that comes with anti-oppressive education fosters a curiosity and a thirst for more understanding. The knowledge base and the research in this field are broad and deep, so if you can't understand something by looking inward, rest assured that you'll find what you're looking for on the outside, in the literature and the work that's been done for you, or from your allies. Just have the confidence to go looking, and to ask when needed. If some of the concepts in the early chapters of this book were new to you, just imagine all the potential for what you can learn about anti-racism from this day forward. Every author, scholar, artist, and activist I've quoted has so much more to say than what I've shared in these pages, and there are countless more whom I didn't quote. With the new knowledge you've yet to acquire, you may just become one of these important thinkers yourself. Imagine it; with the right tools and with determination, with the right attitude and the right strategies, together, we might just be able to change the world.

How empowering a thought. Consider your learning journey as a process of unlocking understanding again and again, removing smoke-screens and veils that our social systems have used to cloud our outlook for years. It is this potential for *newness* in all of our perspectives that gives me hope for the future, and gives me confidence that change is possible. *Confidence* that we can win the war against racism.

And as you do become more and more socially conscious, well, you oughta be confident about your knowledge, too. As Muhammad Ali, one of the world's best boasters, once declared: "It's not bragging if you can back it up." I'm not suggesting that you deliver a mysterious but devastating phantom punch to your opposers, like Ali did to fighter Sonny Liston in 1965. But I am suggesting that, with knowledge, you are well-armed—like Ali was. Forgive the pun, but whether you're in a jab-bing match online or sitting at the dinner table with "that one uncle" at Thanksgiving, know that your ability to critically analyze social power and how it plays out in various situations is ripe ammunition for the fight, should you choose to engage. You may risk being called a buzzkill (like Dill), but if the buzz you're killing is a racist one, would it be so bad to see it die after all?

THE UNLEARNING CHECKLIST

- Read novels and poetry by Black and racialized authors.

- Follow anti-racism accounts or hashtags on social media.

- Attend an anti-oppression workshop in your community.

- Read up on the history of Black and racialized communities and social justice movements in your area.

- Read the autobiographies and teachings of historical social justice leaders.

- Watch biopics and documentaries covering activists, movements, and social change.

- Get involved in organizing work—sometimes the best training is on-the-job training.

- USE WHATEVER GIFTS OR PASSIONS YOU MAY ALREADY HAVE TO CONTRIBUTE TO THE CAUSE.

Strategy is important here too, family. First, in any interpersonal argument, the main concern should be getting to the truth, not taking shots at someone's humanity. Putting others down in order to lift up yourself or your argument doesn't make you come across as a better person than they are; it makes you come across worse. I know because I have been there, getting dragged down into taking the low road. But trust that you will never raise yourself up by doing or saying something low. Whether you're debating online or in person, stick to the facts, or sometimes more effectively, the questions. While even well-constructed arguments are often taken as attacks, questions can only ever be invitations—to think and then respond. Asking rhetorical questions, which you may know the answer to but that the other person may not have yet thought about, is a proven strategy for success. It increases the likelihood that your counterpart will not only see your point, but may actually arrive at it themselves. And *that*, my friends, is how you turn someone into an ally—by making them turn themselves into one. Even posing questions that you may *not* know the answers to but that are still important can push the other party to think deeply about something rather than relying solely on their existing convictions or politics as a guide for relating to the world. Perhaps together, through dialogue, you'll arrive at some new knowledge that can help us all.

Our quest in promoting anti-racism shouldn't be solely about antagonizing our opposers, but rather *changing* them. And in converting our enemies, we may find our friends. Although I support the great orator Malcolm X's declaration that we ought to bring about our recognition as full human beings on this earth "by any means necessary," I also believe that even the most hardened (or polite) racist can be made to see the light through education or dis-education (unlearning). In fact, racists are some of the people with the most potential for radical change. Once we secure that change—that powerful transformation toward a belief in the inherent worth of all human beings—then together, we can all find a new enemy: racism itself. Then, armed with the ammunition of awakened minds, amid a sea of allies, we too will find the confidence to fight forward. Together.

Malcolm X was a fan of rhetorical questions too, asking a predominantly Black crowd in 1962, "Who taught you to hate yourself from the top of your head to the soles of your feet?" It's an important question, because hate is something that nobody, not *anyone*, teaches themselves. And it is only those who hate themselves who tend to hate others, becoming willful but ignorant participants in the many complex systems of oppression that intersect in our society, and that wreak havoc upon our lives and identities.

Before British imperialism and colonization, Black, Indigenous, and racialized peoples were not positioned as inferior. Rather, quite simply, we were people. Powerful people. Intelligent people. Creative people. Beautiful people. Proud people. And not a thing has changed. Except for white supremacy, its transatlantic slave trade, its Jim Crow laws, its Indian residential schools and other genocides. For it's only the illegitimate supremacy of white ways of knowing, doing, and being, that can cause us to see ourselves and our ways as inferior.

For too long, we have been looking at the world and at ourselves through white-colored glasses. The time has come to remove and destroy these imposed lenses and the dangerous optical illusions they create. Once we begin to dismantle the illusion of white supremacy, we begin to dismantle our own self-hatred. Then we can reclaim our self-worth, our power, our brilliance, alongside our joy, our righteous anger, our creativity, and our beauty. We can reclaim our humanness, and in kind, our human rights. As I discussed earlier, once you begin to turn away from the "royal" highness they try to force your allegiance to, you can begin to turn toward your own highness, and your own crown, which as James Baldwin noted, ". . . has already been bought and paid for. All we have to do is wear it." So go on and get *regal* with it.

I'll admit that I was once a victim of a colonized mind. Back when I was brainwashed and busy taking my frustrations out by participating willfully in the oppression of others. Back when I didn't know any better. Back when I didn't know that I actually hated my*self* because of how others hated me. But nah, I know better now. Do not feel bad for me now.

See, today I know myself. I know my history and I know my highness too. I don't hate myself anymore. I consider myself a freedom fighter, a revolutionary, and a warrior for social justice. And you already *know*; I consider myself a *human being*, a real and whole person. I am the bearer of a powerful and creative and invaluable soul; greater than no one, but, *most* importantly, *lesser* than *no* one. I *love* myself, and my Blackness, too.

It ain't pity I seek; it's change.

antivenom 3 — **finding your people**

It's been said that you can only begin to love others once you love yourself. I believe that's true, and it's a good thing too—us loving ourselves, I mean. Because if we are going to win the fight against racism, we're going to need to understand that we are worth fighting for. And we're going to need each *other* to do it. As I said earlier, the enemy is not white people, it's racism. Not just white hoods, but more broadly, white supremacy. Most of us do not want to destroy people *or* property. Well okay, maybe the odd statue of a revered racist can go. But if we are going to transform and improve our society, that's gonna require that some things get broken, including policies, rules, and even laws sometimes. As I've highlighted, many of our past civil rights heroes have broken laws on occasion—the great Rosa Parks is literally famous for it. Besides, if you knew in your heart that the rules were only set in place to try and break people down, wouldn't you *wanna* break the rules?

At the beginning of this book, I talked about the painful shyness I experienced in my early youth. It's true that I was often uncomfortable in situations where I was the only Black person present, which happened a lot. But still, I managed to secure for myself one hell of a good group of friends. It's no wonder that this group is made up of white allies and racialized people alike, with lineages stretching to Central America, the Caribbean, and various parts of Asia. Trust that there weren't a lot of people of color in the schools I grew up in, so it's pretty remarkable that we found each other. Or maybe not. It *could* be that feeling excluded from our broader peer group brought us racialized young people together by default. But if so, I'm glad that it did. It's important to have people in your life who understand what the loneliness that racism induces can feel like. What the pain it brings can feel like. What the self-doubt and the self-hate and the futility of it all can feel like. And even better, having these friends and friends who are allies helps take these difficult feelings away. If some in your friend group aren't invested in your liberation as a full human being, you can work on 'em. But if they don't budge, you may just wanna shop around a little bit. There's no rule that says you've gotta keep the same friends around forever. As you change and grow, you may need to put in work to find friends who you know will be invested in your right to experience the fullness of human life on this planet.

Luckily, activism can open doors to whole communities of good and kind-hearted people—white people and racialized people alike, brave and humble people, outspoken people, and quiet people, all fighting for change in their own ways. So many of the great friends I gained after high school have been Indigenous and racialized people, feminist women, and members of the 2SLGBTQ+ community, all of whom I met through the physical and online networks and armies of activism, allyship, art, poetry, and political organizing. The potential to meet wonderful and compassionate people is another very good reason to engage with social justice work. If progressive people and communities seem hard to find where you live, get online and find them on social media. We out here, and more soldiers are always welcome.

CULTIVATING ALLYSHIP

Talk to your friends about issues that are important to you and those that are important to them. See if you can find common ground.

Research the organizations, collectives, and local politicians and activists who are engaged in social justice work near you. Volunteer and get involved!

If meeting in person is not an option, see if these groups have an online presence and follow them. Their social media pages may be good places to connect with like-minded people.

As a person who experiences oppression, I feel compelled to try and support the liberation of all peoples whenever possible; that only makes sense to me based on the values that I was raised with. If your own values system taught you to treat your neighbor as yourself and you're not involved in social justice work, you may want to ask yourself why that is.

As I mentioned in Chapter 4, I see the movement for Black liberation and the movement for Indigenous liberation as especially interconnected, or adjacent. We have often striven for better futures together. Our shared histories of solidarity, resistance, and compassion stretch back to the days of the Underground Railroad, during which Indigenous people would often help hide formerly enslaved African people from slavecatchers, and at times, welcomed them into their communities for good. Dr. Karina Vernon's work shows evidence of Black–Indigenous intermarriage and solidarity around land sovereignty in pre-Canadian territories dating back to the fur trade. As Erica Violet Lee put it, when it comes to Black and Indigenous peoples, "Our movements are ancient and they are entangled." Our common enemy of colonization makes Black and Indigenous people fitting allies and friends. And there can be no fight for Black liberation without a fight for decolonization—for Indigenous liberation. We are all stronger together. We need solidarity between Black people, Indigenous people, and all people of color; after all, racism and white supremacy are enemies that we share.

antivenom 4 — **finding your ancestors, too**

There is another way to resist isolation, another place in which to find your people, and seek allies, one that I've hinted at throughout this book. It ties back to Chapter 1, where I discussed the value and validity of intuitive experiences, and the importance of spirituality within our lives. In 2006, I had the pleasure of taking my then-girlfriend Carly to my birthplace of Nassau, Bahamas. It was a beautiful trip, which was, in many ways, prophetic. During the trip, my mother took us to meet my great aunt Ruth, the woman who'd helped to raise her on a small homestead on Cat Island, elsewhere in The Bahamas. Aunt Ruth's health was failing, and she'd taken up refuge in the home of my aunt Rose in Nassau. I wasn't sure what to expect out of the meeting, but I was looking forward to it. My mother had always spoken of her aunt Ruth with such reverence, and it would be an honor to finally meet the woman who'd brought my mother up.

When we got to the house, we had to go to a small room in the back to see Great Aunt Ruth, who was seated next to her bed. Her long gray hair was dry but well groomed. Her skin was weathered and her eyes were clouded over with cataracts, to the point that she likely couldn't see our faces at all.

"It's so nice to meet you," Carly and I both said, after my mother introduced us. "I've heard so much about you," I added. But it soon became clear that we wouldn't be engaging in any small talk with Great Aunt Ruth, nor in any dialogue whatsoever. Immediately, she began to pray. "Oh, thank you, Father. Thank you, Lord Jesus." And as soon as she began to pray, her eyes began to well up with tears. "Praise Jesus Christ, almighty Lord. Yes, Jesus. Thank you, oh thank you, Lord!" She went on like that, closing her eyes tight. Before long, the tears were streaming down her face as she continued praying. Carly and I were both frozen—we didn't know what to say or do. My mom wasn't saying much either, but she seemed unsurprised at her aunt's state.

It's hard to describe, but in that moment, something seemed to overtake my great aunt, and the room itself. The energy that emanated from the elder woman was powerful, palpable, and I'll never forget her eyes. For when she opened them and stared in my direction with those clouded irises of hers, she seemed to see within me. She kept on praying too, and I kept on being transfixed, getting completely lost in that moment. Eventually, my mom had to gently redirect us, otherwise Great Aunt Ruth might have prayed with us all day; she had clearly been entranced.

I never forgot that meeting. I never will. Great Aunt Ruth had gone somewhere when she was praying. Where she had gone remains a mystery, but a recent conversation with my aunt Rose, whom Ruth also helped to raise, brought me closer to an answer. I reached out to her after "going somewhere" myself.

When I began having intuitive experiences around 2017, I was feeling rather lost, and again isolated. I didn't know who to tell after I received a nighttime visit from my deceased grandmother, my mom's mother, shortly after the birth of my first child. A "welcome visit," as I like to think of it. There wasn't much drama to it. I think about both of my late grandmothers often, but around the time of this incident, they hadn't been on my mind for some time. Yet I awoke one night in the dark, to the feeling of someone sitting down on the bed beside me. Although I couldn't see who it was, I knew immediately that it was my grandma Lottie. She never said it was her—she didn't say anything at all, in fact. I simply awoke to the shifting of the mattress, felt her sitting there, and knew it was her. I was comforted instantly. We sat for a moment in a reassuring peace, and when I felt her energy fade, I simply cried and said, "Thank you." It wasn't until later that I realized that this visit had come around the anniversary of my grandmother's passing, when some say spirits are more active and likely to make their presence known.

Up until that point, I'd had never had such an intimate spiritual experience before. While I am hesitant to share about experiences like these because of how taboo they can be for some people, I can only write what I know and share what was real to me. So too, I'd like to resist these taboos as much as possible, as they are often the by-products of institutional racism, and are among the intangible forces that coerce us away from knowing and being ourselves. Besides, if you knew in your heart that there was a real way to connect with cherished loved ones who've passed on, wouldn't you want to share that with others?

Not long after Grandma Lottie's visit, I began to have more intuitive experiences. In 2018, I had the honor of taking students to listen to a joint speaking engagement between Holocaust survivor Nate Leipciger and residential school survivor Eugene Arcand. The school-sanctioned event, held uncomfortably at a Catholic cathedral in Saskatoon, drew a large crowd of young people and their teachers. I listened breathlessly as the survivors gave their own accounts of hardship, trauma, and survival, and shared with each other stories, handshakes, and deep respect, acknowledging each other's humanity, dignity, and spirit. Following their powerful lectures and dialogue, a church choir sang. They did so beautifully, and their voices carried upward, reverberating off the cavernous, vaulted ceiling. While most people in the church looked straight ahead at the choir or bowed their heads in reflection, the sound of that choir drew my eye up, and suddenly, I became astonished.

I hadn't been thinking about anything much; rather, I was feeling thoughtless, stunned, empty even, after listening to Arcand's and Leipciger's grim accounts of surviving genocide. But it was in this state of unthinking, and unimagining, that I saw a vision—or rather, that a vision saw me. The experience took whatever breath I did have left clean away. While that choir sang, and while their voices echoed, I saw, hanging from the ceiling above me, dozens of enslaved African people. They wore rags of sullied white and brown, and hung in desperation from the church rafters, as if clinging for life to the masts and booms of a slave ship, huffing determinedly in the act. Even though the building was planted on a firm foundation on the earth, I could feel the vast ship, bobbing in the sea, and felt that I, too, was upon it, adrift.

Everything around me faded—the thousands of people, the voices of the choir—and I knew that whatever was happening then was just for me. My eyes began to well up as I scanned the ceiling. My gaze landed on a young enslaved African man, whose shoulder muscles pulsed as he held onto the rafter from which he hung. He turned his head and looked at me, directly in the eye, and then nodded gravely. *We need you*, his nod seemed to say, and I struggled desperately to maintain any sense of composure in the public setting. The tears sprang from my eyes uncontrollably. Even today, I can never shake the chills that this moment gave me. It was one of the most profound experiences of my life, and nothing that my schooling taught me, at any level, helped prepare me for it (more likely, it kept me unprepared). In that incredible spiritual moment, I fully understood the transcendent kinship that binds together all victims of oppression in this world.

Jewish. Indigenous. Black. Human.

Through all of this, I began to understand that even in my moments of deepest solitude, I was far from alone. A few days later, I asked my mom if she'd ever had any experiences like I did. And while I feel like she may have her own stories to share one day, she was quick to direct me to my aunt Rose. Aunt Rose is a vivacious person, with a strength of character that's matched only by her infectious sense of humor. She's a wise and knowledgeable woman, a skilled Bahamian chef, and a generous soul. I once told her how much I liked an expensive watch she was wearing, and she immediately took it off her wrist and gave it to me for keeps. I trust her.

When I first reached out to Aunt Rose about her own intuitive experiences, she was a little bit evasive. A few unreturned messages on social media left me wondering if she thought I mighta been on something. "Hey, Aunt Rose, I know I haven't talked to you in a long time, but uh, you ever seen a ghost?" My first message went something like that. I got the notification that she had seen the message, but even two weeks later, I hadn't heard back from her. I was feeling pretty paranoid that she might not have been open to my subject of interest at all, or that maybe she was off somewhere praying to God to save my soul from the grips of Satan himself. But finally, with my mom's help, I managed to reach my aunt Rose by phone one evening.

Once we really got to talking, it was like the floodgates had opened. I listened with my jaw dropped as my aunt talked about everything from experiencing premonitions in dreams to seeing random spirits hanging around her house to getting nighttime visits from beloved ancestors. My aunt told me how she could sense if a building was haunted, and she told me about having seen full-bodied apparitions of deceased people out on the street. One spirit in particular used to just chill in her bedroom every night for about a year, watching her, until she told it to get the *hell* on out, and it did.

My aunt spoke with excitement and sincerity, and hearing her explain her truth was exciting for me, as I finally started to understand that intuitive gifts had no doubt been in our family before me. It helped me validate my own experiences. Then, when my aunt Rose went on to talk about Great Aunt Ruth, everything clicked. She told me that Great Aunt Ruth used to "see things." Apparently, she used to go walk the fields near her homestead on Cat Island. Some days, she would come back from walking the fields and report having seen people she knew—loved ones, but who lived far away. Then, Aunt Rose told me, like clockwork, within a few days, Great Aunt Ruth would receive word that whoever she'd last seen in the fields had died around the time of her sighting them.

A whole new level of BSP.

Aunt Rose also told me that, just the same as when Great Aunt Ruth prayed with Carly and me that day, the woman would often sit and sob tearfully, and in that state, at times, she would "visit" people who'd passed, including her late husband.

I was shook. I'd been taken right back to that back room in Aunt Rose's house in Nassau 15 years earlier. I finally understood that wherever my great aunt Ruth had gone during her crying fit then, that it was a place that transcended our physical reality, that perhaps the energy I felt in that moment had been that of my ancestors, welcomed into that back room at my great aunt's invitation. Considering how powerful the energy was, and how powerful my great aunt was, I have no doubt that it could have been so.

I became somewhat saddened that I'd never known of these stories, of the gifts of these powerful women in my family, great spiritual gifts that were unique, profound, awe-inspiring. But they were suppressed by the taboos of a cruel, closed-minded, and overstandardized society. They were part of whole systems of knowledge that have been denied, demeaned, and demonized by colonial arrogance. My great aunt Ruth is gone now, passed on herself, but her gifts and the ways she maintained them alongside a devout Christian identity intrigue me. She stayed true to herself through it all—an inspiration.

And in spite of her passing, I know she is with me.

My aim in sharing these ghostly stories is not to spook you. Nor to convince you that the paranormal is real. Only to share with you that, for me, knowing my ancestors are still somewhere out there, going on thinking and hoping and dreaming and maybe even cheering me on, clinging tight to church rafters high above me, just to help instill me with courage and purpose, even, knowing *that*, for me? Well, it makes me feel a lot less alone in this fight, here, on this earthly plane. In fact, my vision of the enslaved African people in the church may well be one of the major drivers in my writing this book. The experience most certainly renewed and strengthened my resolve for doing anti-racism work. The fact that conversations around these types of experiences remain largely unwelcome in schools, churches, and other public forums is incredibly disappointing, and damaging too. My experiences haven't only helped me to connect with my ancestors, but also with a part of my culture that, through slavery and colonization and their ongoing legacies, had been ripped away from me. Today, my intuition and spirituality have become a remedy for so much pain.

This fight we are in, it can and will alienate you from others. I know full well that the more anti-racism work I do, the more potential there is for people to begin to hate me, including in my places of work, my community, and even within my own family. One thing you'll surely find is that a lot of people don't seem racist at all until you start talking about race. But their propensity to silence issues of racial inequity only perpetuates those issues further. You may lose friends over this fight. Neighbors might stop greeting you in the street. Complete strangers may plot against you from the shadows. But personally, I know that I will always have the strength of my ancestors behind me in this fight, even when I feel like I'm walking alone. I have seen them. I have looked into their eyes and they have looked back into mine, desperately. I have felt them, and I am not the only one. Generations of incredible people within my own family have done the same. Great Black thinkers and writers like Toni Morrison have validated the existence of the ghosts who guide us. Despite what my formal education has taught me, I know these things to be true. I feel them. In spite of my solitude and my uncertainty, in the words of Maya Angelou, "I go forth along, and stand as ten thousand." Imagine the power in that. And know that that power is available to all who are open to wielding it.

That day at the cathedral in Saskatoon, as usual, I was one of very few Black people in attendance. It would have been quite conceivable for me to feel isolated as I often do in the predominantly white spaces of the prairies. But whatever moved me, I decided to go against all I had learned in my devout Lutheran upbringing, where I'd been taught to humble myself, make myself small, and bow my head before the Lord. That day, instead of bowing my head and humbling myself, I decided, just for a minute, to look up. Way up. And had I not done so, I would not have seen what I saw in those rafters. The truth is, I was more humbled by that experience than I would have ever been by simply bowing my head. Hell, I always wondered, if people believe God is up in the sky, what are they lookin' down for anyways?

We are never alone. Sometimes, we've just gotta start looking in order to understand that. Wherever you decide to look, just be sure to look up from time to time. Trust me.

taking power back

As you can see, power is crucial in all the remedies I've explored here, for they all help transform a sense of powerlessness into a sense of empowerment. Spiritually or otherwise, by righting imbalances of power in knowledge, self-confidence, and numbers, each remedy helps to create *social justice*. In today's social justice movements, each one of these remedies is just as important as the next. While we can conjure up the likes of Harriet Tubman, Dr. Martin Luther King Jr., and other almost mythical figures when we think about the movements of the past, it is much harder for the average person to conjure the names and faces of today's great civil rights leaders. And it's not that they aren't there, not by any means. It's that they are many. They are legion, in fact, and they are younger all the time.

Today's freedom movements may appear leaderless to some, but their decentralization actually distributes leadership more evenly than in those of the past. The Black Lives Matter movement has inspired a cross-geographical uprising. Indigenous movements like Idle No More, Land Back, and Wet'suwet'en Strong have taken on a similar dynamic, with Indigenous resistance swelling from coast to coast to coast and beyond. Collectively, these movements have raised the global consciousness around human rights, treaty rights, and environmental and water protection through demonstrations, camps, teach-ins, die-ins, flash mobs, public education, action research, and other important initiatives. And all led not by mythical heroic people, but by real people, just like you. Real grassroots heroes, of the living and breathing sort.

Your engagement with these issues is not only welcome, but crucial, and there are many ways for you to help enact social justice. While some activists use marching, organizing, and fundraising as their main tactics, others offer tech skills and social media influence, public speaking, transportation, security, blogging and op-ed writing, cooking and baking, and art. Take the young and inspirational Amanda Gorman, who helped decolonize Joe Biden's U.S. presidential inauguration ceremony with her gripping performance of her spoken word poem "The Hill We Climb." The young Black poet used her talent for writing and oracy to eloquently scrutinize the "bruised but whole" nation she was likely tasked with acclaiming at the ceremony, and took everyone who was there along for the ride, willingly or not. In her poem, Gorman encouraged us all to have the bravery to *become* the light of the new dawn. "When day comes we step out of the shade," she wrote, "aflame and unafraid." As she so sharply captured, our efforts to illuminate others may in fact require some of us to get burnt sometimes. I mean, she laid it all out: we don't need a Molotov cocktail to get things done. We *are* the Molotov cocktail, family. And we come prepared to light oppression on fire, truly blow it all up, and *destroy* racism using our minds and our words, with breath like restless dragons.

Think you can take the heat?

Today's social justice leaders are countless. Equally mighty and courageous as those of the past, they are more than ready to light up our lives and our society. They are brave, powerful, and widespread, and among them, there is a space for you. You can be a leader too, just by your example of working for change. In today's landscape, I do not believe that it will be the role of any singular speaker, thinker, or persona to help move our countries toward justice for all. Trust that no one is coming to save us. The truth is that just as you can lead a horse to water but cannot force it to drink, you can lead people toward freedom but cannot force them to be free. They must want it. And so, the hard work of securing freedom will be up to all of us. We must engage in it *together*. We must lead each other, all the way, whoever we may be and at whatever age.

My parents have always supported my anti-racism work; indeed they helped me form many of my own values and beliefs around social justice issues, but they never really engaged in what we call "the work," at least not for decades. It wasn't until the spring of 2020 that they decided to get involved, following the brutal police murder of George Floyd in Minnesota, the same state in which police had killed Philando Castile, whom I mentioned in the introduction of this book. The ubiquitous media coverage of the deaths of Floyd, Breonna Taylor, and many others around that time was a catalyst for change, with calls to divert portions of police funds to community support services being taken seriously for once, and even implemented in some places. My parents, then in their sixties and seventies, attended their first ever social justice rally in the wake of those events, a Black Lives Matter gathering in my old hometown of Moose Jaw, Saskatchewan. Around them were many of the longstanding members of the town's Caribbean Association, and a remarkable crowd of non-Black allies. As I said early on, anti-racism is for everyone, of every age, race, culture, and identity.

Moose Jaw was where I grew up; I experienced immense joys there, but it was also the place in which I suffered some of the most immense racial hostility of my life, even without realizing it. As welcoming as the people there often seemed toward me, many of them were at the same time often violent toward my Blackness, politely coercing me to try and erase it. Seeing the BLM rally in that town, though, reminded me that everyone on this planet has the potential to become awakened. And it doesn't work the other way around—for once you see injustice, and even your role in upholding it, you cannot unsee it. That makes everyone in your family and everyone in your life a potential ally in this movement toward freedom. And we must find a way to reach them, even the most hardened of colonial or colonized minds.

It's easy to resent such people and move into antagonism. But again, the true aim of our quest must not be only to fight against those whom we may view as bigots, nor wait for them to die off, as some have promoted, but to help them see the light, and to find their inner compassion. When I'm gone, I don't want the measure of my work to be how many people I angered and radicalized *against* the liberation of my people, but rather, how many people I riled up and radicalized *for* the liberation of my people. I don't want to antagonize or harm or kill anyone in the fight for social justice; I want to disrupt and kill harmful beliefs. I want to end racist policies and kill violent practices that have been designed and perpetrated against my people. I want to kill racism, kill oppression.

And I want to *transform* people, and our society, too.

resist.

While many have labeled social activists as provocative, they may not understand that it is in fact *us* who have been provoked. We wouldn't need to say "Black lives matter" if society and its police forces didn't constantly tell us through their actions that our lives *don't* matter at all. In using this somehow now controversial mantra, we are simply doing what Robyn Maynard has called "refusing the expendability of Black life," an expendability that is so *clear* in the social messaging all around us. I wouldn't need to speak to my boss at school about my concerns over fundraising activities if those activities didn't reinforce the narrative that my racial group is subhuman and deserving of cruel mockery.

The problem with racism is that it is so normalized in North America

239

that it is often invisible to those who participate in and benefit from it. And while racism and other forms of oppression remain our only targets in the work of resistance, the difficulty that some people have in *seeing* racism often makes them see us as troublemakers—meaning some of those folks will then try to make targets out of *us*. After all, so very *many* martyrs have been made of Black people: too many to name here, although their names will not be forgotten, and too many to count, though their collective deaths will *not* be ignored.

The ubiquity of Black murder might make the work of anti-racism seem dangerous, and it may well be, but please, don't be deterred, for there is safety in numbers. The more of us who join the fight, the less likely we are to lose, or lose our lives. With a whole army, we are well positioned to win, and to thrive. Even more so if we pick the right battles and fight with the right strategies. For me, writing has become a way not only to resist the everyday inequities that persist all around us, but also to confront past instances of racism that I didn't have the understanding, confidence, or strategies to properly deal with at the time. Watching that slave auction in grade school, getting harassed by the police as a young man—many of these experiences shook me too much to respond properly in the moment. So I respond to them today, in my poetry and my writing. And each time I do, I hope to curb the chances of these sorts of things happening to other young Black people in the future. One of my greatest hopes is for you to be free from the troubling notions of death that our people have carried as burdens for so long. As the great artist and activist Nina Simone once said, "I'll tell you what freedom means to me: no fear."

My hope is for you to be fearless.

Anti-racism is meant to work as both a response *and* a preventative measure. As I said in Chapter 2, when it comes to racism, we all have the ability to respond. If you're ready and willing to take on that responsibility, pick your team, pick your battles, and pick your lane. Expect that the work will be exhausting. It will likely require the support of a community, strategically chosen periods of rest, and a consistent spiritual practice or artistic outlet (in my belief, these two are connected). Sometimes, you will be the one supporting while others require rest. This work will require *un*learning, *re*learning, and more unlearning again. It will require humility, bravery, and *humility* again. It will challenge your identity. It will put you through crises. It will require self-care and mental health care too. The work may require a large portion of your time, a small price to pay when many have lost their lives to this work, and when you may prevent others in the future from going the same way. Because of your work, little kids, parents and grandparents, students, teachers, musicians, poets, dancers, lovers, and visionaries will get to go on breathing. Anti-racism doesn't just destroy racism; it saves lives.

In short, you are needed. Whoever, wherever, and whenever you are.

Social justice is a complex puzzle, and we all have a part to play. For some of us, the stakes are high; it can feel a lot like we're playing with guns to our heads. Others, though they hold a piece to play, are hardly paying attention. That makes solving this a lot more difficult than it needs to be. Worse still, no one knows what the final picture is supposed to look like. Let's just say that somebody threw out the box, or is hiding it at least. But we can't let that stop us from trying, from continuing to fight for that vision of true equity in our society, from continuing to fight for our lives.

Perhaps the puzzle metaphor is a bit simple, but I feel it's a good parable for our current reality. Nobody truly knows what the just society that we're fighting for truly looks like. And the haters can miss me with their constant demands to have it described in detail. We only know that right now, it's heavy out here, and we all have a role to play in making the lives of racialized people a little less burdensome. Finding our roles doesn't mean checking items or actions off a list either; it means fundamentally changing who we are inside and how we see the world around us, so that our responses to racism are proactive, ongoing, and automatic. So that we can help *change* the world around us. We don't need to know exactly how we want things to be in order to start fighting for that change; we just have to decide that we want things to be better, fairer than they are right now. Can we at least start with that?

Racism is a weight that pushes us down. And there's no anti-gravity gun for that. No magic solution. Only history's lessons. Only our ancestors cheering us on, and our future descendants' solemn thanks. There is only responsibility, commitment, hard work. There is only all of us, together, our collective will and might and fight, and our wildest imaginings of freedom and jubilation for each other, for all people. Damn, maybe there is some magic to it after all. But it can't fall solely onto Black people, Indigenous people, and people of color to overturn racism. As some of the biggest perpetrators of systemic racism, schools, colleges, and other institutions and organizations must become leaders in decolonizing their operations, redesigning their structures, reimagining their goals, and fighting to achieve true equity within their spaces. White allies must join this fight and must be unwavering in two things: leading others by example and holding each other to account. Allies, too, must co-conspire and *participate*.

By taking on the quest to find our own avenues toward fighting oppression, our own gifts and ways of contributing, we can help make things a little lighter for everyone else. As we work to put together the social justice jigsaw puzzle, we work to restore humanity, blocking bullets from backs and removing nooses and knees from necks in the street. We can do that. We can solve this strange and complex puzzle . . . together.

So, what piece you got, family?

conclu∫ion

No matter your racial identity, anti-racism changes your whole perspective, and once you change that, your whole life changes too— your past, your present, even your future. The transformation can be jarring, even crisis-inducing. I mentioned earlier in this book that, during its writing, I entered something of a crisis myself.

One day at school, I asked my students to write a journal entry using a quote from Elizabeth Acevedo's brilliant novel *The Poet X:* "When was the last time you felt free?" I always try to write whenever my students write, so I sat down right there with them and tried to begin journaling too. I always tell my students not to think too hard about the prompt, but to just let their pens or their keyboards go and see what happens (this advice is a seed of a dream, perhaps, for a more intuitive kind of education). Like any good teacher, I try to model my own advice and just let the writing flow. Only this time, I couldn't do it. I couldn't get to writing; I was stuck. The problem was that I couldn't actually *think* of a single recent time in my life when I'd felt free. Realizing that, I was immediately devastated, and became sullen. My journal that day was only one line long, and I later shared it with my students shortly before I took my leave from teaching: "It's been a long time since I've felt free."

In writing this book and reviewing my life through the lens of anti-racism, I began to understand that so much of what I'd done in my life, and *with* my life, including becoming an English teacher, had been done subconsciously in response to white supremacy and to racism. Having internalized the fact that my Blackness was unacceptable in most spaces here, it seems I had done whatever I could to distance myself from it, making most of my life up to this point a response to the trauma of racism. Talk about a jarring realization.

Today, I'm still working out how my daily experiences, encounters, and movements through the world have been marked by both restrictions and projections imposed upon me and my Blackness by white supremacy, having inevitable impacts on my life and its direction. In writing this book, in all my remembering, I realized that I'd forgotten myself . . . somewhere, long ago. To gain this sort of true sight, though it may be *hindsight*, is world-shattering. I know now that our everyday experiences of white supremacy can amount to more than just microaggressions, but rather to micro-coercions, which, stacked on top of each other, can become almost insurmountable. I would never have come to this realization without anti-racism, and without the role that writing has played in my life. To make a crucial distinction, the crisis I've been experiencing isn't the writing's fault—it's racism's. The brutal honesty that writing inspires just helped me wake up to it, and that's the healthiest move I've ever made.

You see, now, I've found the *source* of my pain.

Like I said before, I would much rather see this source and try to change it, than not see it at all but be altered and confined by it still. In other words, I've never been happier to be so sad. My middle-aged epiphany may help steer some of you younger readers clear of the same bait traps of white supremacy that I fell into, might help you avoid letting that supremacy shape you, your view of yourself, and of the person who you are every day becoming. At any rate, as it is in the world around us, my own personal recovery from white supremacy is ongoing. After all, it's difficult to heal from a trauma that's still there. But trust that one step better than not being free is *realizing* that you're not free, and that you deserve to be. Perhaps most important to my healing journey is the understanding that the negative feelings I've been carrying about myself for so long are unfounded, and are, again, not my own fault.

As a teacher, I am one of the few people in this world who never truly left the institution of school. As such, for my entire life, I have been living and working in an environment that, at a systemic level, actively upholds white supremacy, that silences and punishes its detractors, and that rewards and upholds its proponents and followers. This, to prepare us all for life in a world where all the same rules and dynamics apply. For a racialized person, and even as an adult in such a setting, it is difficult not to want to make yourself small. So small, sometimes, that you may disappear entirely. Despite my shy demeanor as a child and despite all the powerlessness I experienced in my youth, the reality is that I never truly *lost* my voice or my power; they were taken from me, by a system and by people who refused to acknowledge my words, my will, and, at times, my existence.

But in the words of Haudenosaunee writer Alicia Elliott, "Things that were stolen once can be stolen back."

I cannot begin to express the feelings of freedom and gratitude that come in taking back both my voice and my agency. In taking back my identity, my self-worth. In taking back my Blackness. For me,

247

anti-racism has proven the most effective of mental health treatments; I am undergoing a profoundly positive personal transformation of the truly radical sort.

I believe that we must all go to these places of radical change before we can begin to sow the seeds of love where they are needed most, and begin the daunting but crucial task of changing our society. Trust that as more and more of us change ourselves, the more our society will begin to transform. After all, our society is little more than . . . us, all put together. The concrete steps that need to be taken may not be immediately apparent, but with a renewed disposition and a functioning critical lens for injustice, we will be able to recognize where and how to start. I believe that our friends, elders, allies, experts, and even our ancestors who've passed on can help guide us in this work. I have witnessed their immense strength and determination, their hope and their desperation too, and I know that they are counting on *us* to keep their dreams for our freedom alive. Without question, it is our ancestors who fought fiercely for our own survival, and it's our future descendants whose quality of life will depend on the work we do today. Knowing as much should help us to, in the words of Iraqi-Canadian rapper Mualla, ". . . understand this is our moment and the product must be brilliant."

There is a fire in Mualla's words, in his voice, as he raps. And it's true that fire creates brilliance in our environments. Sometimes, as it is in the great forests of our continent, the destruction that fire brings is the very power that is needed to renew and transform whole ecosystems. We must prepare to bring that same power to our fight for justice, even at the risk of getting burned ourselves. You will carry this fire, this flame and this power, within your very bones, within your proud postures, and within the fortitude of your knowledge and the strength of your adamant voices. It will help to shed light upon a stagnant and unjust ecosystem, an entire forest that was built upon a bed of racism that has persisted unchecked for too long. A forest that is ready for renewal. The flame you carry holds within it the potential to destroy, renew, and transform old ways of thinking and doing. And the fires we light with our flames will help to heal us, heal others, and warm the collective spirit of all humanity, so long as we are willing to take the torch. If we are willing, then we got this. To my young people out there, please, I implore you, take all of your angst and any rebelliousness you may have within your spirit and join with others to apply it here: to *this* rebellion, this *resistance*. To justice. To a world and to a future worth fighting for. So go on and reach each other. Teach each other.

Spread your firelight.

And remember: while the colonized mind may indeed be a dangerous weapon, the awakened mind is far more powerful. Stay up.

—KD

epilogue

"You have to decide who you are and force the world
to deal with you, not with its idea of you."
—James Baldwin

acknowledgments

I was not alone in writing this book. So very many people contributed to its making in so very many ways. I will forever be in gratitude to all of them. To my parents, Alan and Daphanie Dill, thank you for raising me in a way that encouraged my hobbies of thinking and writing to blossom and grow, and for being there for me always. Dad, thank you for your work sourcing photos for the imagery in this book. Thank you to my sister Chrissy for being my early guide and my protector in this life, and for continuing to guide and to look out for me now. To Carly Brown, thank you for your incredible support, your partnership, your assistance in editing early drafts, and for all of the sacrifices you made to help make the dream of this book a reality. To my two kids, Hazel and Ezrah, my queen and my king, you are the reason I do it all. I love you now and always; I love you infinitely, more than anything in the whole universe and beyond. All my inspiration comes from you two. To Glendyne Brown, thank you for the all the ways in which you have supported and continue to support our family as one who gives love and care.

To my highly gifted editors, Claire Caldwell and Khary Mathurin at Annick Press, I am extremely grateful to you for taking a chance on me, for trusting me, for guiding me, and for supporting me. You and all the incredible staff at Annick have helped to make my dreams a reality. Truly, I am humbled by your powerful kindness, by your professionalism and your acumen, and by your inspiring commitment to excellence. To

Karina Vernon, I will be forever in gratitude for the brilliant and crucial guidance you offered in helping to shape this book as an expert reader. Thank you. To stylo starr, words can't describe how well you saw my spirit in the words of this book and made it come alive in your imagery. Your artistry is phenomenal and takes this book to the next level. Deepest thanks. To Cleopatria, thank you for your incredible vision for the overall design of this book; it is simply beautiful.

A special shout-out goes to my wonderful aunt Rose of Nassau, Bahamas, whose reflections on intuition and whose recollections about my incredible great aunt Ruth helped me to better know myself, my history, and my gifts. Thank you to all of my extended family back home and close by. Thanks to my homies and friends, my day-ones and new ones, from MJ to Saskatoon, for the heart-to-hearts and even the head-to-heads that helped me grow over all these years. To all the good teachers I had back at King George School and Central Collegiate in Moose Jaw, I thank y'all for pushing me, for believing in me, and for inspiring me to pursue everything that this life had in store for me.

To the brilliant university professors and educators who have guided me toward a critical race consciousness through the courses you taught and the mentorship you offered, I owe so much to the paths you paved, and to the work that you did and shared with me and so many others. Verna St. Denis, Carol Schick, Alex Wilson, Dianne Miller, Marie Battiste, Mike Capello, Sheelah McLean, and others, thank you for helping me to truly see and to question the world that we live in. You taught me that it can be better, and that we can make it so. To my principal, Tammy Girolami, thank you for supporting me, for raising me up, and for centering the work of anti-racism in our amazing school. To all of my incredible colleagues at Nutana Collegiate, thank you for your allyship and your bravery in supporting Indigenous and racialized students, even when the conditions and systems we work within can make it challenging to do so. Special recognition goes to Cheryl Ermine and Darryl Isbister for your help with the land acknowledgment for this book, and for all the crucial work you do for students in Saskatoon. To my own students today and over the last 17 years, I give you my sincere thanks for listening to me, for teaching me, and for keeping my spirit young. You are all powerful and beautiful beings with the potential to change the world.

To the spoken word poetry community of Saskatoon and across this country, I will forever be grateful for the space you made for voices like mine to find themselves, assert themselves, and thrive, when traditional institutions would not let us in the door. Thank you to the youth poets and rappers of today, the young griots, whose courageous voices are helping to change the world, one poetry slam and one track at a time. To the small but mighty writing community in Saskatoon, and across the province, much thanks for making space for this kid from Moose Jaw. To Alice Kuipers and Yann Martel, thank you for cheering for me and helping to promote my work. To all who contributed to this book in your own important ways, like Bruce Fairman, Jan Radwanski, Rachel Funk, Dr. Kellen Baptiste, Mercedes Acosta, Dana Hopkins, Erin Chan, Dorothy Visser, and Siusan Moffat, thank you. To my wonderful agent Carly Watters, deepest gratitude for your support and your faith in me.

I'd also like to acknowledge the Black literary community in Canada, which is firmly planted here and is decidedly here to stay. Thank you for lifting me up. Jael Richardson, thank you so much for your generosity of spirit and for your support of my career and that of so many others who face roadblocks in this industry. To every racialized writer or rapper who ever put their critical perspectives and stories on paper and shared them with the world, I see you, just as you have helped me feel seen. Jael Richardson, Robyn Maynard, Desmond Cole, Kendrick Lamar, Eternity Martis, the late James Baldwin, Ian Williams, Alicia Elliott, George M. Johnson, Dallas Hunt, Gina Starblanket, Lawrence Hill, Ibram X. Kendi, Assata Shakur, the late DMX, the late Toni Morrison, Rapsody, Jamila

Lyiscott, Elizabeth Acevedo, J. Cole, Noname, Jason Reynolds, the late Richard Wagamese, Asha Bandele, Patrisse Cullors, Bryan Stevenson, the late Tupac Shakur, Karina Vernon, and so many others, thank you. Your powerful words inspired this book directly. To those still just dreaming of becoming writers of the resistance one day, I am grateful for your dreams. Please chase them; we need you.

I would like to extend a special thanks to my higher power, and to all the ancestors who guided me in the writing of this book, from my own grandmother to those ancestors looking down on me from the stars and from church rafters, and the ones whispering ideas and fully formed paragraphs in my ears as I walked through the wilderness. I saw you, I heard you, I told about you, and I hope you never stop speaking to me. Malcolm X, I heard your voice lilt and roll in my head as I read your life-changing autobiography. Through the records you have left, your words and ideas will reverberate in my mind and throughout all the earth forevermore. I will forever be thankful for your spirit and your activism.

To my readers, young, old, and in between, it has been my honor to get your attention and to keep it. From the deepest place in my heart, thank you for stickin' with me. Please, whatever you can do with any shred of inspiration these words might have given you, go do it, family. We will all be ancestors one day. With each new day that passes, let us try our best to be good ones.

Sincerely,
—KD

Deep thanks to the entire Annick team, past and present, especially Paul Covello, Claire Caldwell, Khary Mathurin, and Sam Tse—what a dream team! Thank you for stewarding this process with such care, space, and grace, and especially for seeing me. I couldn't have asked for a better first creative experience!

Thank you also and of course to Khodi Dill; I appreciate you for trusting in the process and for trusting your work with my creative interpretation. Magic made!

Giving thanks.

—S.S.

the unlearning library

Dear Reader,

The following articles, novels, films, anthologies, poems, songs, speeches, and non-fiction books represent a whole battery of anti-racist knowledge from which I have benefitted greatly. I use the word *battery* intentionally because, as I noted in this book, when it comes to the resistance against racism, our knowledge of anti-racist ideas is power, plain and simple. That's why many of these books have already been banned by institutions, and why many more will continue to be challenged. Those at the helm of these institutions also know the power of these works, and fear its ability to diminish their own power, which is often both unearned and extremely precarious.

I've included works from a variety of genres here because I know that while some people can learn enthusiastically by studying factual information, for others, it is the magnetic pull of art and story that may eventually change their minds. And whether those stories are true, as in the transfixing autobiographies of Malcolm X and Assata Shakur, or imagined, as in Lawrence Hill's gripping work *The Book of Negroes* and Richard Wagamese's important and painful novel *Indian Horse*, the impact of their teachings is palpable to the seeking mind and spirit.

So seek, and you shall find power and awakening.

—KD

fiction (novels and short stories)

The Poet X by Elizabeth Acevedo

The Book of Negroes by Lawrence Hill

"Meet You at the Door" by Lawrence Hill, originally published in The
Walrus

Gutter Child by Jael Richardson

Indian Horse by Richard Wagamese

non-fiction (books and articles)

When They Call You a Terrorist: A Black Lives Matter Memoir
by Asha Bandele and Patrisse Cullors

The Skin We're In by Desmond Cole

Eloquent Rage: A Black Feminist Discovers Her Superpower by
Brittney Cooper

A Mind Spread Out on the Ground by Alicia Elliott

All Boys Aren't Blue by George M. Johnson

How to Be an Antiracist by Ibram X. Kendi

They Said This Would Be Fun by Eternity Martis

**Policing Black Lives: State Violence in Canada from Slavery to
the Present** by Robyn Maynard

"Canada 150 is a celebration of Indigenous genocide" by Pam
Palmater, published in *Now Toronto*

Stamped: Racism, Antiracism and You by Jason Reynolds and
Ibram X. Kendi

Assata: An Autobiography by Assata Shakur

**"Silencing Aboriginal Curricular Content and Perspectives
Through Multiculturalism: 'There Are Other Children
Here,'"** by Verna St. Denis, published in the *Review of Education,
Pedagogy, and Cultural Studies*

Storying Violence: Unravelling Colonial Narratives in the Stanley Trial by Gina Starblanket and Dallas Hunt

Just Mercy: A Story of Justice and Redemption by Bryan Stevenson

"Black sleeping car porters: The struggle for Black labour rights on CanadA's railways" by Travis Tomchuk, published online by the Canadian Museum for Human Rights (humanrights.ca)

The Black Prairie Archives: An Anthology edited by Karina Vernon

Disorientation: Being Black in the World by Ian Williams

The Autobiography of Malcolm X by Malcolm X, as told to Alex Haley

poetry

The Hill We Climb by Amanda Gorman

"Dream Variations" by Langston Hughes

films, videos and multimedia content

Black on the Prairies. Interactive project edited by Ify Chiwetelu and Omayra Issa, from the Canadian Broadcasting Corporation: https://www.cbc.ca/newsinteractives/features/black-on-the-prairies

Judas and the Black Messiah. Film directed by Shaka King.

Malcolm X. Film directed by Spike Lee.

"3 Ways to Speak English." TED Talk by Jamila Lyiscott.

"Why English Class Is Silencing Students of Color." TEDx Talk by Jamila Lyiscott.

sources

Epigraph
Shakur, Assata. *The Eyes of the Rainbow*. Directed by Gloria Rolando. Images of the Caribbean, 1997. YouTube video, 46:19. https://youtu.be/0jItg69Hnq8.

Introduction
[Introduction, p. 3: Cree origin of "Saskatchewan"]
Office of the Treaty Commissioner and the Saskatchewan Ministry of Education. "kisiskāciwani-sīpiy," section 9 of introduction to *Kindergarten to Grade 9 Treaty Education Learning Resource*. Saskatoon, SK: Office of the Treaty Commissioner, 2018. https://www.edonline.sk.ca/courses/1/2016_Truth_and_Reconciliation_and_Residential_Schools_Experience_Teaching_Supports_sanderjoa/content/_311764_1/scormdriver/indexAPI.html.

[Introduction, p. 3]
Dill, Khodi. "'The safest place': Anti-oppression in Spoken Word Poetry." Master's thesis, University of Saskatchewan, 2013. https://harvest.usask.ca/bitstream/handle/10388/ETD-2013-01-873/DILL-THESIS.pdf?sequence=4&isAllowed=y.

[Introduction, p. 4]
St. Denis, Verna. "Aboriginal Education and Anti-racist Education: Building Alliances across Cultural and Racial Identity." In "Coalition Work in Indigenous Educational Contexts," special issue, *Canadian Journal of Education* 30, no. 4 (December 2007): 1068–92. https://doi.org/10.2307/20466679.

[Introduction, p. 6: "cease fleeing . . ."]
Baldwin, James. *The Fire Next Time*. Reissue ed. New York: Vintage International, 1992. First published 1963 by Dial Press (New York).

Chapter 1
[Ch. 1, p. 10: Origin of "Moose Jaw" name: Cree term "moscâstani-sîpiy"]
City of Moose Jaw. "Welcome to Moose Jaw – 'Canada's Most Notorious City.'" City of Moosejaw. Accessed January 11, 2022. https://moosejaw.ca/business-development/welcome-to-moose-jaw/.

[Ch. 1, pp. 16–17: Examples of gaslighting and how to respond]
Huizen, Jennifer. "What Is Gaslighting?" Medical News Today, updated July 14, 2022. https://www.medicalnewstoday.com/articles/gaslighting.

[Ch. 1, p. 18]
Nicholas, George. "When Scientists 'Discover' What Indigenous People Have Known for Centuries." *Smithsonian*, Smithsonian Institution, February 21, 2018. Originally published on *The Conversation*, February 14, 2018. https://www.smithsonianmag.com/science-nature/why-science-takes-so-long-catch-up-traditional-knowledge-180968216/.

[Ch. 1, pp. 28–29]
Haug, Frigga. "Memory-work as a Method of Social Science Research: A Detailed Rendering of Memory-Work Method." In *Dissecting the Mundane: International Perspectives on Memory-work*, edited by Adrienne E. Hyle, Margaret S. Ewing, Diane Montgomery, and Judith S. Kaufman, 21–44. Lanham, MD: University Press of America. http://www.friggahaug.inkrit.de/documents/memorywork-researchguidei7.pdf.

SOURCES

Chapter 2

[Ch. 2, pp. 37–38: Linnaeus, Karl, referencing systema naturae]

Kendi, Ibram X. *How to Be an Antiracist*. New York: One World, 2019.

[Ch. 2, p. 37: Blumenbach]

Gordon, Linda. "Who's White?" *New York Times*, March 25, 2010. https://www.nytimes.com/2010/03/28/books/review/Gordon-t.html.

[Ch. 2, p. 38: Eugenics]

National Human Genome Research Institute. "Eugenics and Scientific Racism." National Human Genome Research Institute, updated May 18, 2022. https://www.genome.gov/about-genomics/fact-sheets/Eugenics-and-Scientific-Racism.

[Ch. 2, p. 38: Eugenics]

Samson, Amy. "Karl Binding and Alfred Hoche Publish Die Freigabe Der Vernichtung Lebensunwerten Lebens." The Eugenics Archives, September 13, 2013. https://eugenicsarchive.ca/.

[Ch. 2, p. 38: Sterilization of Indigenous women]

The Canadian Press. "'Heinous' Forced and Coerced Sterilization of Indigenous Women Ongoing: Senate Report." *Star Phoenix*, June 4, 2021. https://thestarphoenix.com/news/local-news/heinous-forced-and-coerced-sterilization-of-indigenous-women-ongoing-senate-report.

[Ch. 2, p. 42, 48: Wealth distribution in Canada]

Di Matteo, Livio. "Wealth Inequality: A Long-Term View." Finances of the Nation, July 28, 2020. https://financesofthenation.ca/2020/07/28/wealth-inequality-long-term-view/.

[Ch. 2, p. 44: South Africa]

Dammam: South African Department of Agriculture, Forestry, and Fisheries. "Population of South Africa by population group." Dammam: South African Department of Agriculture, Forestry, and Fisheries, 2004. Archived from the original on February 28, 2005. Wayback Machine, Internet Archive. https://web.archive.org/web/20050228135335/http://www.nda.agric.za/docs/abstract04/Population.pdf.

[Ch. 2, p. 44: Apartheid – system, definition and facts]

HISTORY. S.v. "Apartheid." By History.com Editors. Updated November 22, 2022. A&E Television Networks. https://www.history.com/topics/africa/apartheid.

[Ch. 2, p. 44–45: Apartheid, Canada as model]

Galloway, Gloria. "Chiefs Reflect on Apartheid and First Nations as Atleo Visits Mandela Memorial." *Globe and Mail*, December 11, 2013. https://www.theglobeandmail.com/news/politics/chiefs-reflect-on-apartheid-and-first-nations-as-atleo-visits-mandela-memorial/article15902124/.

[Ch. 2, p. 45: Deficit thinking]

Valencia, Richard R. *Dismantling Contemporary Deficit Thinking: Educational Thought and Practice*. London: Routledge, 2010.

[Ch. 2, p. 45: Meritocracy]

Young, Michael Dunlop. *The Rise of the Meritocracy*. 2nd ed. London: Routledge, 2017.

[Ch. 2, p. 46: Pay gaps]

Statistics Canada. "Table 14-10-0324-01 Average and Median Gender Pay Ratio in Annual Wages, Salaries and Commissions." Statistics Canada, March 23, 2022. https://doi.org/10.25318/1410032401-eng.

[Ch. 2, p. 46–47: Wealth distribution in Canada]

Parliamentary Budget Officer. *Estimating the Top Tail of the Family Wealth Distribution in*

Canada. Ottawa: Office of the Parliamentary Budget Officer, June 17, 2020. https:// www.pbo-dpb.gc.ca/web/default/files/Documents/Reports/RP-2021-007-S/ RP-2021-007-S_en.pdf.

[Ch. 2, p. 47: Poverty disproportionately affects race]

Ontario Council of Agencies Serving Immigrants. "New Fact Sheets Show Growing Racial Disparities in Canada." OCASI, March 21, 2019. https://ocasi.org/ new-fact-sheets-show-growing-racial-disparities-canada.

[Ch. 2, p. 49–50: Dress codes]

Perry, Andre. "Dress Codes in Schools Are the New 'Whites Only' Signs." The Hechinger Report, February 5, 2020. https://hechingerreport.org/ dress-codes-are-the-new-whites-only-signs/.

[Ch. 2, pp. 50–51: Distraction]

Noguchi, Sharon. "Short Shorts, Spaghetti Straps, Halter Tops No Longer No-Nos at San Jose Unified." *Mercury News*, July 17, 2017. https://www.mercurynews.com/2017/07/17/ san-jose-unified-dumps-restrictive-dress-codes/.

[Ch. 2, p. 51: Utah dress code law – Richards, Jeff]

Richards, Jeff. "Bill Permitting Native American Students to Wear Tribal Regalia at Graduation Passes Legislature Unanimously." St George News, February 9, 2022. https://www.stgeorgeutah.com/news/archive/2022/02/09/jmr-lgl22-bill-permitting- native-american-students-to-wear-tribal-regalia-at-graduation-passes-legislature- unanimously/#.Y01wwNfMJPY.

[Ch. 2, p. 51: Braided extensions]

Nittle, Nadra. "Students Are Waging War on Sexist and Racist School Dress Codes — And They're Winning." *Vox*, September 13, 2018. https://www.vox.com/the-goods/2018/9/13/17847542/ students-waging-war-sexist-racist-school-dress-codes.

[Ch. 2, p. 53: Christian Cooper, Black bird-watcher]

Booker, Brakkton. "Amy Cooper, White Woman Who Called Police on Black Bird-Watcher, Has Charge Dismissed." NPR, February 16, 2021. https://www.npr.org/2021/02/16/968372253/ white-woman-who-called-police-on-black-man-bird-watching-has-charges-dismissed.

[Ch. 2, pp. 54–55, 60, 62: Peggy McIntosh]

Alliance for Healthier Communities. "Notisha Massaquoi and Peggy McIntosh." YouTube, June 11, 2010. Video, 6:06. https://www.youtube.com/watch?v=-3zHygcFeTk.

McIntosh, Peggy. "Some Notes for Facilitators on Presenting My White Privilege Papers." Wellesley Centers for Women, Wellesley, MA, 2010.

McIntosh, Peggy. "White Privilege: Unpacking the Invisible Knapsack." National SEED Project, 2022. First appeared in *Peace and Freedom Magazine* (July/August 1989): 10–12.

W.K. Kellogg Foundation. "Peggy McIntosh on Facing Her Own Race." YouTube, March 12, 2012. Video, 1:40. https://www.youtube.com/watch?v=a4mjw2cVaDY.

[Ch. 2, p. 55: Hate crimes – Black Muslim women]

Yourex-West, Heather. "Why Are Alberta's Black, Muslim Women Being Attacked?" Global News, March 26, 2021. https://globalnews.ca/news/7721850/ hate-crime-alberta-attacks-black-muslim-women/.

[Ch. 2, pp. 57–58: Residential schools]

The Canadian Encyclopedia. S.v. "Residential Schools in Canada." By J.R. Miller. Updated by Tabitha De Bruin, David Gallant, and Michelle Filice, January 6, 2023. https://www. thecanadianencyclopedia.ca/en/article/residential-schools.

SOURCES

Ch. 2, pp. 57–58: Residential schools]

Hanson, Eric. "The Residential School System." Indigenous Foundations. Updated by Daniel P. Gamez and Alexa Manuel, September 2020. https://indigenousfoundations.arts.ubc.ca/residential-school-system-2020/.

[Ch. 2, p. 57: Wente, Jesse on reconciliation]

Skinner, Laura. "What Canada Needs Is Conciliation, Not Reconciliation." *The Argosy*, November 28, 2018. https://www.since1872.ca/active-sections/1-news/what-canada-needs-is-conciliation-not-reconciliation/.

[Ch. 2, p. 58: Palmater, Pam]

Palmater, Pamela. "Canada 150 Is a Celebration of Indigenous Genocide." NOW Toronto, March 29, 2017. https://nowtoronto.com/news/canada-150-is-a-celebration-of-indigenous-genocide/.

[Ch. 2, p. 58: Yerxa, Jana-Rae]

Yerxa, Jana-Rae, and Leo Yerxa. "We Need to Stop Calling Them 'Schools.'" Seven Generations Education Institute, June 30, 2021. https://www.7generations.org/we-need-to-stop-calling-them-schools/.

[Ch. 2, p. 59: Arrests – Wet'suwet'en]

Bracken, Amber. "In Photos: A View of RCMP Arrests of Media, Indigenous Land Defenders on Wet'suwet'en Territory." The Narwhal, November 25, 2021. https://thenarwhal.ca/rcmp-arrests-wetsuweten-media-photos/.

[Ch. 2, p. 60: Co-conspiratorship]

Habtom, Sefanit, and Megan Scribe. "To Breathe Together: Co-Conspirators for Decolonial Futures." Yellowhead Institute, June 2, 2022. https://yellowheadinstitute.org/2020/06/02/to-breathe-together/.

[Ch. 2, p. 61: King Jr., Dr. Martin Luther]

Blow, Charles M. "Reparations: Reasonable and Right." *New York Times*, June 19, 2019. https://www.nytimes.com/2019/06/19/opinion/reparations-reasonable-and-right.html.

[Ch. 2, p. 61: Proposed federal legislation barring Black people from Canada]

Canadian Museum of Immigration at Pier 21. "Order-in-Council PC 1911-1324." Canadian Museum of Immigration at Pier 21. Accessed July 2021. https://pier21.ca/research/immigration-history/order-in-council-pc-1911-1324.

[Ch. 2, p. 61: McLean, Sheelah]

McLean, Sheelah. "'We Built a Life from Nothing': White Settler Colonialism and the Myth of Meritocracy." In *Our Schools/Our Selves* (Fall/Winter 2018): 32–33. Canadian Centre for Policy Alternatives. https://www.policyalternatives.ca/sites/default/files/uploads/publications/National%20Office/2017/12/McLean.pdf.

[Ch. 2, pp. 61–62: Intersectionality]

Coaston, Jane. "The Intersectionality Wars." *Vox*, May 28, 2019. https://www.vox.com/the-highlight/2019/5/20/18542843/intersectionality-conservatism-law-race-gender-discrimination.

[Ch. 2, pp. 63–64: Kumashiro, Kevin – discourse citation, etc.]

Kumashiro, Kevin K. "Toward a Theory of Anti-Oppressive Education." *Review of Educational Research* 70, no. 1 (Spring 2000): 25–53. https://doi.org/10.3102/00346543070001025.

[Ch. 2, p. 65: Stats – police killings]

Washington Post. Fatal Force Database. Washington Post, originally published May 30, 2015; re-released with department data December 5, 2022; updated May 13, 2023. https://www.washingtonpost.com/graphics/investigations/police-shootings-database/.

[Ch. 2, p. 65: Stats – police killings]

Clayton, Aubrey. "The Statistical Paradox of Police Killings." *Boston Globe*, updated June 11, 2020. https://www.bostonglobe.com/2020/06/11/opinion/statistical-paradox-police-killings/.

[Ch. 2, p. 65: Stats – police killings in Canada]

Singh, Inayat. "2020 Already a Particularly Deadly Year for People Killed in Police Encounters, CBC Research Shows." CBC News, updated July 23, 2020. https://newsinteractives.cbc.ca/features/2020/fatalpoliceencounters/.

[Ch. 2, p. 67: Decolonizing mental health]

Khúc, Mimi. Quoted in Karina Zapata, "Decolonizing Mental Health: The Importance of an Oppression-Focused Mental Health System." *Calgary Journal*, February 27, 2020. https://calgaryjournal.ca/2020/02/27/decolonizing-mental-health-the-importance-of-an-oppression-focused-mental-health-system/.

Chapter 3

[Ch. 3, pp. 74–75: Pierce, Chester M.]

Pierce, Chester M. Quoted in Jenée Desmond-Harris, "What Exactly Is a Microaggression?" Vox, February 16, 2015. https://www.vox.com/2015/2/16/8031073/what-are-microaggressions.

[Ch. 3, p. 75: X, Malcolm – Autobiography of (p. 372)]

X, Malcolm, and Alex Haley. *The Autobiography of Malcolm X*. Reissue ed. New York: Ballantine Books, 2015.

[Ch. 3, p. 77: Skin-bleaching]

Allen, Maya. "The Reality of Skin Bleaching and the History behind It." Byrdie, updated May 13, 2022. https://www.byrdie.com/skin-bleaching.

[Ch. 3, p. 77: Skin-bleaching]

Santos-Longhurst, Adrienne. "Skin Bleaching Products and Procedures: Side Effects and Benefits." Healthline, July 22, 2019. https://www.healthline.com/health/skin-bleaching#side-effects.

[Ch. 3, p. 77: Richardson, Jael]

Richardson, Jael. *Gutter Child: A Novel*. Toronto: Harper Avenue, 2021.

[Ch. 3, p. 79: Biko, Steve]

Biko, Steve. Quote. "The most potent weapon in the hands of the oppressor is the mind of the oppressed." Quoted in Takudzwa Hillary Chiwanza, "'The Most Potent Weapon in the Hands of the Oppressor Is the Mind of the Oppressed' – Steve Biko." The African Exponent, September 12, 2017. https://www.africanexponent.com/post/8569-steve-biko-was-a-prominent-and-eminent-activist-in-the-fight-against-apartheid.

[Ch. 3, p. 81: Linguists, th sounds]

Rickford, John R. "What Is Ebonics (African American English)?" Linguistic Society of America. Accessed January 24, 2022. https://www.linguisticsociety.org/content/what-ebonics-african-american-english.

[Ch. 3, p. 82: Chomsky, Noam]

Chomsky, Noam. Interview. "Linguist Noam Chomsky on Black English, AAVE, Ebonics, Etc." IRL Server, YouTube, June 14, 2019. Video, 2:29. https://www.youtube.com/watch?v=jWIkES_4Gfk.

[Ch. 3, p. 87: Kendi, Ibram X.]

Kendi, Ibram X. *How to Be an Antiracist*. New York: One World, 2019.

SOURCES

[Ch. 3, p. 89: Desmond, Viola]

The Canadian Encyclopedia. S.v. "Viola Desmond." By Russell Bingham. Updated by Eli Yarhi, April 16, 2021. https://www.thecanadianencyclopedia.ca/en/article/viola-desmond.

[Ch. 3, p. 91: Waxman, Olivia]

Waxman, Olivia B. "How the U.S. Got Its Police Force." *Time*, May 18, 2017. https://time.com/4779112/police-history-origins/.

[Ch. 3, p. 91: Ahmaud Arbery killing]

Cohen, Rebecca. "The Judge Who Sentenced Ahmaud Arbery's Killers Made the Courtroom Sit in Silence for 1 Minute to Put 'Into Context' How Long the Men Chased Arbery." Insider, January 7, 2022. https://www.insider.com/ahmaud-arbery-judge-makes-courtroom-sit-silence-sentencing-2022-1.

[Ch. 3, p. 91: Ahmaud Arbery killing]

McLaughlin, Eliott C. "Ahmaud Arbery Was Hit with a Truck before He Died, and His Killer Allegedly Used a Racial Slur, Investigator Testifies." CNN, June 4, 2020. https://www.cnn.com/2020/06/04/us/mcmichaels-hearing-ahmaud-arbery/index.html.

[Ch. 3, p. 91: RCMP control and displace]

Gerster, Jane. "The RCMP Was Created to Control Indigenous People. Can That Relationship Be Reset?" Global News, June 27, 2019. https://globalnews.ca/news/5381480/rcmp-indigenous-relationship/.

[Ch. 3, p. 92: Vox.com coded language]

Lopez, German. "The Sneaky Language Today's Politicians Use to Get Away with Racism and Sexism." *Vox*, February 1, 2016. https://www.vox.com/2016/2/1/10889138/coded-language-thug-bossy.

[Ch. 3, pp. 92–93: Canadian citizenship oath]

Immigration, Refugees and Citizenship Canada. "Oath of Citizenship." Immigration, Refugees and Citizenship Canada, updated July 8, 2021. https://www.canada.ca/en/immigration-refugees-citizenship/corporate/publications-manuals/operational-bulletins-manuals/canadian-citizenship/ceremony/oath.html.

[Ch. 3, p. 93: Scout's pledge]

Scouts Canada. "The Scout Promise." Quoted in US Scouting Service Project, "Scout Oaths, Promises, Mottos, and Slogans – Canada." USSSP. Accessed July 2021. http://www.usscouts.org/profbvr/oath_promise/canada.asp.

[Ch. 3, p. 93: Nelson, Kadir]

Nelson, Kadir. Quoted in The Root, "Kadir Nelson Puts Iconic Moments in Black History on Canvas." The Root, February 13, 2019. Video, 5:11. https://www.theroot.com/kadir-nelson-puts-iconic-moments-in-black-history-on-ca-1832594303#.

[Ch. 3, p. 97: Ali, Muhammad – affirmations quote]

Ali, Muhammad. Quote. "Muhammad Ali In His Own Words: Six of His Best Quotes to Live By." Quoted by Jeff Johnson, NBC News. June 4, 2016. https://www.nbcnews.com/news/nbcblk/remembering-muhammad-ali-six-quotes-pack-punch-n585571

[Ch. 3, p. 94: Dirty Dozens game]

Lewis, Gregory. "Dozens Is Oral Legacy Rooted in Survival." *Baltimore Sun*, February 11, 1994. https://www.baltimoresun.com/news/bs-xpm-1994-02-11-1994042244-story.html.

[Ch. 3, p. 94: Ancestors' wildest dreams quote]

Labat, Sydney (@_botttt). "Standing in front of the slave quarters of our ancestors, at The Whitney Plantation, with my medical school classmates. We are truly our ancestors' wildest dreams." Twitter, December 14, 2019, 3:39 p.m. https://twitter.com/_botttt/status/1205995679014891525. Quoted in Philip Lewis, "Photo of

Black Medical Students at Plantation Goes Viral: 'We Are Truly Our Ancestors' Wildest
Dreams.'" Complex, December 19, 2019. https://www.complex.com/life/2019/12/
black-medical-students-plantation-viral-photo.

[Ch. 3, p. 95: Douglass, Frederick, from Booker T Washington Auto-bio]

Douglass, Frederick. Quoted in Booker T. Washington, "Black Race and Red Race." In *Up from
Slavery: An Autobiography*. 1901. Literature Page. Accessed September 2021. http://www.
literaturepage.com/read/upfromslavery-66.html.

[Ch. 3, p. 96: Shakur, Assata]

Rolando, Gloria, dir. *The Eyes of the Rainbow*. Images of the Caribbean, 1997. YouTube video,
46:19. https://youtu.be/0jItg69Hnq8.

[Ch. 3, p. 96: Tubman, Harriet – how many freed?]

Maranzani, Barbara. "Harriet Tubman: 8 Facts about the Daring Abolitionist." HISTORY.
A&E Television Networks, May 31, 2013. https://www.history.com/news/
harriet-tubman-facts-daring-raid.

[Ch. 3, p. 96: Tubman, Harriet – last words]

Tubman, Harriet. Quote. "I go to prepare a place for you." From the ending chyron text in
Harriet. Directed by Kasi Lemmons. Focus Features, 2019. Quoted in Kate Aurthur, "Why
'Harriet' Doesn't Mention the $20 Bill." *Variety*, November 11, 2019. https://variety.
com/2019/film/news/harriet-movie-20-bill-kasi-lemmons-1203400681/.

[Ch. 3, p. 99: Trump, Donald – divisive concepts ban]

Exec. Order No. 13950. Combating Race and Sex Stereotyping. 85 Fed.
Reg. 60683. September 22, 2020. https://www.federalregister.gov/
documents/2020/09/28/2020-21534/combating-race-and-sex-stereotyping.

[Ch. 3, p. 99: Trump, Donald]

Guynn, Jessica. "President Joe Biden Rescinds Donald Trump Ban on Diversity Training
about Systemic Racism." USA Today, published January 20, 2021; updated
January 26, 2021. https://www.usatoday.com/story/money/2021/01/20/
biden-executive-order-overturns-trump-diversity-training-ban/4236891001/.

[Ch. 3, p. 99: Oklahoma ban]

H.B. 1775, 58th Leg., 1st Sess. Oklahoma, 2021. As approved by Gov. Kevin Stitt,
May 7, 2021. Oklahoma Secretary of State. https://www.sos.ok.gov/documents/
legislation/58th/2021/1R/HB/1775.pdf.

[Ch. 3, p. 100: Love, Bettina]

Downey, Maureen. "Opinion: Turning Equity Lens on Schools Exposes White Unhappiness."
Atlanta Journal-Constitution, May 23, 2021. https://www.ajc.com/education/get-
schooled-blog/opinion-turning-equity-lens-on-schools-exposes-white-unhappiness/5
YUPAKNZPRHONJP6JGEF4553AQ/.

[Ch. 3, pp. 100–101: X, Malcolm – quote]

X, Malcolm. Speech at the founding rally of the Organization of Afro-American Unity,
New York, NY, June 28, 1964. Quoted in BlackPast, "(1964) Malcolm X's Speech at
the Founding Rally of the Organization of Afro-American Unity. BlackPast, October
15, 2007. https://www.blackpast.org/african-american-history/speeches-african-
american-history/1964-malcolm-x-s-speech-founding-rally-organization-afro-
american-unity/.

[Ch 3, p. 101: Asante, Molefi]

Institute for Educational Leadership. *Learning Exchange Protocol: The Power of Nommo in Learning
Exchanges*. Institute for Educational Leadership. Accessed January 24, 2022. https://iel.
org/wp-content/uploads/2015/12/iel-lt2-power-of-nommo.pdf.

SOURCES

[Ch. 3, p. 101 footnote: Asante, Molefi – Afrocentricity]
Asante, Molefi Kete. *An Afrocentric Manifesto: Toward an African Renaissance*. Cambridge: Polity, 2007.

Chapter 4
[Ch. 4, p. 111: Clinton, Bill – crime law]
Ofer, Udi. "How the 1994 Crime Bill Fed the Mass Incarceration Crisis." American Civil Liberties Union, June 4, 2019. https://www.aclu.org/blog/smart-justice/mass-incarceration/how-1994-crime-bill-fed-mass-incarceration-crisis.

[Ch. 4, p. 111: Clinton, Hillary]
Clinton, Hillary. Speech referencing "superpredators" at Keene State College, 1996, Keene, NH. "1996: Hillary Clinton on 'Superpredators' (C-SPAN)." YouTube Video, 2:02. https://youtu.be/j0uCrA7ePno?t=58.

[Ch. 4, pp. 111–112: US Incarceration Rate – Black people]
NAACP. "Criminal Justice Fact Sheet." NAACP. Accessed July 2021. https://naacp.org/resources/criminal-justice-factsheet#:~:text=32%25%20of%20the%20US%20population,total%206.8%20million%20correctional%20population.

[Ch. 4, p. 112: Incarceration Rate – Black people]
"Blacks, Hispanics make up larger shares of prisoners than of U.S. population." Pew Research Center. May 2020. https://www.pewresearch.org/short-reads/2020/05/06/share-of-black-white-hispanic-americans-in-prison-2018-vs-2006/ft_20-05-05_imprisonmentrates_2a/

*Blacks and whites include those who report being only one race and are non-Hispanic. Hispanics are of any race. Prison population is defined as inmates sentenced to more than a year in a state or federal prison. Source: U.S. Census Bureau, Bureau of Justice Statistics, 2018.

[Ch. 4, p. 112, 123: Cole, Desmond]
Cole, Desmond. *The Skin We're In: A Year of Black Resistance and Power*. Toronto: Doubleday Canada, 2020.

[Ch. 4, p. 113: "To be a negro . . ."]
"To Be in a Rage, Almost All the Time." Produced by Paige Osburn. *1A*, June 1, 2020. Podcast, MP3 audio, 34:39. https://www.npr.org/2020/06/01/867153918/-to-be-in-a-rage-almost-all-the-time.

[Ch. 4, p. 113: Cooper, Brittney]
Cooper, Brittney. *Eloquent Rage: A Black Feminist Discovers Her Superpower*. New York: St. Martin's Press, 2018.

[Ch. 4, pp. 110–11: Dilulio, John]
DiLulio, John. "The Coming of the Super – Predators." *Washington Examiner*, November 27, 1995. https://www.washingtonexaminer.com/weekly-standard/the-coming-of-the-super-predators.

[Ch. 4, pp. 111–112: Prison population – US]
Lopez, German. "Mass Incarceration in America, Explained in 22 Maps and Charts." Vox, October 11, 2016. https://www.vox.com/2015/7/13/8913297/mass-incarceration-maps-charts.

[Ch. 4, p. 113: Hill, Lauryn – Black Rage]
Hill, Ms. Lauryn. "Black Rage (Sketch)." MsLaurynHill, SoundCloud, August 20, 2014. Audio, 3:46. https://soundcloud.com/mslaurynhill/black-rage-sketch.

[Ch. 4, p. 118: Health inequity, Black Canadians]

Public Health Agency of Canada. *Social Determinants and Inequities in Health for Black Canadians: A Snapshot*. Written by Ifrah Abdillahi and Ashley Shaw. Ottawa: Public Health Agency of Canada, September 8, 2020. https://www.canada.ca/en/public-health/services/health-promotion/population-health/what-determines-health/social-determinants-inequities-black-canadians-snapshot.html.

[Ch. 4, p. 118: Health inequity (mental health), Black Americans]

Vance, Thomas A. "Addressing Mental Health in the Black Community." Columbia University Department of Psychiatry, February 8, 2019. https://www.columbiapsychiatry.org/news/addressing-mental-health-black-community.

[Ch. 4, pp. 118–19: Mental health disparity, Indigenous people]

Public Health Agency of Canada. *Key Health Inequalities in Canada: A National Portrait*. Ottawa: Public Health Agency of Canada, 2018. https://www.canada.ca/en/public-health/services/publications/science-research-data/inequalities-mental-illness-hospitalization-infographic.html.

[Ch 4, pp. 119–120: Suicide risk and rates for Indigenous people]

Public Health Agency of Canada. *Key Health Inequalities in Canada: A National Portrait*. Ottawa: Public Health Agency of Canada, 2018. https://www.canada.ca/en/public-health/services/publications/science-research-data/inequalities-death-suicide-canada-infographic.html.

[Ch. 4, pp. 121–122: Stigma, mental health]

Mental Health Commission of Canada. "Shining a Light on Mental Health in Black Communities." Mental Health Commission of Canada, Health Canada. Accessed June 23, 2021. https://www.mentalhealthcommission.ca/wp-content/uploads/drupal/2021-02/covid_and_suicide_tip_sheet_eng.pdf.

Vance, Thomas. "Addressing Mental Health in the Black Community." Columbia University Department of Psychiatry, February 8, 2019. https://www.columbiapsychiatry.org/news/addressing-mental-health-black-community.

Mental Health America. "Black and African American Communities and Mental Health." Mental Health America. Accessed February 23, 2022. https://www.mhanational.org/issues/black-and-african-american-communities-and-mental-health.

Dictionary.com. S.v. "Stigma." Accessed February 23, 2022. https://www.dictionary.com/browse/stigma.

[Ch. 4, p. 122: *New York Times* – Curse of Ham]

Lee, Felicia R. "From Noah's Curse to Slavery's Rationale." *New York Times*, November 1, 2003. https://www.nytimes.com/2003/11/01/arts/from-noah-s-curse-to-slavery-s-rationale.html.

[Ch. 4, p. 123: Baldwin, James]

WayWayBack TV. "Nikki Giovanni and James Baldwin." January 30, 2019. Youtube. Video, 5:33. All credits to Soul! and ShoutFactoryTV.com. https://www.youtube.com/watch?v=zdR0PVznL4o&t=308s.

[Ch. 4, p. 123: X, Malcolm]

X, Malcolm, and Alex Haley. *The Autobiography of Malcolm X*. Reissue ed. New York: Ballantine Books, 2015.

[Ch. 4, p. 124: Roderique, Hadiya]

Roderique, Hadiya. "The Case for Black Joy." *FASHION*, February 1, 2019. https://fashionmagazine.com/flare/the-case-for-black-joy/.

SOURCES

[Ch. 4, p. 124: Martis, Eternity]

Martis, Eternity. *They Said This Would Be Fun: Race, Campus Life, and Growing Up*. Toronto: McClelland & Stewart, 2021.

[Ch. 4, p. 126: Williams, Ian]

Williams, Ian. *Disorientation: Being Black in the World*. Toronto: Random House Canada, 2021.

[Ch. 4, p. 126–27: Upset Homegirls]

Upset Homegirls of California. https://web.archive.org/web/20211129050810

[Ch. 4, p. 127: TIME – BLM protests 93% peaceful]

Mansoor, Sanya. "93% Of Black Lives Matter Protests Have Been Peaceful, New Report Finds," *TIME*, September 5, 2020. https://time.com/5886348/report-peaceful-protests/.

[Ch. 4, p. 127: Factory, Brandy, Upset Homegirls]

Pham, Kim. "Celebrating Black Joy as an Alternative Form of Resistance and Reclaiming of Humanity." Voice of OC, February 1, 2021. https://voiceofoc.org/2021/02/celebrating-black-joy-as-an-alternative-form-of-resistance-and-reclaiming-of-humanity/.

[Ch. 4, p. 128: Lee, Erica Violet]

From Erica Violet Lee's September 20, 2017, talk, "NDN Girls at the End of the World," as reported by *The McGill Daily*. Grenier, Claire. "Erica Violet Lee on Indigenous Feminism." *The McGill Daily*, September 27, 2017. https://www.mcgilldaily.com/2017/09/erica-violet-lee-on-indigenous-feminism/.

[Ch. 4, p. 128: Davis, Angela]

Davis, Angela. Foreword to *When They Call You a Terrorist: A Black Lives Matter Memoir*, by Patrisse Khan-Cullors and Asha Bandele, xiv. Reprint ed. New York: St Martin's Press, 2020.

[Ch. 4, p. 132: Ban, on rap, congressional hearing]

Harrington, Linda M., and Tribune Staff Writer. "On Capitol Hill, a Real Rap Session." *Chicago Tribune*, February 24, 1994. https://www.chicagotribune.com/news/ct-xpm-1994-02-24-9402240240-story.html.

[Ch. 4, p. 139: Lorde, Audre]

Caraballo, Jor-El. "Self-Care Is an Act of Revolution When You Are Black." Essence, June 17, 2020. https://www.essence.com/feature/self-care-is-an-act-of-revolution-when-you-are-black/.

Chapter 5

[Ch. 5, p. 144: 1997 Top 100 songs]

Top40-Charts. "1997: Year-End USA Charts (Singles)." Top40-Charts. Accessed August 2021. https://top40-charts.com/features/YearEnd/yearend1997.php.

[Ch. 5, p. 147: Dubois, WEB]

Du Bois, William Edward Burghardt. "Strivings of the Negro People." *Atlantic Monthly*, August 1897. Reprinted in "The Civil War," special issue, *Atlantic*, 2011. https://www.theatlantic.com/magazine/archive/1897/08/strivings-of-the-negro-people/305446/.

[Ch. 5, pp. 147, 156–57: Minstrel Shows]

Encyclopaedia Britannica Online. S.v. "Minstrel Show." By the Editors of Encyclopaedia Britannica. Updated September 2, 2020, https://www.britannica.com/art/minstrel-show.

[Ch. 5, pp. 147–148, 159–160: Kendi, Ibram X.]

Kendi, Ibram X. "This Is the Black Renaissance." *TIME*, February 3, 2021. https://time.com/5932842/ibram-kendi-black-renaissance/.

[Ch. 5, p. 152: Savage, Candace – *The Nature of Wolves*]

Savage, Candace. *The Nature of Wolves: An Intimate Portrait*. Vancouver: Greystone Books, 1996.

[Ch. 5, p. 155: Doctrine of Discovery and Terra Nullius, concepts]

Assembly of First Nations. *Dismantling the Doctrine of Discovery*. Ottawa: January 2018. https://
www.afn.ca/wp-content/uploads/2018/02/18-01-22-Dismantling-the-Doctrine-of-
Discovery-EN.pdf.

[Ch. 5, p. 155: Terra Nullius definition]

Australian Law Dictionary, 1st ed. S.v. "*terra nullius*." Edited by Trischa Mann and Audrey
Blunden. Oxford University Press, 2010. Oxford Reference. https://www.
oxfordreference.com/view/10.1093/oi/authority.20110803103157982.

[Ch. 5, p. 155: Non-Christians in terra nullius]

Indigenous Corporate Training. "Indigenous Title and the Doctrine of Discovery." Indigenous
Corporate Training Inc., March 30, 2023. https://www.ictinc.ca/blog/indigenous-
title-and-the-doctrine-of-discovery#:~:text=The%20Doctrine%20of%20Discovery%20
was%20the%20international%20law%20that%20gave,was%20not%20populated%20
by%20Christians.

[Ch. 5, p. 155: *The Pass System* (film)]

Williams, Alex, dir. *The Pass System*. VTape, 2015. http://thepasssystem.ca/.

[Ch. 5, p. 155: McLean, Sheelah]

McLean, Sheelah. "The Whiteness of Green: Racialization and Environmental Education." In
"Critical Geographies of Education," edited by Tyler McCreary, Ranu Basu, and Anne
Godlewska, special issue, *The Canadian Geographer*, 57, no. 3 (Autumn 2013): 354–62.
https://doi.org/10.1111/cag.12025.

[Ch. 5, p. 156: Ashini, Daniel]

Ashini, Daniel. "David Confronts Goliath: The Innu of Ungava Versus the NATO Alliance."
In *Drumbeat: Anger and Renewal in Indian Country*, edited by Boyce Richardson, 46.
Toronto: Summerhill Press, 1989. Quoted in Bruce W. Hodgins and Kerry A. Cannon,
eds., *On the Land: Confronting the Challenges to Aboriginal Self-Determination in Northern
Quebec and Labrador*. Toronto: Betelgeuse Books, 1995. Google Books. https://books.
google.ca/books?id=gmiQolqtx7kC&pg=PA20-IA4&lpg=PA20-IA4&dq=how+did+w
e+become+strangers+in+our+own+land+canada&source=bl&ots=dea2JYH4dk&sig=A
CfU3U3js1z7n9xYx08vNip7I3jWooW-yg&hl=en&sa=X&ved=2ahUKEwjn15GC2_
TxAhUN3p4KHbioAKQ4ChDoATAJegQICRAD#v=onepage&q=how%20did%20we%20
become%20strangers%20in%20our%20own%20land%20canada&f=false.

[Ch. 5, pp. 156–57: Griffin, John Howard – *Black Like Me*]

Griffin, John Howard. *Black Like Me*. 50th anniversary ed. New York: Berkley, 2010.

[Ch. 5, p. 157: Hughes, Langston – "Dream Variations"]

Hughes, Langston. "Dream Variations." *The Collected Poems of Langston Hughes*. New York:
Alfred A. Knopf, 1994. Poets.org, Academy of American Poets, https://poets.org/poem/
dream-variations.

[Ch. 5, pp. 157–58: Grey Owl]

Grey Owl's Strange Quest. Youtube, December 2, 2008. Video, 8:33. https://www.youtube.com/
watch?v=D0ye0KXuF00&t=513s

[Ch. 5, p. 159: Mass shootings – race and gender demographics]

Statista Research Department. "Mass Shootings by Shooter's Race in the U.S. 2023."
Statista, as of February 20, 2023. https://www.statista.com/statistics/476456/
mass-shootings-in-the-us-by-shooter-s-race/.

SOURCES

[Ch. 5, p. 164: DMX – Golden Girls fan]

Kubota, Samantha. "Late Rapper DMX Was Apparently a Huge Fan of 'The Golden Girls.'" TODAY, April 9, 2021. https://www.today.com/popculture/dmx-was-apparently-huge-fan-golden-girls-t214528.

[Ch. 5, p. 164: DMX – Grandma lyric]

DMX. "What's My Name?" Track 3 on *And Then There Was X*, 1999. Written by Self Service, Irv Gotti, and DMX. Genius. https://genius.com/Dmx-whats-my-name-lyrics.

[Ch. 5, p. 168: Angelou, Maya]

Angelou, Maya. Quote. "When you know better, you do better." Quoted by Oprah Winfrey in an October 2011 interview. In "The Powerful Lesson Maya Angelou Taught Oprah." Oprah Winfrey Network. Video, 4:16. https://www.oprah.com/oprahs-lifeclass/the-powerful-lesson-maya-angelou-taught-oprah-video.

[Ch. 5, p. 168: Blackthought]

The Roots. "What They Do." Track 8 on *Illadelph Halflife*, 1996. Written by Leonard "Hub" Hubbard, Black Thought, Raphael Saadiq, ?uestlove, and Kamal Gray. Genius. https://genius.com/The-roots-what-they-do-lyrics.

[Ch. 5, p. 168: hooks, bell]

hooks, bell. Quote. "I will not have my life narrowed down. I will not bow down to somebody else's whim or to someone else's ignorance." Conversation between bell hooks and Maya Angelou, *Shambhala Sun*, January 1998. http://www.hartford-hwp.com/archives/45a/249.html.

Chapter 6

[Ch. 6, p. 175: St Denis, Verna]

St. Denis, Verna. "Silencing Aboriginal Curricular Content and Perspectives Through Multiculturalism: 'There Are Other Children Here.'" In "Racism, Colonialism, and Film in Canada," edited by Jennifer S. Simpson, special issue, *Review of Education, Pedagogy, and Cultural Studies* 33, no. 4 (2011): 303–317. https://doi.org/10.1080/10714413.2011.597637.

[Ch. 6, p. 176: Colorblindness stat]

Colour Blind Awareness. "About Colour Blindness." Colour Blind Awareness. Accessed September 2021. https://www.colourblindawareness.org/colour-blindness/.

[Ch. 6, p. 178: Streaming students in schools – Black students]

Draaisma, Muriel. "Black Students in Toronto Streamed into Courses below Their Ability, Report Finds." CBC News, April 24, 2017. https://www.cbc.ca/news/canada/toronto/study-black-students-toronto-york-university-1.4082463.

[Ch. 6, p. 178: Black and Indigenous students]

Canadian Women's Foundation. "Ending Systemic Racism in School Isn't Just about Ending Streaming." Canadian Women's Foundation, August 6, 2020. https://canadianwomen.org/blog/ending-streaming/.

[Ch. 6, pp. 178–79: Lyiscott, Jamila – TED Talk]

Lyiscott, Jamila. "Why English Class Is Silencing Students of Color." "Liberation Literacies in the Classroom" presentation filmed at TEDxTheBenjaminSchool Sapir-Whorf, April 21, 2018, Palm Beach Gardens, FL. TEDx Talks video, 22:05. YouTube, May 23, 2018. https://youtu.be/u4dc1axRwE4.

[Ch. 6, p. 179: Timberlake, Justin]

Timberlake, Justin. "I'm Lovin' It." Jingle for McDonald's, 2003. YouTube video, 1:01. https://www.youtube.com/watch?v=ZhXt3v5rYnE.

[Ch. 6, p. 179: Johnson, George M. – *All Boys Aren't Blue*]

Johnson, George M. *All Boys Aren't Blue: A Memoir-Manifesto*. Illustrated ed. New York: Farrar Straus Giroux Books for Young Readers, 2020.

[Ch. 6, p. 179: Johnson, George M. – quote]

Johnson, George M. "An Interview with George M. Johnson." In "The Gender Issue," edited by Bettina Judd, special issue, *Auburn Avenue*, no. 7 (April 27–May 25, 2020). https://www. theauburnavenue.com/george-m-johnson-interview.

[Ch. 6, pp. 179–80: Jackson, Lauren Michele – Teen Vogue]

Jackson, Lauren Michele. "We Need to Talk about Digital Blackface in Reaction GIFs." *Teen Vogue*, August 2, 2017. https://www.teenvogue.com/story/ digital-blackface-reaction-gifs.

[Ch. 6, p. 180: Chavez, Felicia Rose]

Chavez, Felicia Rose. *The Anti-Racist Writing Workshop: How to Decolonize the Creative Classroom*. Chicago: Haymarket Books, 2021.

[Ch. 6, p. 181: Brigham, Carl C – Eugenics support and SAT development]

FRONTLINE. "Americans Instrumental in Establishing Standardized Tests." In "Secrets of the SAT." PBS. Supplementary online material to *FRONTLINE* episode "Secrets of the SAT." Written, produced, and directed by Michael Chandler. Aired October 1999, on PBS. Accessed August 2021. https://www.pbs.org/wgbh/pages/frontline/shows/sats/where/ three.html.

[Ch. 6, p. 181: Common Core standards]

Council of Chief State School Officers. "Common Core State Standards." The Learning Portal. Accessed July 2021. http://www.corestandards.org/.

[Ch. 6, p. 181: Common Core standards]

National Governors Association. "Forty-Nine States and Territories Join Common Core Standards Initiative." National Governors Association, June 1, 2009. Archived from the original on October 4, 2013. Wayback Machine, Internet Archive. https://web. archive.org/web/20131004230129/http://www.nga.org/cms/home/news-room/ news-releases/page_2009/col2-content/main-content-list/title_forty-nine-states-and- territories-join-common-core-standards-initiative.html.

[Ch. 6, p. 181: SAT and Common Core Standards]

Lewin, Tamar. "A New Sat Aims to Realign with Schoolwork." *New York Times*, March 5, 2014. https://www.nytimes.com/2014/03/06/education/major-changes-in-sat-announced- by-college-board.html.

[Ch. 6, p. 181: History of the SAT]

Ben. "A Brief History of the SAT and How It Changes." Peterson's, December 20, 2017. https:// www.petersons.com/blog/a-brief-history-of-the-sat-and-how-it-changes/.

[Ch. 6, p. 181: University of California SAT]

Watanabe, Teresa. "UC Slams the Door on Standardized Admissions Tests, Nixing Any SAT Alternative." *Los Angeles Times*, November 18, 2021. https://www.latimes.com/california/ story/2021-11-18/uc-slams-door-on-sat-and-all-standardized-admissions-tests.

[Ch. 6, p. 182: St. Denis, Verna]

St. Denis, Verna. "Silencing Aboriginal Curricular Content and Perspectives Through Multiculturalism: 'There Are Other Children Here.'" In "Racism, Colonialism, and Film in Canada," edited by Jennifer S. Simpson, special issue, *Review of Education, Pedagogy, and Cultural Studies* 33, no. 4 (2011): 303–317. https://doi.org/10.1080/10714413.2011.5 97637.

SOURCES

[Ch. 6, p. 183: Freire – Pedagogy of the Oppressed]
Freire, Paulo. *Pedagogy of the Oppressed*. 50th anniversary ed. Translated by Myra Bergman Ramos. New York: Bloomsbury Academic, 2018.

[Ch. 6, p. 183: Freire – jailed]
Los Angeles Times. "Paulo Freire; Brazilian Author, Literacy Educator." *Los Angeles Times*, May 9, 1997. https://www.latimes.com/archives/la-xpm-1997-05-09-me-57209-story. html#:~:text=Freire%20was%20arrested%20for%20preaching,were%20translated%20 into%2035%20languages.

[Ch. 6, p. 185: Canadian Anti-Hate Network toolkit (SK govt discourages use)]
Sciarpelletti, Laura. "Sask. Gov't Discourages Use of Federally Funded Canadian Anti-Hate Network Toolkit in Classrooms." CBC News, updated October 24, 2022. https://www. cbc.ca/news/canada/saskatchewan/sask-govt-discouraging-use-of-federally-funded- canadian-anti-hate-network-toolkit-in-classrooms-1.6626217.

[Ch. 6, p. 185: Stop WOKE Act]
Jones, Zoe Christen. "Florida Legislature Passes 'Stop Woke Act,' Second Controversial Education Bill This Week." CBS News, March 10, 2022. https://www.cbsnews.com/ news/florida-critical-race-theory-education-stop-woke-act/.

[Ch. 6, p. 185: Critical Race Theory bans]
Ellingwood, Susan. "What Is Critical Race Theory, and Why Is Everyone Talking About It?" Columbia News, July 1, 2021. https://news.columbia.edu/news/ what-critical-race-theory-and-why-everyone-talking-about-it-0.

[Ch. 6, p. 186: hooks, bell]
hooks, bell. *Teaching to Transgress: Education as the Practice of Freedom*. Milton Park, Abingdon Oxon, UK: Routledge, 1994.

[Ch. 6, p. 186: Anti-literacy laws, slavery, Missouri example]
General Assembly of the State of Missouri. An Act Respecting Slaves, Free Negroes and Mulattoes, passed February 16, 1847. Missouri Secretary of State. Uploaded February 7, 2005. https://www.sos.mo.gov/CMSImages/MDH/AnActRespectingSlaves,1847.pdf.

[Ch. 6, p. 186: White nationalism]
Facing History & Ourselves. "White Nationalism." Facing History & Ourselves, last updated August 9, 2019. https://www.facinghistory.org/educator-resources/current-events/ explainer/white-nationalism.

[Ch. 6, p. 187: NY state grad rate]
New York State Education Department. "NY State Graduation Rate Data 4 Year Outcome as of August 2019." NYSED Data Site. Accessed August 2021. https://data.nysed.gov/ gradrate.php?year=2019&state=yes.

[Ch. 6, p. 187: Grade rate, 2020 Wisconsin]
Johnson, Annysa. "Wisconsin, Milwaukee Graduation Rates Increase, but Disparities Remain." *Milwaukee Journal Sentinel*, March 11, 2020. https://www.jsonline.com/story/ news/education/2020/03/11/wisconsin-milwaukee-graduation-rates-increase-but- disparities-remain/5013712002/.

[Ch. 6, p. 187: Grad rate, 2020 SK]
Saskatchewan Ministry of Education. *Ministry of Education Annual Report for 2020-21*. Government of Saskatchewan. Accessed July 2021. https://pubsaskdev.blob.core. windows.net/pubsask-prod/128170/2020-21EducationAnnualReport.pdf.

[Ch. 6, p. 189: ACLU School to prison pipeline]
American Civil Liberties Union. "School-to-Prison Pipeline." American Civil Liberties Union. Accessed August 2021. https://www.aclu.org/issues/juvenile-justice/school-prison-pipeline.

SOURCES

[Ch. 6, p. 190–91: Maynard, Robyn excerpt from]
Maynard, Robyn. *Policing Black Lives: State Violence in Canada from Slavery to the Present*. Fernwood Publishing, 2017. Excerpted in *The Walrus*, published November 29, 2017; updated January 30, 2022. https://thewalrus.ca/canadian-education-is-steeped-in-anti-black-racism/.

[Ch. 6, p. 191: Ekong, Jane, report to RPSB]
Ekong, Jane. "Report from the Regina Black/African Canadian Community." Report for the Regina Public School Board presented on September 8, 2020, Regina, SK. In "Notice: Meeting of the Board of Education of the Regina School Division No. 4 of Saskatchewan, September 8, 2020, at 5:30 p.m." Regina, SK: Regina Public School Board, 23–27. https://drive.google.com/file/d/1_EVamK4PgKmCxSnAbcKae-KM7Aj2e8tr/view.

[Ch. 6, p. 191: Giesbrecht, Lynn, report to RPSB]
Giesbrecht, Lynn. "Report on Issues Facing Black Students Presented to Regina Public Schools." *Regina Leader-Post*, September 14, 2020. https://leaderpost.com/news/local-news/report-on-issues-facing-black-students-presented-to-regina-public-schools.

[Ch. 6, p. 191: Cole, Desmond – p. 64, pp 178–179, p. 191]
Cole, Desmond. *The Skin We're In: A Year of Black Resistance and Power*. Toronto: Doubleday Canada, 2020.

[Ch. 6, p. 192: Edmonton SRO study]
Da Costa, Alexandre, and Bashir Mohamed. "The Numbers." *The Edmonton SRO Research Project.* Accessed August 2022. https://www.sroresearchproject.ca/research/thenumbers.

[Ch. 6, p. 192: TDSB SRO program cancelled]
Nasser, Shanifa. "Canada's Largest School Board Votes to End Armed Police Presence in Schools." CBC News, November 22, 2017. https://www.cbc.ca/news/canada/toronto/school-resource-officers-toronto-board-police-1.4415064.

[Ch. 6, p. 193: Peel Regional Police Budget, SRO program]
Duxbury, Linda E., and Craig Bennell. *Assigning Value to Peel's Regional Police's School Resource Officer Program*. Ottawa: Carleton University, January 2018. chrome-extension://efaidnbmnnnibpcajpcglclefindmkaj/https://www.peelpoliceboard.ca/en/board-meetings/resources/Presentations/Dr.-Duxbury-Presentation---Assigning-Value-To-Peel-Regional-Polices-School-Resource-Officer-Program.pdf

[Ch. 6, p. 193: BLM youth vanguard – random searches ended]
Twersky, Carolyn. "Thandiwe Abdullah Is Leading the Next Generation of the Black Lives Matter Movement." *Seventeen*, December 1, 2020. https://www.seventeen.com/life/a34717855/thandiwe-abdullah-black-lives-matter-voices-of-the-year-2020/.

[Ch. 6, p. 193: Abdullah, Thandiwe, Anya Dillard, and Sophie Ming]
Abdullah, Thandiwe, Anya Dillard, and Sophie Ming. "These Teen Black Lives Matter Activists Are Writing the Future." As told to Madison Feller. *Elle*, July 20, 2020. https://www.elle.com/culture/career-politics/a33329403/black-lives-matter-teen-activists/.

[Ch. 6, p. 194: Oakland School District Example]
Woo, Elaine, and Mary Curtius. "Oakland School District Recognizes Black English." *Los Angeles Times*, December 20, 1996. https://www.latimes.com/archives/la-xpm-1996-12-20-mn-11042-story.html.

[Ch. 6, p. 194: Linguistics Society of America]
Linguistics Society of America. "Resolution on the Oakland 'Ebonics' Issue Unanimously Adopted at the Annual Meeting of the Linguistic Society of America, Chicago, Illinois, January 3, 1997." Linguistics Society of America, updated October 9, 2008. http://www-personal.umich.edu/~jlawler/ebonics.lsa.html.

[Ch. 6, p. 194: Jackson, Jesse]

Sun Sentinel. "Jackson: Black English Not Separate Language." *Sun Sentinel*, December 23, 1996. Updated September 24, 2021. https://www.sun-sentinel.com/news/fl-xpm-1996-12-23-9612230011-story.html.

[Ch. 6, p. 194: Cenoz and Gorter – translanguaging]

Cenoz, Jasone, and Durk Gorter. "Teaching English through Pedagogical Translanguaging." In "World Englishes and Translanguaging," edited by Christopher Jenks and Jerry Won Lee, special issue, *World Englishes* 39, no. 2 (June 2020): 300–311. https://onlinelibrary.wiley.com/doi/full/10.1111/weng.12462.

[Ch. 6, p. 198: Shakur, Assata – autobio, p. 29]

Shakur, Assata. *Assata: An Autobiography.* Chicago: Lawrence Hill Books, 1999.

[Ch. 6, p. 199: Hill, Lawrence]

Hill, Lawrence. *The Book of Negroes.* Toronto: HarperCollins, 2007.

[Ch. 6, p. 199: Vernon, Karina]

Vernon, Karina. "I Grew up a Black Girl in Alberta without Ever Hearing of Amber Valley. How Does History Go Missing?" For CBC First Person, CBC News, published April 25, 2021; last updated April 29, 2021. https://www.cbc.ca/news/canada/calgary/bop-pov-whitewashing-prairies-1.5880367.

[Ch. 6, p. 199–200: Vernon, Karina]

Karina Vernon, ed. *The Black Prairie Archives: An Anthology.* Waterloo, ON: Wilfrid Laurier University Press, 2020.

[Ch. 6, p. 200: Removing references to residential schools, Alberta]

Bench, Allison. "UCP under Fire for K-4 Curriculum Plans That Suggest Leaving Out Residential Schools." Global News, published October 21, 2020; updated October 22, 2020. https://globalnews.ca/news/7410812/alberta-curriculum-education-residential-schools/.

[Ch. 6, p. 200: Alberta curriculum advisor issues]

French, Janet. "Alberta Social Studies Curriculum Adviser Calls Inclusion of First Nations Perspectives a Fad." CBC News, August 18, 2020. https://www.cbc.ca/news/canada/edmonton/alberta-social-studies-curriculum-adviser-calls-inclusion-of-first-nations-perspectives-a-fad-1.5690187.

[Ch. 6, p. 201: Garlic Heights]

Kossick, Don. "The Hall." In *Moose Jaw: People, Places, History*, by John Larsen and Maurice Richard Libby, 114–21. Moose Jaw, SK: Coteau Books, 2001. Google Books. https://books.google.ca/books?id=3MDXtHm0nYcC&lpg=PA123&pg=PA114#v=onepage&q&f=false.

[Ch. 6, p. 202: Black Porters – Canada]

Tomchuk, Travis. "Black Sleeping Car Porters." Canadian Museum for Human Rights, February 27, 2014. https://humanrights.ca/story/sleeping-car-porters.

[Ch. 6, p. 202: KKK]

Latimer, Kendall. "KKK History Challenges Idea Sask. Always Welcomed Newcomers: Expert." CBC News, August 18, 2017. https://www.cbc.ca/news/canada/saskatchewan/ku-klux-klan-saskatchewan-history-1.4251309.

[Ch. 6, pp. 203–4: Hampton, Fred – in Regina]

Ahearn, Victoria. "Black Panther Party Leader Fred Hampton Visited Regina Weeks before His 1969 Murder." Global News, February 11, 2021. https://globalnews.ca/news/7634506/judas-and-the-black-messiahs-fred-hampton-black-panthers-regina/.

[Ch. 6, p. 206: Pledge of Allegiance – requirement]

Caruso, Catherine. "The Pledge of Allegiance and 9/11: How It Was Used to Enforce Patriotism." *Teen Vogue*, September 8, 2021. https://www.teenvogue.com/story/pledge-of-allegiance-schools-911.

[Ch. 6, p. 206: Arrest – 11-year-old re: pledge of allegiance]

Stelloh, Tim. "Sixth-Grader Arrested in Florida after Refusal to Participate in Pledge of Allegiance Led to Confrontation." *NBC News*, February 17, 2019. https://www.nbcnews.com/news/us-news/sixth-grader-arrested-florida-after-refusal-participate-pledge-allegiance-led-n972671.

[Ch. 6, p. 206: Harry Potter books]

Elliott, Josh K. "Harry Potter Banned from School Library for Including 'Actual' Spells." Global News, September 3, 2019. https://globalnews.ca/news/5848190/harry-potter-banned-catholic-school-library-spells/.

[Ch. 6, p. 207: Glinton-Meicholas, Patricia]

Glinton-Meicholas, Patricia. *An Evening in Guanima: A Treasury of Folktales from the Bahamas*. 2nd ed. Nassau, NP: Guanima Press, 1994.

[Ch. 6, p. 209: Hill, Lawrence – "Meet you at the door" story in Vernon, Karina]

Hill, Lawrence. "Meet You at the Door." In *The Black Prairie Archives: An Anthology*, edited by Karina Vernon, 253–66. Waterloo, ON: Wilfrid Laurier University Press, 2020.

Chapter 7

[Ch. 7, p. 221: Wagamese, Richard, p 65]

Wagamese, Richard. *Indian Horse*. Vancouver: Douglas & McIntyre, 2012.

[Ch. 7, p. 223: Ali, Muhammad]

Ali, Muhammad. Quote. "It's not bragging if you can back it up." Quoted by Hilary Whiteman, "'Float like a butterfly, sting like a bee': Best quotes from Muhammad Ali," CNN Sports. June 2016. https://www.cnn.com/2016/06/04/sport/best-quotes-muhammad-ali/index.html.

[Ch. 7, p. 224: X, Malcolm – By any means necessary]

"Malcolm X's Speech at the Founding Rally of the Organization of Afro-American Unity." *Black Past*, 15 October 15, 2007. Accessed June 2023. www.blackpast.org/african-american-history/speeches-african-american-history/1964-malcolm-x-s-speech-founding-rally-organization-afro-american-unity/#:~:text=We%20declare%20our%20right%20on,existence%20by%20any%20means%20necessary.

[Ch. 7, p. 225: National Inquiry – MMIWG:]

Barrera, Jorge. "National Inquiry Calls Murders and Disappearances of Indigenous Women a 'Canadian Genocide.'" CBC News, May 31, 2019. https://www.cbc.ca/news/indigenous/genocide-murdered-missing-indigenous-women-inquiry-report-1.5157580.

[Ch. 7, p. 225: Baldwin, James]

Baldwin, James. Quote. "Our crown has already been bought and paid for. All we have to do is wear it." Quoted by Toni Morrison, "James Baldwin: His Voice Remembered; Life in His Language," *The New York Times*. December 20, 1987. https://archive.nytimes.com/www.nytimes.com/books/98/03/29/specials/baldwin-morrison.html

[Ch. 7, p. 235: Morrison, Toni – on ghosts (18:25)]

Morrison, Toni. Interview by Mavis Nicholson. *Mavis on 4*, February 24, 1988. YouTube video, 22:15. https://youtu.be/UAqB1SgVaC4?t=1105.

SOURCES

[Ch. 7, p. 235: Angelou, Maya]

Angelou, Maya. "Our Grandmothers." In *I Shall Not Be Moved*. New York: Random House, 1990. AfroPoets. Accessed September 2021. https://www.afropoets.net/mayaangelou25.html

[Ch. 7, p. 237: Gorman, Amanda]

Gorman, Amanda. "The Hill We Climb." Recited by the author at the inauguration of Joe Biden, Washington, DC, January 20, 2021. "Youth Poet Laureate Amanda Gorman's Inaugural Poem," CNN, January 20, 2021. Video, 5:32. https://www.cnn.com/2021/01/20/politics/amanda-gorman-inaugural-poem-transcript/index.html.

[Ch. 7, p. 239: Maynard, Robyn]

Maynard, Robyn. "Police Abolition/Black Revolt." *TOPIA* 41 (Fall 2020): 70–78. https://www.academia.edu/44664129/Police_Abolition_Black_Revolt?email_work_card=view-paper.

[Ch. 7, p. 240: Simone, Nina]

Moran, Lee. "Street Artist Honors Protesters with Nina Simone's Iconic Quote about Freedom." HuffPost, published June 5, 2020; updated June 23, 2020. https://www.huffpost.com/entry/nina-simone-pegasus-street-art-protests_n_5ed8fc0ec5b69b39db20c4b9.

[Ch. 7, p. 240: Simone, Nina]

Simone, Nina. *Nina Simone: A Historical Perspective*. Edited by Frederick D. Charney, produced by Peter Aristotle Rodis, and directed and photographed by Joel Gold. Cinemagic, 1970. YouTube video, 1:20. https://youtu.be/nPD8f2m8WGI.

[Ch. 7, p. 236: Black Lives Matter]

Black Lives Matter. "Herstory." Black Lives Matter. Accessed July 2021. https://blacklivesmatter.com/herstory/.

[Ch. 7, p. 228: Vernon, Karina]

Karina Vernon, ed. *The Black Prairie Archives: An Anthology*. Waterloo, ON: Wilfrid Laurier University Press, 2020.

[Ch. 7, p. 228: Lee, Erica]

Lee, Erica Violet. "Treaties beyond the State: Honouring Our Responsibilities to Each Other." For CBC First Person, CBC News, published April 25, 2021; last updated April 27, 2021. https://www.cbc.ca/news/canada/saskatchewan/black-on-the-prairies-treaties-beyond-the-state-1.5986994.

Conclusion

[Conclusion, p. 245: Acevedo, Elizabeth – *The Poet X*]

Acevedo, Elizabeth. *The Poet X*. New York: Quill Tree Books, 2018.

[Conclusion, p. 247: Elliot, Alicia – p. 12]

Elliot, Alicia. *A Mind Spread Out on the Ground*. Toronto: Doubleday Canada, 2019.

[Conclusion, p. 248: Mualla]

Mualla. "From the Heart to the Fist." Track 10 on *From the Heart to the Fist*, 2012. YouTube video, 4:17. https://www.youtube.com/watch?v=FnbKBkBfmRE.

Epilogue

[Epilogue, p. 250]

Baldwin, James. Quote. "You have to decide who you are and force the world to deal with you, not with its idea of you." Quoted in "James Baldwin debates William F. Buckley," Melville House. June 19, 2020. https://www.mhpbooks.com/james-baldwin-debates-william-f-buckley/.

General references

Angelou, Maya. "Still I Rise." In *And Still I Rise*. New York: Random House, 1978. Poets.org. Academy of American Poets. Accessed January 24, 2022. https://poets.org/poem/still-i-rise.

Armstrong, Patricia. "Bloom's Taxonomy." Vanderbilt University Center for Teaching, 2010. https://cft.vanderbilt.edu/guides-sub-pages/blooms-taxonomy/.

Boisvert, Nick. "Toronto's Africentric School Draws Consistent Praise — So Why Is Enrolment Flagging?" CBC News, February 5, 2019. https://www.cbc.ca/news/canada/toronto/africentric-school-anniversary-1.5005262.

brown, adrienne maree. *Pleasure Activism: The Politics of Feeling Good*. Chico, CA: AK Press, 2019.

The Canadian Press. "Remorse a Factor in Hate Speech Charges Not Being Laid after Shooting of Colten Boushie: Document." CBC News, February 10, 2021. https://www.cbc.ca/news/canada/saskatchewan/remorse-factor-no-hate-speech-charges-after-colten-boushie-shooting-1.5908317.

Cole, Desmond. *The Skin We're In: A Year of Black Resistance and Power*. Toronto: Doubleday Canada, 2020.

Eagle Feather News Staff. "Saskatoon's Oskayak High School Receives National Award." *Eagle Feather News*, May 13, 2014. https://eaglefeathernews.com/archive/saskatoons-oskayak-high-school-receives-national-award.

García, Ofelia, and Kleifgen, Jo Anne. "Translanguaging and Literacies." In *Reading Research Quarterly* 55, no. 4 (October/November/December 2020): 553–571. International Literacy Association. https://doi.org/10.1002/rrq.286.

Guffy, Ossie, and Caryl Ledner. *Ossie: The Autobiography of a Black Woman*. New York: Norton, 1971.

Issa, Omayra, and Ify Chiwetelu. *Black on the Prairies*. 1st ed. CBC, April 25, 2021. https://www.cbc.ca/newsinteractives/features/black-on-the-prairies.

Joseph, Chante. "What Black Joy Means — And Why It's More Important than Ever." *British Vogue*, July 29, 2020. https://www.vogue.co.uk/arts-and-lifestyle/article/what-is-black-joy.

Kendi, Ibram X. *How to Be an Antiracist*. New York: One World, 2019.

"Kyle Rittenhouse: Who Is US Teen Cleared of Protest Killings?" *BBC News*, November 19, 2021. https://www.bbc.com/news/world-us-canada-53934109.

Los Angeles Times. "Nelson Mandela Transformed Himself and Then His Nation." *Los Angeles Times*, December 6, 2013. https://www.latimes.com/opinion/topoftheticket/la-xpm-2013-dec-06-la-na-tt-nelson-mandela-20131206-story.html.

Lyiscott, Jamila. "3 Ways to Speak English." Filmed February 2014 in New York, NY. TED video, 4:29. YouTube, June 19, 2014. https://youtu.be/k9fmJ5xQ_mc.

Martis, Eternity. *They Said This Would Be Fun: Race, Campus Life, and Growing Up*. Toronto: McClelland & Stewart, 2021.

Maveal, Alexander. "Man Who Threw Shoe at George W. Bush Is Running for Iraqi Parliament." Global News, May 2, 2018. https://globalnews.ca/news/4181933/iraq-shoe-throw-george-w-bush/.

Mckesson, DeRay (@deray). "I love my blackness. And yours." Twitter, February 27, 2019, 9:55 p.m. https://twitter.com/deray/status/1100997905488347141.

me too. International. "Get to Know Us: Tarana Burke, Founder." me too. Movement, July 17, 2020. https://metoomvmt.org/get-to-know-us/tarana-burke-founder/.

Mexal, Stephen J. "The Roots of 'Wilding': Black Literary Naturalism, the Language of Wilderness, and Hip Hop in the Central Park Jogger Rape." *African American Review* 46, no. 1 (Spring 2023): 101–115. https://doi.org/10.1353/afa.2013.0010.

SOURCES

Mock, Brentin. "How Our Fear of 'Wilding' Colored the Central Park Five Case." Grist, July 8, 2014. https://grist.org/cities/how-our-fear-of-wilding-colored-the-central-park-five-case/.

Modjeski, Morgan. "Evan Penner Healing with Family after Arrest by Saskatoon Police Caught on Video: FSIN." CBC News, July 8, 2020. https://www.cbc.ca/news/canada/saskatoon/evan-penner-arrest-follow-1.5642393.

Montpetit, Dominique. "Women in the Parliament of Canada." HillNotes, January 23, 2020. https://hillnotes.ca/2020/01/23/women-in-the-parliament-of-canada/.

Rockett, Caitlin. "HEAVY ROTATION: The Revolution Will Not Be Televised." *Boulder Weekly*, June 4, 2020. https://www.boulderweekly.com/entertainment/music/heavy-rotation-the-revolution-will-not-be-televised/.

Starblanket, Gina, and Dallas Hunt. *Storying Violence: Unravelling Colonial Narratives in the Stanley Trial*. Winnipeg: ARP Books, 2020.

St. Denis, Verna, and Carol Schick. "What Makes Anti-Racist Pedagogy in Teacher Education Difficult? Three Popular Ideological Assumptions." *Alberta Journal of Educational Research* 49, no. 1 (Spring 2003): 55–69. https://doi.org/10.11575/ajer.v49i1.54959.

U.S. Constitution. Amend. XIII, §1 and §2. Constitution Annotated. "Thirteenth Amendment." *Constitution of the United States of America: Analysis and Interpretation*. Library of Congress. Accessed January 24, 2022. https://constitution.congress.gov/constitution/amendment-13/.

Web MD Editorial Contributors. "Stockholm Syndrome: What Causes It and How to Treat It." WebMD, April 13, 2021. https://www.webmd.com/mental-health/what-is-stockholm-syndrome.

X, Malcolm, and Alex Haley. *The Autobiography of Malcolm X*. Reissue ed. New York: Ballantine Books, 2015.

image credits

Cover: Moon, © ryuichi niisaka /Adobe Stock; Amethyst © Minakryn Ruslan/Adobe Stock; Raised hand © Jacob Lund/Adobe Stock, Vine leaves © Ammak/Adobe Stock; Heart-shaped leaves, © Chansom Pantip/Adobe Stock; Black man reaching up, © Nektarstock/Adobe Stock; Chrysanthemum flower heads, © Natika/Adobe Stock; Purple quartz geode, © xiao/Adobe Stock; Various images sourced from unsplash.com; Various images sourced from pexels.com; Various images courtesy of stylo starr © 2023.

Introduction (pages x−1): Various images sourced from unsplash.com; Various images sourced from pexels.com.

Chapter 1 (pages 8−9): Heart-shaped leaves, © Chansom Pantip/Adobe Stock; Pink agate crystal, © Sebastian/Adobe Stock; Striped leaf, © Odua Images/ Adobe Stock; Citrine, © Minakryn Ruslan/Adobe Stock; Various images sourced from unsplash.com; Various images sourced from pexels.com; Various images courtesy of stylo starr © 2023.

(Page 12): Various images sourced from unsplash.com; image sourced from pexels.com; Various images courtesy of Alan Dill © 2023.

Chapter 2 (pages 32−33): Hibiscus flower, black rose, © sommai/Adobe Stock; Black clematis flowers, © Анастасія Шатирова/Adobe Stock; Magnoliaceae evergreen flower, © tamu/Adobe Stock; Black violet flowers, © Marina/Adobe Stock; Marsh-mallow flower, © OK Stock/Adobe Stock; Picture frame, © zurbagan/Adobe Stock; Nemophila, © roichi tamago/Adobe Stock; Black Poppy, © hadot/Adobe Stock; Green plant shrubbery, Monstera jungle plant, © sakdam/Adobe Stock; Black calla flowers, © agneskantaruk/Adobe Stock; Quartz crystal cluster, Smoky quartz crystal, © Sebastian/Adobe Stock; White orchid flower, © JiriD/Adobe Stock; Tangled cord, © cooperr/Adobe Stock; Various images sourced from unsplash.com; Various images courtesy of Alan Dill © 2023.

(Page 50): Flowers head collection, © Flower Studio/ Adobe Stock; Black man in tracksuit, © kiuikson tamago/Adobe Stock; Chrysanthemum flower heads, © Natika/Adobe Stock; Various images sourced from unsplash.com; Image sourced from pexels.com.

Chapter 3 (pages 72−73): Lemurian crystal, © Minakryn Ruslan/Adobe Stock; Two young women embracing, © Raul Mellado/Adobe Stock; Purple quartz geode, © xiao/Adobe Stock; Vine leaves © Ammak/Adobe Stock; Zombie hands, © meen_na/ Adobe Stock; Zombie hand, © aekkorn/Adobe Stock; Woman covering eyes, © olly/Adobe Stock; Human hand, © Africa Studio/Adobe Stock; Two lilac tulip flowers, © Prostock-studio/Adobe Stock; Colorful quartz rainbow, © Sebastian/Adobe Stock; Grüne Wiese, © Thaut Images/Adobe Stock; Various images sourced from unsplash.com; Image sourced from pexels. com; Various images courtesy of Alan Dill © 2023.

(Page 76): Various images sourced from unsplash.com; Various images sourced from pexels.com.

(Page 85): Sun, © lukszczepanski/Adobe Stock; Various images sourced from unsplash.com; Various images sourced from pexels.com; Various images courtesy of Alan Dill © 2023.

Chapter 4 (pages 104−105): Jupiter, © Stockbym/ Adobe Stock; Hand gestures, © Rawpixel.com/ Adobe Stock; Amethyst crystal, © Minakryn Ruslan/Adobe Stock; Heart-shaped leaves, © Chansom Pantip/Adobe Stock; Monstera leaves © sakdam/Adobe Stock; Sunflower, © Venus/Adobe Stock; Tropical plants, © eakarat/Adobe Stock; Quartz crystals, © Daniel/Adobe Stock; Various images sourced from unsplash.com; Various images sourced from pexels.com.

(page 127): Jupiter, © Stockbym/Adobe Stock; Chrysanthemum flower heads, © Natika/Adobe Stock; Morpho butterfly, © Oleksii/Adobe Stock; Jumping amazed guy, © Look!/Adobe Stock; Amethyst crystal © Minakryn Ruslan/Adobe Stock; Heart-shaped leaves, © Chansom Pantip/ Adobe Stock; Vine leaves © Ammak/Adobe Stock; Tropical plants, © eakarat/Adobe Stock; Image sourced from unsplash.com; Various images sourced from pexels.com.

Chapter 5 (pages 142−143): Grey wolf, © AB Photography/Adobe Stock; Ametrine quartz crystals, © Daniel/Adobe Stock; Colorful butterflies, © Maksim Shmeljov/Adobe Stock; Morpho butterfly, © Oleksii/Adobe Stock; Dancer, © snaptitude/Adobe Stock; Image sourced from unsplash.com; Various images sourced from pexels.com.

IMAGE CREDITS

(Page 149): Diamonds, © neirfy/Adobe Stock; Amethyst quartz crystals, © Sebastian/Adobe Stock; Various images sourced from unsplash.com; Various images sourced from pexels.com.

(Page 154): Man holding white mask, © zephyr_p/Adobe Stock; Sick African man, © 9nong/Adobe Stock; Pensive youg woman, © Fotosushi/Adobe Stock; Succulent, © Regina Foster/Adobe Stock; Rose stems, © Yevhenii/Adobe Stock; Euphorbia cactus, © sakdam/Adobe Stock; Smoky quartz crystal, © Sebastian/Adobe Stock; Image sourced from pexels.com.

(Page 165): Monstera leaf, © Pixel-Shot/Adobe Stock; Snapdragon flower, © ksena32/Adobe Stock; Trefoil flower, Chrysanthemum flower heads, © Natika/Adobe Stock; Blue cornflower, © ulkan/Adobe Stock; Clematis flower, © Irina Fischer/Adobe Stock; Various images sourced from pexels.com.

Chapter 6 (pages 170–171): Opuntia Cactus © visitr/Adobe Stock; Opuntia microdasys, © Solomiia/Adobe Stock; Succulent, © Regina Foster/Adobe Stock; Prison facility interior, High school lobby, Vintage books, © Rawf8/Adobe Stock; Scheelite mineral, Citrine, © Minakryn Ruslan/Adobe Stock; Quartz crystals, © Daniel/Adobe Stock; Purple quartz geode © xiao/Adobe Stock; Vine leaves © Ammak/Adobe Stock; Heart-shaped leaves, © Chansom Pantip/Adobe Stock; Collection of flowers, © Flower Studio/Adobe Stock; Black rose, © Юлия Усикова/Adobe Stock; Black flowers of surfinia, © Sergey/Adobe Stock; Black clematis flowers, © Анастасія Шатирова/Adobe Stock; Black violet flowers, © Marina/Adobe Stock; Various images sourced from pexels.com.

(Page 177): Flags of South Africa, © Rawpixel.com/ Adobe Stock; Green Leaf, © sakdam/Adobe Stock; Monstera plant leaves, © Bowonpat/Adobe Stock; Olive branch leaves, © missty/Adobe Stock; Citrine, © Minakryn Ruslan/Adobe Stock; Open notebook, © imagedb.com/Adobe Stock; Various images sourced from pexels.com.

(Page 207): Pandan green leaves, © suwanb/Adobe Stock; Green palm coconut leaves, © Yellow Boat/Adobe Stock; Young man praying, © master1305/Adobe Stock; Various images sourced from pexels.com.

Chapter 7 (pages 212–213): Collection of flowers, © Flower Studio/Adobe Stock; Easter lily, © Jennie/ Adobe Stock; Pink gerbera flower, © Leonid Nyshko/ Adobe Stock; Two-tailed swallowtail, © Claudiu Mladin/Adobe Stock; Monstera leaf, © Pixel-Shot/ Adobe Stock; Pink or red gerbera, © boule1301/ Adobe Stock; Feuille de palmier © Unclesam/Adobe Stock; Various images sourced from unsplash.com; Various images sourced from pexels.com.

(Page 216): Fresh green sprigs of rosemary, © sucharat/Adobe Stock; Young tomato plant with soil, © WDnet Studio/Adobe Stock; Snapdragon flower, © ksena32/Adobe Stock; Pink or red gerbera, © boule1301/Adobe Stock; Various images sourced from unsplash.com; Various images sourced from pexels.com.

(Page 243): Wild morning glory leaves, © Venus/ Adobe Stock; Chrysanthemum flower heads, Clover or trefoil flower, Pink rose flower bouquet, © Natika/Adobe Stock; Two-tailed swallowtail, © Claudiu Mladin/Adobe Stock; Snapdragon flower, © ksena32/Adobe Stock; Blue cornflower, © ulkan/Adobe Stock; Flag of Cameroon, © Carsten Reisinger/Adobe Stock; Image sourced from unsplash.com; Various images sourced from pexels.com.

Conclusion (pages 244–245): Tropical plants, © eakarat/Adobe Stock; Lemurian Crystal, © Minakryn Ruslan/Adobe Stock; Cupped hands, © WavebreakMediaMicro/Adobe Stock; Various images sourced from unsplash.com; Image sourced from pexels.com; Various images courtesy of stylo starr © 2023.

index

Page numbers in **bold** mean definitions.

Photo credit: Carly Brown Photography

KHODI DILL is a Bahamian-Canadian writer, rapper, spoken word artist, and anti-racist educator. He is a sought-after public speaker known for his engaging lectures on issues of race, oppression, and education. Khodi lives in Saskatoon, Saskatchewan.

Photo credit: Nathalie Cortes

STYLO STARR is a Jamaican-Canadian collage artist whose work centers nature, fantasy, and notions of the Afrofuture. She is an emerging curator and arts educator with interests in exploring hand-cut collage as a grounding and healing creative modality. stylo lives and works in her hometown of Hamilton, Ontario.